Columbia Studies in the History of U.S. Capitalism

Series Editors: Devin Fergus, Louis Hyman, Bethany Moreton, and Julia Ott

Capitalism has served as an engine of growth, a source of inequality, and a catalyst for conflict in American history. While remaking our material world, capitalism's myriad forms have altered—and been shaped by—our most fundamental experiences of race, gender, sexuality, nation, and citizenship. This series takes the full measure of the complexity and significance of capitalism, placing it squarely back at the center of the American experience. By drawing insight and inspiration from a range of disciplines and alloying novel methods of social and cultural analysis with the traditions of labor and business history, our authors take history "from the bottom up" all the way to the top.

Capital of Capital: Money, Banking, and Power in New York City, by Steven H. Jaffe and Jessica Lautin

From Head Shops to Whole Foods: The Rise and Fall of Activist Entrepreneurs, by Joshua Clark Davis

Creditworthy: A History of Credit Surveillance and Financial Identity in America, by Josh Lauer

American Capitalism: New Histories, by Sven Beckert and Christine Desan, editors

Buying Gay: How Physique Entrepreneurs Sparked a Movement, by David K. Johnson

BANKING ON FREEDOM

Black Women in U.S. Finance Before the New Deal

Shennette Garrett-Scott

Columbia University Press New York

Columbia University Press
Publishers Since 1893
New York   Chichester, West Sussex
cup.columbia.edu

Library of Congress Cataloging-in-Publication Data
Names: Garrett-Scott, Shennette, author.
Title: Banking on freedom : black women in U.S. finance before the New Deal / Shennette Garrett-Scott.
Description: New York : Columbia University Press, [2019] | Series: Columbia studies in the history of U.S. capitalism | Includes bibliographical references and index.
Identifiers: LCCN 2018045341| ISBN 9780231183901 (cloth : alk. paper) | ISBN 9780231183918 (pbk. : alk. paper) | ISBN 9780231545211 (ebook)
Subjects: LCSH: Women in finance—United States—History. | African American bankers—History. | African American women—History. | Women bankers—United States—History. | African American banks—History.
Classification: LCC HG181 .G357 2019 | DDC 332.1092/520973—dc23

LC record available at https://lccn.loc.gov/2018045341

Columbia University Press books are printed on permanent and durable acid-free paper.

Printed in the United States of America

Cover design: Lisa Hamm
Cover image: Courtesy of the National Park Service, Maggie L Walker National Historic Site

To my wind, Malcolm, Dominique, and Malik,
and my wings, Vincent

Contents

Acknowledgments

I owe far more than I can ever repay. I cannot hope to recount fully my myriad debts here. I would like to thank the following institutions and entities for financial support that allowed me to complete key research for this book: the Alfred Chandler Research Grant, Baker Business Library, Harvard University; the Arch Dalrymple III Department of History Faculty Research Grant and the College of Liberal Arts Summer Research Stipend, University of Mississippi; the Center for Black Business History Research Grant and the Dora Bonham Research Grant, Department of History, University of Texas; the John Hope Franklin Center Research Grant, Duke University; the Mellon Research Grant, Virginia Historical Society; the Postdoctoral Fellowship in African American Studies, Case Western Reserve University; and Shelby C. Davis Center for Historical Studies, Princeton University.

This book would not have been possible without the scraps left in the archival record, tended and cared for by patient and open-hearted archivists such as Dana Chandler at Tuskegee University, Selecia Gregory Allen at Virginia Union University, and (from years ago) Klydie Thomas at the Maggie Lena Walker National Historic Site.

At various academic posts, scholars generously poured into me, which gave me the courage to tell the stories of thousands of women whose names we may never know. I am especially indebted to Juliet Walker, Tiffany Gill, Rhonda Y. Williams, and Charles K. Ross. At Princeton, conversations with the Davis Center Fellows in our Wednesday lunches and Friday seminars as well as over dinner expanded my historical third eye. Warm thank-yous to my cohort—Giovanni Ceccarelli, Jacco Dieleman, Pablo F. Gómez, Caley Horan, Vanessa Ogle, and Carl Wennerlind—and the thoughtful and supportive Davis Center unofficial League of Extraordinary People: Angela Creager, Jennifer Goodman, and Jack Tannous. (Extra-special thanks to Caley for the St. Luke pin; it is one of my most treasured possessions.)

The executive board of the Association of Black Women Historians has enriched my work and spirit beyond measure. Over the years, my cohort of sister scholars has been an inspiration and model of scholarly excellence. Special thanks to LaShawn Harris, Talitha Leflouria, Ula Y. Taylor, and Francille Rusan Wilson.

I would also like to thank my editor, Bridget Flannery-McCoy, and the History of Capitalism (HOC) series editors at Columbia University Press. In 2013, when Louis Hyman asked me to send him a book proposal, I was flattered—and convinced he was bonkers. I had just started a new position, and the book seemed so far away. He was persistent, and I am glad he did not give up on me. Columbia Press's HOC series editors, Julia Ott (my writing doula!), Bethany Moreton, Devin Fergus, and Louis Hyman, must have made a pact to save their authors from every bad experience they might ever have. I appreciate your time, expertise, and enthusiasm for this project.

I am so grateful to everyone who ever shared insights on various incarnations of this work. You pushed me to become a better vessel for these women's stories. For any names I missed, charge it to my head and not my heart. I send my deepest gratitude to every member of the Delta Women Writers for reading (and rereading) various drafts and for the good times over wine and dinner across the Arkansas-Louisiana-Mississippi Delta. Thanks as well to University of Mississippi faculty and graduate students who participated in my department colloquium as well as participants in the Governing Women in Capitalism on Three Continents workshop and panel at the 2017 Berkshire Conference on the History of Women, Genders, and Sexualities.

I can never repay the many kindnesses shown by Telisha Dionne Bailey, William Miller Boyd III, Deirdre Cooper Owens, Susan Grayzel, Mary Heen, Elizabeth Higginbotham, Tera Hunter, Cherisse Jones-Branch, Rebecca Marchiel, Elizabeth Payne, Jessica Wilkerson, and Brandon K. Winford.

My family has been so supportive over the years as I went to school, stopped, and went back again. I have been blessed by the three most important women in my life: my aunts Gennie Gilmore and Daisy Elder and my mother, Johnnie Brossman. Thanks for the love and support over the years to my siblings, Curtis Sanders Jr., Keisha Hall, and Mac Garrett; my father-in-law, Curtis Scott; his wife, Lynn; my mother-in-law, Alberta Jordan; and my sister-in-law, Kelly Scott. Thanks to my three little lights who inspire me to leave a positive legacy: Kyndall, Mason, and Katana. I am always far away, but you are ever in my heart. I am deeply grateful to the wonderful women who brought you into the world, Jazzmine MacMillan, Lunden Whitfield, and Kelsea Salone. I love you all.

Last but not least, thank you to my own little family. Words cannot express my feelings for you. Malcolm, Dominique, and Malik: *everything* I do, I do for you. Finally, to my soul mate and best friend, Vincent: I just love you.

BANKING ON FREEDOM

Introduction

"Shennette, you are going to make me a millionaire!" Daniel shouted, his smile cracking open something inside of me.[1] It was 2002, the height of the subprime mortgage industry, and I worked as a loan processor for a mortgage banker in Dallas. Founded two years before I came on board, Daniel's company was ready to burst out of a two-office suite in a storefront office complex. By the time I had clocked a year at the job, we had moved to the top two floors of a gleaming high-rise office building in North Dallas. I saw small fortunes made—and a few lost. Some loan officers went from living out of their cars or with relatives to earning more than $20,000 a month. New crowns and veneers lit up smiles like tiny electric lights. Luxury cars and new motorcycles filled the parking lot. Some took out creative loans themselves, purchasing their own minimansions.

Fortune eluded me, however. I earned a base salary and made a small commission on any loans I closed over my quota. Loans that paid loan officers upwards of $4,000 each (sometimes tipping up into the five-figure range) paid me only fifty dollars apiece. I worked seventy-plus-hour weeks. My family often came to the office with me in the evenings and on weekends. I imagined that I was part of a team—that is, until the words that Daniel had meant as praise shattered my delusion. I was decidedly the overworked, underpaid cog in a machine that made the riches of others possible. The moment I realized this, I vowed to pursue my own dream: a PhD.

What I did not realize until much later was that those high-interest, high loan-to-value loans we were peddling would destroy the dreams of the home buyers we believed we were helping. The very first firm I worked for innovated the kinds of loans that would eventually cripple the industry. Its commercials and direct-mail marketing materials featured a superstar athlete spokesperson. People gobbled up the thirty-year, fixed, 18 percent interest home refinance loans we promoted for 25 percent over the home's value. When I was in graduate school, I learned that an FBI probe had uncovered the firm's alleged mafia connections. Daniel, who had sworn I would make him a millionaire, had allegedly embezzled more than $350,000, which he gave to the Church of Scientology. These abuses joined thousands of others and contributed to the subprime mortgage market crash that began in 2007 and brought the entire U.S. financial system to its knees in 2008.

Pundits looking to root blame for the crisis and its ripple effects sought flesh and blood, often blaming the victims rather than the perpetrators. "Subprime" became a way to describe not just risky financial products but also the individuals who utilized them, painting them as incapable, rationally and ethically, to perform as responsible actors in the modern economy and society. The crisis deeply implicated racial and gendered disparities. The subprime mortgage debacle in many ways became a black woman.

Even so, my own personal experience as a loan processor led me to understand that black women, especially unmarried ones with children, had been particularly susceptible. Slick, targeted marketing promised the American dream of homeownership, achievable through any number of creative financing options: 100 percent financing with no money down and, in some cases, with no requirement to prove your income or even how much money you had in the bank; adjustable-rate mortgage (ARM) loans with ridiculously low teaser rates; interest-only ARM loans, where borrowers could choose every month to pay only the interest on their mortgages at cents on the dollar. Very few of my black women clients utilized the most maniacally imaginative loans, but many did receive ARMs and loans with very low or no down payments.

During federal investigations into the subprime crisis, witnesses described bank employees' racially insensitive comments, including characterizations of subprime loans as "ghetto loans" and black borrowers as "mud people."[2] Race and gender were key indicators of which customers received high-cost mortgage loans, even when controlling for credit and neighborhood. Black women were two times more likely than white women and three to five times more likely than white men, depending on the part of the country, to receive a subprime mortgage.[3]

When the market crashed, millions of mortgage holders lost their homes to foreclosure. Given the already-precarious accumulated wealth of black communities, the effect on black families and neighborhoods had to be described in terms of magnitude. *Generational. Cataclysmic.* Because home equity makes up the greatest percentage of black wealth, by various estimates blacks lost between $71 billion and $93 billion through foreclosures and from higher fees and interest rates associated with subprime loans. Not surprisingly, black women were prominent among the hardest-hit victims. They figured disproportionately high in the number of foreclosures. Even high-earning black women buyers, who might be expected to weather financial crises, were 80 percent more likely to lose their properties than whites. Foreclosures decimated predominantly black subdivisions and neighborhoods, from million-dollar subdivisions in places like Prince George's County, Maryland, to modest working-class developments like Belair-Edison in Baltimore.[4]

The so-called subprime crisis of 2007–2008 was far from the first episode in which African Americans—especially black women—grappled with the perils and promises of the financial industry in an effort to improve their lives. In the antebellum years, free and enslaved women created secret societies with clever names like the Sisters of Usefulness and the Sisters of the Mysterious Ten. These societies pooled meager resources to care for the sick, bury the dead, and buy the most important thing of all: freedom—for themselves, a child, or an ailing relative. The dislocations of the Civil War forced them to rely on each other again, especially given the often-trifling charity of aid societies and Union officers whose priorities placed Bible lessons, cotton bales, and cookstoves above black women's freedom dreams. After the Civil War, experiments to turn supposedly indolent women into industrious and thrifty workers privileged paychecks and passbooks as markers of their capacity for citizenship. Women continued to resist economic exploitation and limited opportunities to build wealth by creating their own financial institutions, but the problems of low wages, high-cost credit, and segregation dogged them at every turn. Disparities and exploitation in access, lending, and income have consistently underscored black women's credit experiences to the present day.

Banking on Freedom considers the black women who created webs of formal and informal banking and savings institutions from the eve of the Civil War to the New Deal. These institutions included building and loan associations; credit unions; burial, mutual aid, and secret societies; formal banks; and insurance corporations. Black women played essential roles in blacks' efforts to use finance to carve out possibilities within U.S. capitalism and society. As black women created, maintained, and used their own financial institutions and networks, they forged their own definitions of economic opportunity and citizenship. Those definitions refuted stereotypes about black women's sexuality and intellect as well as assumptions about women's ability to assume and manage economic risk. Black women also asserted their important financial roles in their families and communities, linking political demands, such as equal access to public accommodations, with other demands for reparative justice, such as access to credit, fair prices, and better housing.

Black women's complicated entanglements with U.S. finance reveal how race and gender mutually reinforce each other as categories of exclusion and difference—and inclusion and participation—in U.S. capitalism. Black women responded to these challenges and opportunities in multifaceted ways. They molded wealth-building strategies, banking practices, and evaluations of creditworthiness around gendered economic practices—not only the individual ways women made and used their money but also the collective values attached to building institutions, opportunities, and security for others. Financial institutions and practices represented a terrain upon which black women worked out familial and community strategies to achieve economic and social justice under the Jim Crow system of racial apartheid—even as those same institutions and practices constrained their vision of what constituted justice.

In many ways, black women's experiences with finance were similar to those of ethnic immigrants during the same period. Both groups operated within circumscribed enclaves defined by those who were recognized as "white"—a designation that conferred power in the market. Both immigrants from overseas and blacks—many of them migrants—developed creative strategies for survival in a segregated marketplace. Market exclusion explains in part why many black and ethnic businesses remained small but often espoused politicized, group-help, and nationalist philosophies. While poor, working-class, and aspiring-class blacks; ethnic immigrants; and whites sometimes shared similar values and wealth-building strategies—even utilized the same institutions and practices—enterprising blacks faced particular challenges.[5]

Although ethnic immigrants certainly suffered discrimination, racism and white supremacy presented harsher challenges for blacks. Under Jim Crow, legal, cultural, and social proscriptions kept people who supposedly had even one drop of Negro blood in a subordinate status. At the same time, it legitimated the privileges and opportunities of people with white skin—a privilege and opportunity that ethnic immigrants would ultimately claim for themselves. For blacks, community-based financial institutions were a bulwark against Jim Crow, but they could not erase the color line. Whitened ethnics, by contrast, used the tools of finance—especially residential mortgages and consumer credit—to gain access to and wrest benefits from U.S. capitalism in ways that blacks simply could not.

The limitations imposed by capitalism, sexism, and white supremacy, however, posed a real and ever-present threat, thwarting even the best-intentioned possibilities. Capitalism itself was a double-edged sword, built on the exploitation of others' labor and shaped by the racial exclusionary logics of Jim Crow. Jim Crow was a system of laws and customs that blocked blacks' ambition and progress through segregation and discrimination, denial of education and civil rights, economic repression, and violence.[6] Emerging in the late nineteenth century, Jim Crow segregation had, by the early twentieth century, opened up niche markets marked by racial difference. Black entrepreneurs capitalized on the separate black economy but were simultaneously limited in their access to and ability to compete in wider markets.[7] Pseudoscientific theories of racial and gender differences undergirded Jim Crow and sexism, fueling assumptions about blacks' and women's spending habits, capacity to assume and manage risk, and ability to save and invest. These theories reinforced actuarial and business practices that blocked blacks' ability to purchase life insurance, get credit, and make investments, especially in real estate.[8] They also blocked blacks' access to professional networks and education that would have helped them stay competitive in the U.S. financial industry.

Between 1888 and 1930, black Americans opened and controlled more than one hundred banks, which served an almost exclusively black clientele. They organized thousands of insurance companies and associations. *Banking on Freedom* examines this period of African American financial innovation through the story of the St. Luke Bank in Richmond, Virginia, opened by the members of the Independent Order of St. Luke (IOSL) in 1903. Maggie Lena Walker, the first black woman to organize and lead a bank, served as president of the St. Luke Bank for more than three decades.[9]

As Gertrude Marlowe, Elsa Barkley Brown, and Angel Kwolek-Folland have documented, Walker, the IOSL, and the St. Luke Bank provided women with jobs and opportunities in the financial industry. The IOSL was the largest white-collar employer for black women in the early twentieth century. By the early 1920s, bank customers had paid in full more than 650 mortgage loans, and the St. Luke Bank provided credit and loans to small and large businesses as well as individuals. *Banking on Freedom* recognizes the St. Luke Bank as not only a financial but also a political institution for the black communities it served, especially regarding issues such as jobs, housing, and community development.[10]

The St. Luke and other black banks operated as successful economic and political institutions, in part because whites favorably perceived them. Conservatives, moderates, and even extremists could support segregated economic achievement because they believed it kept black political ambitions in check by championing achievement in other areas. In addition, business seemed to be a reasonable, civil, and beneficent solution to the ubiquitous "Negro problem" while effectively eliminating black competition. However, black banks became targets of state surveillance and policing in the years before and after World War I.

Every cent saved, every nickel loaned, and every dollar invested through women-controlled institutions like the St. Luke Bank presented possibilities. As black women built, ran, and patronized the St. Luke Bank, they helped construct and alternately deconstruct discourses about race, risk, and rights. However, negative discourses devalued black women's morality, intellect, and fitness for citizenship in the context of Jim Crow, industrialization, and imperialism, and they discouraged women from taking financial risks and practicing economic autonomy, which were often constructed as markers of masculine privilege and male rights.

From the perspective of black women themselves, financial institutions presented a means to both accommodate and challenge capitalist accumulation, sexism, and white supremacy. For example, under Walker's leadership, the St. Luke Bank accommodated rigid lines of residential segregation by granting mortgages to blacks only in limited areas of the city. However, Walker challenged Jim Crow by mobilizing black homeowners to pay poll taxes and support black candidates for public office, especially black women homeowners after the passage of the Nineteenth Amendment. Black women used the St. Luke Bank as a site for developing a political culture. As Glenda Gilmore has recognized, the intertwined and mutually reinforcing gender and racial norms of Jim Crow ironically permitted black women to redefine the political; they transformed the teller cage and boardroom into sites of activism and resistance.[11]

The club, church, field, factory floor, and private home were not the only spaces for women to work out meanings of respectability, identity, and power. Connections forged among black women at the St. Luke Bank allowed them to draw from fraternal ritual and bureaucratic structure to create practical and workable solutions for assessing creditworthiness and mitigating risks. The money they lent was often a last resort to protect hard-won assets like homes and commercial spaces or to maintain hard-fought-for efforts like completing education or migrating north. St. Luke women also held both leadership and rank-and-file positions in multiple other organizations. They were thus able to mobilize support for movements concerning economic rights and empowerment such as streetcar boycotts and women's suffrage. These connections spilled well beyond the confines of what we might imagine as "legitimate" financial institutions and "formal" politics. Christmas savings accounts, loan amounts as small as five dollars, and affordable rents represent the kinds of banking practices that had real-world—I daresay, liberatory—potential.

Like many prominent black women who challenged Jim Crow racial and gender stereotypes, the women connected to the St. Luke relied on strategies of racial uplift and politics of respectability. They framed their activities as economic self-help, and they viewed their role in extending credit to working black women as almost a duty of their leadership in the black community. Uplift and respectability were, however, to borrow Erin Chapman's characterization, "deeply class-based, ultimately self-defeating strateg[ies] . . . to combat white supremacy."[12] Even so, black women's financial strategies and choices cannot be understood apart from the imperatives of uplift and respectability. Capitalism and respectability complicated the exercise, intention, and direction of black women's financial strategies. For example, encouraging wives to be endorsers for their husbands' loans acknowledged women's economic importance to their families, but it also committed them to repaying debts that they could not afford if the husband reneged.

Banking on Freedom recovers black women in the histories of U.S. finance and political economy because their stories illustrate how race and gender shaped modern capitalism. Black intellectuals like W. E. B. Du Bois, C. L. R. James, and Eric Williams positioned enslaved people and race formation at the center of their historical explanations of the rise and development of capitalism, and they interrogated race in their analyses of configurations of global capitalism.[13] Scholars have extended their analyses of twentieth-century racial capitalism to examine mortgage redlining, consumer credit access, actuarial criminology, and social impact bonds. These works recognize racial exclusion in the development of finance, and they point to the role of race in destabilizing wealth building in black communities.[14]

Too often, however, historians of capitalism miss opportunities to emphasize gender. The problem is not merely one of locating women. It is the challenge of articulating the ways in which gender shapes and is shaped by economic practices and concepts. Admittedly, the number of black women working in financial institutions dwarfs the number working in agricultural labor and domestic service. By the 1920s, St. Luke women stood at the vanguard of an emerging black white-collar class. Yet the St. Luke was not an exclusive domain for the elite and aspiring classes. Thousands of washerwomen, tobacco factory workers, domestics, teachers, businesswomen, and others held stock certificates, passbooks, and promissory notes that sustained and made the St. Luke an essential community—and national—institution. While Jim Crow placed some limitations on the St. Luke Bank, it relied on gendered economic practices to push back and shape the bank's practices and values around their needs and desires.

In the mid-1850s, Mary Ann Prout, a free black woman in Baltimore, organized the St. Luke Society in the Bethel African Methodist Episcopal Church. She intended the St. Luke to be a society created by women for women and children. St. Luke women collected dues and raised money to provide for funerals, to support schools and other community- and church-related institutions, and to care for the vulnerable and needy. As thousands of African Americans poured into Baltimore to escape the dislocations of the Civil War, Prout formally organized the Grand United Order of St. Luke in 1867 to expand the order and, in part, to capitalize on a new market. It was also the first time she allowed men to join the order. A Virginia faction broke off in 1869 and formed the Independent Order of the Sons and Daughters of St. Luke (IOSL). In the 1880s, the IOSL experimented with offering modest life insurance policies, but it struggled to create viable and affordable long-term financial products in which black communities were willing to trust and invest.

Maggie Lena Walker took over the reins of the IOSL in 1899 as right worthy grand secretary-treasurer. She shifted the centerpiece of the order away from social reform and service work and toward offering financial services, refined the IOSL's financial products, and expanded the order in various parts of the country. In 1903, she organized the St. Luke Penny Savings Bank. In the early years of the twentieth century, the St. Luke Bank experimented with small-scale consumer lending, much like other banks that catered to working-class depositors in the period. The bank rejected emerging scientific assumptions about black deviance and degeneracy; instead, it relied on the IOSL's bureaucratic structure and institutional values to evaluate individuals' risk and creditworthiness. The St. Luke Bank faced mounting regulatory and extralegal harassment in the 1910s and 1920s, which forced it to adopt industry standards and practices. However, it never completely abandoned its unique practices and values. And in the years following World War I, the Great Migration created new challenges to meeting the complex needs of black women in both northern and southern cities.

Banking on Freedom reveals the ways that black women's saving, spending, and lending practices challenge understandings of success and security, notions of risk, and the possibilities of citizenship in the U.S. economy and society. The first chapter, "'I Am Yet Waitin': African American Women and Free Labor Banking Experiments in the Emancipation-Era South, 1860s–1900," highlights savings experiments created for freedpeople by white northern reformers and Union military leaders during and after the Civil War. Freedmen's funds, military and free labor banks, and the Freedman's Bank represented federal versions of racial paternalism and economic exploitation that undermined much of the economic autonomy that free black and formerly enslaved women struggled to carve out in the transformation to free labor. These experiments interfered with long-standing networks created and utilized by black women, individually and collectively, to manage their economic futures. Black women who utilized the free labor banks and the Freedman's Bank resisted appeals that privileged male breadwinners as the proper savers and providers, a model that actively undercut and ignored the circumstances, needs, and challenges facing women depositors.

Chapter 2, "'Who Is So Helpless as the Negro Woman?': The Independent Order of St. Luke and the Quest for Economic Security, 1856–1902," chronicles the growth of the IOSL from the mid-nineteenth century through the opening of the St. Luke Bank in 1903. In its early years, the IOSL responded to the challenges that tested black women and their families in freedom. They continued their long tradition of economic provision and activism, community building, and communal enterprise that had been begun by enslaved and free black women. The IOSL would succeed in creating and maintaining important financial institutions, such as a bank and an insurance company. In the decades after emancipation, however, the IOSL's success was hardly a foregone conclusion. It struggled to create viable and affordable long-term investment and related financial products in which black communities were willing to trust and invest.

Chapter 3, "'Let Us Have a Bank': St. Luke Penny Savings Bank, Economic Activism, and State Regulation, 1903 to World War I," explores the organization and operations of the bank from its opening in 1903 to the late 1910s. The bank's opening proved to be more successful than its president, Maggie Lena Walker, could have imagined in large part due to the working-class black women who invested in the bank as stockholders, depositors, and executives. Walker fought tenaciously to align her vision of economic empowerment for women with the bank's success, but the bank's first decade reflects the tension between its ideals and reality. With the bank's success came increased threats to its future, particularly extralegal harassment from the white business community and aggressive state oversight. It succeeded where others failed, in part because of the visionary leadership of Walker and in part because of the hard work of women in the IOSL who kept the organization grounded in meeting the social and economic needs of working black women.

Chapter 4, "Rituals of Risk and Respectability: Gendered Economic Practices, Credit, and Debt to World War I," explores the bank's lending practices through the late 1910s. The young St. Luke Bank found opportunities and challenges in the emerging market for small, short-term lending. While saving remained paramount, the bank also worked to increase blacks' wealth, especially through home, business, and property ownership. The bank negotiated a place for itself both within the world of quotidian credit and in contradistinction to it. Mitigating risk was crucial, but race, gender, and class shaped what constituted risk. One of the bank's most important missions acknowledged women's important economic roles in their families and communities, and so the bank strove to increase women's financial literacy and make borrowing a respectable activity. To these ends, mutuality and obligation proved to be useful and protean resources to negotiate risk, link respectability and profit, and promote individual benefit and collective good. Obligation, though, held inherent tensions, tensions that were revealed in the tactics that borrowers relied on to press their cases for loans, the limitations that respectability placed on women borrowers, and the bank's efforts to collect from delinquent debtors.

Finally, chapter 5, "'A Good, Strong, Hustling Woman': Financing the New Negro in the New Era, 1920–1929," turns our attention to the women working in the IOSL and the world of black finance in New Negro cities like Harlem before the 1929 stock market crash. The young women working in the IOSL appreciated the advantages of working in the financial industry but struggled under the weight of the work and expectations that some found old-fashioned. Women and men moving to and living in cities both north and south stretched the capacity of black banks alone to address their needs in new contexts. Anxieties about black women's bodies in urban spaces necessitated cultural, economic, and political responses to rebut public discourses painting black women as both victims and sources of social problems, as in need of both financial protections and also new economic opportunities. In financial institutions that women led and controlled, they experimented with innovative ways to raise capital but struggled with inexperience and the intractable problems of racial and sexual discrimination. Thus, black financial institutions became highly contested spaces—and conduits of resistance.

I

"I Am Yet Waitin"

AFRICAN AMERICAN WOMEN AND FREE LABOR BANKING EXPERIMENTS IN THE EMANCIPATION-ERA SOUTH, 1860s–1900

"I am yet waitin." Matilda Scott's crude handwriting rose off the page, more an accusation than an observation. By 1920, Scott felt frustrated inquiring about the eighteen-dollar refund from her mother's Freedman's Bank account. As commissioner of the defunct Freedman's Savings and Trust Company, John Skelton Williams had received hundreds—probably thousands—of letters like hers during his six years in the position. His main responsibility as commissioner was to help depositors recover some of their money. When the Freedman's Bank shut its doors in 1874, tens of thousands of African Americans lost an accumulated wealth of more than $63 million (in 2017 dollars). One of them was Adaline Washington, Matilda Scott's mother. A former slave, Adaline did not know her age, could neither read nor write, and mentioned no husband, dead or alive, when she opened her account in the fall of 1872 at the Freedman's Bank branch in Shreveport, Louisiana. She lived about a mile outside the city with her six children. Young Matilda helped her mother with the children and her farming work, so much so that Adaline instructed the bank clerk that Matilda could make deposits in and withdrawals from the account. Nearly fifty years later, Adaline's daughter continued to speak for her mother. She pressed Commissioner Williams, wanting to know "hoo you paid my money too." An insistent Scott ended her note not with a request but a demand: "Anser at once."[1]

Scott felt emboldened to make demands rather than requests but not because the amount her mother left was significant. Scott belonged to a generation of African American women who had lived with both slavery and emancipation but sometimes questioned the essential differences between the two. They had grown accustomed to fighting: fighting dishonest planters, marauding vigilantes, and tightfisted bureaucrats in their efforts to provide for their families. Black women's insistent claims for economic independence fulfilled bureaucrats', reformers', and philanthropists' expectations that black women be prudent with money, but these women did not intend to rely on compliant, meek, and dependent behavior to achieve financial self-sufficiency.

This chapter explores how the transformation from slavery to free labor from just after the Civil War until the end of the nineteenth century influenced the various strategies that black women pursued and contested in their search for economic security. The iteration of free labor promoted by northern military officers, philanthropists, and politicians extolled the pay slip and passbook as the truest tests of blacks' capacity for citizenship. The "free" in free labor did not mean the opposite of slavery—nor did it mean that blacks were, as Willie Lee Rose notes, "free to do just as they pleased."[2] Black labor remained essential to revitalizing the southern economy and maintaining the United States' predominance in the global economy, but these officers, philanthropists, and politicians seldom described free labor in such crass, free-market terms. They preferred to imagine that they were offering blacks a path to citizenship through economic responsibility by promoting approaches that combined some form of paid wage labor with various money management and savings schemes. The key economic experiments included the Freedmen's Fund, free labor and military savings banks, and the capstone institution: the Freedman's Bank.[3]

These experiments, however, preserved an ideological commitment to black subservience, leaving most blacks economically vulnerable and with little in the way of civic or political rights. The Freedmen's Fund collected the wages of black workers, and military officials maintained control over that money—undermining the very lessons of self-sufficiency that the fund purported to instill. The three free labor and military banks that were opened during the last years of the war were intended to overcome the inherent paradox of the Freedmen's Fund, which paid blacks but did not allow them free access to their wages. The banks offered black soldiers and workers more autonomy over their funds; however, both the free labor banks and the Freedman's Bank espoused a version of male liberal breadwinner subjectivity that actively undercut and ignored the circumstances, needs, and challenges facing women depositors.

None of the savings and banking experiments shared or even reflected black women's expansive vision of freedom. Rather, these experiments sat at the uncomfortable juncture of labor and ideology, which compelled black women to work but placed them outside the bounds of propriety for doing so. In addition to devaluing black womanhood, these experiments interfered with and disrupted long-standing informal networks and formal institutions that had been created and utilized by black women, individually and collectively, to manage their economic futures. In practice, they offered few advantages for freedwomen and often relied on coercion and compliance.

THE FREEDMEN'S FUND

In late 1862, Major General Ulysses Grant enlisted his new chaplain John Eaton Jr. to deal with the growing numbers of self-emancipated men and women flocking to Union lines at Grand Junction, Tennessee. Grant's General Orders No. 15 called for putting freedpeople to work and "see[ing] that they are properly cared for."[4] Grant believed that blacks should work, and in exchange for their labor, they could receive provisions and protection from the army. He did not feel it advisable to pay freedpeople wages, but Eaton disagreed. Eaton advocated modest salaries for blacks who were working for the army as teamsters, servants, cooks, nurses, and in other capacities. In addition to performing such services for the military, he also hired freedpeople to grow and pick cotton on abandoned, confiscated, and embargoed farms and plantations.[5]

Contraband camps were encampments of self-emancipated slaves who had escaped to Union lines or had been captured by Union troops. The army considered escaped slaves as contraband, or enemy property.[6] Eaton, in his new role as superintendent of contrabands in the Mississippi Valley, created the Freedmen's Fund to help care for freedpeople. The Freedmen's Fund, representing one of the earliest experiments to manage freedpeople's labor, served as a depository for the wages they earned working for and under the direction of the army. Rather than allow freedpeople individual control over their wages, Eaton used the money to provide food, shelter, and other needs for freedpeople collectively. The Freedmen's Fund reflected Eaton's high-minded ideals about the supposed rehabilitative powers of wage labor over the enslaved, but it also highlighted tensions between ideals and the practice of free labor. Eaton's belief that it was necessary to inculcate the work ethic and habit of thrift, which he and many other northerners believed that formerly enslaved people lacked, informed his practical efforts to deal with the self-emancipated blacks who were placed under his care. In some cases, he followed the lead of other generals, for instance, putting the thousands of refugees behind Union lines to work. In many other ways, however, Eaton initiated economic programs that other military officers duplicated during the Civil War, foreshadowing federal approaches to Reconstruction.[7]

Eaton not only deposited freedpeople's wages in the Freedmen's Fund, he also took all their wealth. Soldiers confiscated horses, wagons, money, and other valuables that self-emancipated blacks brought with them to the Union lines. What soldiers and the quartermasters did not steal for themselves, Eaton commandeered for the fund. He also placed money, clothing, blankets, and other items that had been donated by northern churches, aid societies, and individuals in the fund. Freedpeople thus had no individual access to their wages or savings, nor did they have any say in how their own wages or the money that was donated for their benefit would be used.[8]

Eaton, and other military officials who followed his example, believed that such free labor and savings experiments would inculcate a work ethic and sense of thrift in the formerly enslaved and break them of the dependence that they believed a lifetime of servitude had stamped into their very beings. Demeaning assumptions about blacks' intellect, character, and capacity for work shaped the military's economic experiments. Though Eaton thought it advisable that freedpeople work, he never thought it advisable to allow them access to "undirected resources." He believed that, as formerly enslaved people, freedpeople had never made the "connection between their industry and their comfort." They never understood, he decided, that it was "not their labor but their masters [who] clothed and fed them."[9] Eaton styled himself as their new master, boasting that he "expended judiciously [from the fund] . . . to supply them with many comforts they had never known."[10] It is baffling why Eaton thought freedpeople might better make the connection between their labor and comfort if he denied them access to their wages. For all his talk of teaching the value of self-sufficiency, Eaton blinded himself to the ways that his own policies undermined the lesson he hoped to teach. In addition, blacks' industry and their strong commitment to self-help belied reformers' demeaning assumptions. Eaton and other military officials who controlled freedpeople's wages through experiments like the Freedmen's Fund defined them as independent laborers rather than free citizens.

Exploitative practices significantly fattened the fund's coffers and further undermined black economic autonomy. By the last years of the war, Eaton controlled a wider network of contraband camps throughout the Mississippi Valley, and by 1864, he formalized his contract labor system. The government leased abandoned plantations to northerners and to some southerners who supported the Union, and Eaton negotiated contracts for and hired out black workers on these leased plantations. Any profits from the cash crops that former bondspeople grew and harvested were placed in the Freedmen's Fund.

Black women's labor added to these funds because they comprised a significant part of the workers on leased plantations. In most instances, the military enlisted able-bodied men to serve as soldiers and to work on the battlefront and used women, children, the elderly, and the disabled to fulfill labor contracts. These exploitative contracts often left women little to show for their labors. A military official noted that a black woman who earned seventy dollars for seven months' labor on a leased plantation was lucky to profit nine dollars after deducting supplies. She earned even less if she had dependent children. Apprenticeship arrangements often bound women to the land. Further, lessors and other whites legally took ownership of children to perform work until the children reached adulthood, so mothers, desperate to recover or stay near their children, performed agricultural labor. Women also suffered forced separation from loved ones—not only children but husbands, sons, fathers, and other relatives—on these leased plantations. They often worked with inadequate food and provisions and under dangerous conditions. Many of the leased plantations lay in isolated, rural areas that were vulnerable to Confederate raids, and Confederate soldiers and civilians would perpetrate acts of physical and sexual violence and then sell women and children back into slavery. In addition to laboring on plantations and farms, women also worked loading, unloading, and cording wood in timber yards.[11]

In cities, military officials and white-led charitable associations shuttled black women into the work they had performed during slavery, such as cooking and domestic work. Working in whites' homes, women sometimes suffered physical violence at the hands of employer-mistresses and sexual harassment from men connected to those households. Women also provided low-skill and unskilled labor in canneries, tobacco factories, and other southern industries where the work was sometimes dangerous and often dirty and tedious.

Black women earned less than male workers and soldiers, but women's labor produced incredible wealth for the army and the federal government. For example, at Grand Junction, Tennessee, a workforce of only women and children grew and harvested $20,000 worth of cotton (about $319,000 in 2017 dollars) during the first season. Eaton boasted that in one year, $103,000 (about $1.6 million in 2017 dollars) from the fund not only provided food, clothing, and housing for freedpeople but also "met all the incidental expenses of [the army's] widespread operations; paid $5,000 for hospitals; [paid] the salaries of all hospital stewards and medical assistants . . . ; and enabled us to supply implements of industry to the [Negroes]."[12] Near the war's end, Eaton used the fund to pay and board teachers, and Freedmen's Bureau officials tapped the fund to build schools. The true lessons of the Freedmen's Fund experiment escaped most of the officers, politicians, and philanthropists who patted themselves on the back for their own magnanimity and foresight in directing the resources of former bondspeople.

Black women, in particular, deserved to feel proud of their economic impact in building up and sustaining their communities. The wealth they helped produce built homes, hospitals, and schools. Their labor sustained entire communities. Under the Freedmen's Fund experiment, however, women personally controlled almost none of the wealth they produced. Subsequent experiments continued to prove both bitter and sweet.[13]

FREE LABOR AND MILITARY BANKS

Other military leaders borrowed liberally from Eaton's programs, and some improved on them. Rather than oversee a central fund, they went a significant step further to allow blacks more autonomy over their income by creating banks for black soldiers and workers. General Nathaniel Banks created the first free labor and military bank in New Orleans in early 1864.[14] Banks used a system of contracting black people's labor similar to Eaton's, but Banks was not as committed to the freedmen's fund model of managing formerly enslaved people's wages. Historian Jonathan Levy notes that the New Orleans free labor and military bank represented an "ideological and practical solution to the shortcomings" of Banks's system of contracting black labor.[15] The free labor bank also represented efforts to deal with shortcomings of the Freedmen's Fund experiments.

The free labor banks served as an institutional arm of savings and banking experiments and complemented contract labor experiments. However, contemporaries criticized Banks's contract labor system. Like Eaton's and other military officers' programs, his authorized below-market wages and required lengthy contracts that returned blacks to a system of slavery at worst and serfdom at best. Banks addressed his critics in a speech before the Young Men's Christian Commission in Boston in late 1864. He argued that provisions supplemented the paltry monthly wage of four to ten dollars. Workers received food rations, clothes, housing, medical care, schools, and acre-and-a-half plots of land (when feasible) to grow their own food or cotton. Regarding the length of contracts, Banks argued that it took continuous labor over time to raise and harvest crops effectively. More important, the long-term contracts compelled blacks; he reminded the audience, "It had never been demonstrated by actual experiment that the negro would subject himself to continuous labor by any engagement or choice of his own."[16]

Other high-ranking army officers followed Banks's experiment by creating banks expressly for black laborers and soldiers. General Benjamin Butler opened a bank in Norfolk soon after Banks started his, and General

Rufus Saxton followed suit in Beaufort, South Carolina. Saxton opened the South Carolina Freedmans [*sic*] Bank in the summer of 1864 (see fig. 1.1). The free labor and military banks offered distinct advantages over a centralized fund and even over the army quartermaster. Unlike the Freedmen's Fund, banks gave workers some measure of control over their money. They could decide for themselves how much to save and how much to keep for personal expenses and wants. They could also build up their individual wealth rather than contribute to collective expenses. Army quartermasters issued passbooks in which soldiers and civilian workers kept records of their deposits. The army, however, limited a soldier's single deposit to five dollars, which placed considerable constraints on individuals who wanted to save more. Further, soldiers could not withdraw funds until their enlistment ended, which placed another constraint on how they could use their own savings. Nor did the accounts earn interest. Finally, the army provided no fiduciary oversight; it assumed no responsibility to protect the soldiers' deposits from loss. Indeed, not all quartermasters proved trustworthy. They sometimes mismanaged and outright absconded with soldiers' savings.[17]

Savings banks created specifically for black soldiers and workers constituted part of a wider savings bank movement focused on working-class men and women. First created in the 1810s as a way to inculcate middle-class values of thrift and hard work, the number of industrial savings banks

FIGURE 1.1 A black child sits on the steps of the South Carolina Freedmans Bank in Beaufort, c. 1863–1866.
Source: LC-DIG-stereo-1s07095, Library of Congress.

increased exponentially after the Civil War. These banks accepted small deposits, paid interest, and discouraged borrowing for and investing in anything but the most secure risks, such as a home or education. Savings accounts represented, in the estimation of the organizers, security, a hedge against the inevitable vagaries of working-class life, and a way to avoid charity. Often headed by civic-minded wealthy elites and successful businessmen, these banks institutionalized a paternalistic model of banking and savings for laborers and small farmers.[18]

The military officers who modeled their free labor and military banks on these northern institutions shared some of the paternalist attitudes that animated reform-minded business and civic leaders who created savings banks for working-class people. For example, Saxton explained that he created the bank in Beaufort for instruction, yes, but for protection as well: "to protect the Freedmen from being defrauded by sharpers, ever ready to prey on their simplicity, and chiefly to induce in them habits of carefulness and prudence," he wrote to Secretary of War Edwin M. Stanton.[19] Concerns about black dependency motivated Butler as well. Unlike Eaton, he did not want to act as an intermediary; he wanted to make it clear to blacks that they were responsible for their own food, shelter, and clothing: "I think the labor of the negroes, with the savings of their earnings, will be sufficient to meet [blacks' housing and other] expenses."[20] To be sure, the practical problems associated with managing the large amounts of money earned by black soldiers and workers, coupled with the lack of a clear federal policy or a mandate from the president or Congress, fueled officers' willingness to experiment with different ways to manage black people's money.

Yet it is critical to understand that the hundreds of thousands of black soldiers and freedpeople also exerted pressure against officers and reformers. They demanded more autonomy over their lives as free people. With regard to the Freedmen's Fund, they complained about low wages and slow payment of wages. They also demanded more control over their wages. As long as freedpeople's pay was saved and doled out by patrons to meet their necessities, they could never truly be masters of their own lives. Soldiers, too, complained about unpaid wages. Freedpeople, soldiers, and others with access to the three free labor banks won some assurance that wages would be paid; fearing labor conflict or even a strike, General Butler decided to discontinue his Refugee and Freedmen's Fund and open a freestanding bank.[21]

Despite assumptions that black people could not connect their own industry to their comfort, they clearly understood the power inherent in their cash wages. Wages reinforced their claims as free people and as citizens, particularly in the economic and social dislocations of war. Where they were located, the free labor banks kept more U.S. greenbacks in the cities and nearby areas, and the amounts could be significant. By the end of 1864, after only a few months of operation, the bank in Norfolk held $65,000; by the end of the war in mid-1865, estimates for deposits ranged from $170,000 to $200,000 (or about $2.8 to $3.3 million in 2017 dollars). Northeastern banks backed the money that black people kept in and withdrew from the free labor banks. In a local market where questionable Confederate currency and scrip circulated, the cash that freedpeople saved and spent gave them tremendous power to direct their everyday lives and futures, even if their wages were low.[22] The free labor banks presented some challenges for their black customers, but blacks still wrested some utility out of them.

Beyond the heresies of free labor, these savings experiments ignored an obvious fact: blacks were not unbanked. Both enslaved and free blacks actively participated in both the informal and the formal antebellum market economy. Even enslaved people saved money in banks, with local merchants, and with their masters. Free blacks served as informal lenders and, in addition to charging interest, made money by discounting notes, and free people of color invested in bank stock. Well before the Civil War, black people were, as one historian observes, "conversant with the operation of a credit economy" and the free market.[23] Free and enslaved blacks had a long tradition creating financial institutions as well. In addition to investing in and utilizing banks, they created money clubs, rotating credit associations, and savings and loan associations, and they saved and managed money in church, mutual aid, and secret societies.[24]

They also stashed money away under beds, in private chests, and in other hiding places. At war's end, most black people were impoverished, but a few freedpeople managed to bring the wealth they had accumulated during slavery with them to the contraband camps. One astounded observer's comments regarding freedpeople in South Carolina around 1862 deserves extended quotation: "Those who were best acquainted with the condition of the freedmen were surprised at the amount of savings brought from their hiding-places by the recent auction sales. The negroes competed with white men almost everywhere, and often successfully, especially for land, horses, and carriages. . . . Still better proofs of prosperity are the plantations and lots of land bought by freedmen at the regular auction sales—in most cases bought by combination, and held in undivided shares."[25]

As the observer notes, the money that blacks used typically represented pooled resources. This collective savings strategy was not new. Free and enslaved black communities often pooled resources from overwork, self-hire, and market activities to accumulate, protect, and pass on assets.[26] Blacks also fought to get back the wealth that Union and Confederate soldiers stole and impounded. They sought recompense for livestock, goods, and money through the Southern Claims Commission at the end of the war.[27]

No extant evidence exists, but it is very probable that black women made use of the free labor banks, though in a limited way. Black women should have counted among free labor banks' most active users for three reasons. First, savings banks proved extremely popular among women. The self-made-man mythology that was so popular in the United States during the late nineteenth century obscures the fact that women were the primary depositors in savings banks. Gendered appeals to the virtues of saving and the domestic economy created new categories of savers in women and children despite savings banks' aggressive marketing centered on men's roles as the primary providers. Second, black women earned wages. The army could not spare too many able-bodied men for agricultural work; they served as soldiers and aided army and navy operations on the front lines. Therefore, freedwomen and girls comprised the significant majority of laborers on leased plantations, as in Mississippi and South Carolina, and a near-equal ratio on others, as in Louisiana. They also earned wages from the army, working as nurses and cooks and in other capacities. Third, enterprising women earned money on the side, selling goods and services to soldiers, washing clothes and selling pies and other food and produce.[28]

Black women needed safe places to keep their wages and profits but may have felt uncomfortable placing their hard-won money under the supervision of the very people who demanded that they only earn money from sources and activities that the military approved, arranged, and supervised. These sources and activities paid women below-market wages and sometimes forced them to work under dangerous and trying conditions. Just as reformers' free labor experiments undermined women's economic independence, their banking and savings experiments were met with mixed emotions. Reformers' mangled motives reflected their anxiety that blacks might not ever become economically independent, a concern that often trumped considerations of blacks' civil and economic rights.

Reformers had reason to feel anxious—not because black women were incapable of understanding free labor but because black women workers disrupted the logic undergirding their carefully planned economic experiments. For black women, being free meant acting free, and they asserted their right to be treated fairly and to be paid what they were owed. They resisted being commodified as ticks on a ledger in which only other people profited.[29] For example, black women working on leased plantations made shrewd calculations, not only asserting but affirming their rights and economic importance in the free labor system by openly protesting, slowing down their work, and inspiring others to strike until their demands were met. They also continued to support and invest their money in networks they controlled, especially churches and secret societies.

To be sure, black women did not achieve their expansive definition and vision of freedom. Few received land, and they did not even get the right to vote. However, they stood squarely at the center of the vision that reformers, military officials, politicians, and business-minded men had of the reconstructed fields, factories, and households of the South. Black women's actions changed few official policies, and it was evident that the free market would not create parity between blacks and whites. Black women's resistance did reveal, however, that they would not allow those in charge of these savings and banking experiments to ignore the moral dilemmas that were inherent in their policies. Black women still held on to a part of their freedom dream: economic freedom. At the war's end, reformers and Freedmen's Bureau leaders continued to hold great faith in the possibilities of banks that were set aside for freedpeople.

"NIGGER HAINT GOT NO FRIENDS, NO HOW": THE FREEDMAN'S BANK, 1865–1874

The Freedman's Bank and Trust Company, created by an act of Congress in 1865, represented the culmination of various experiments in which whites managed and directed the wages of freedpeople in the tumultuous era of emancipation. Dormant accounts from free labor savings banks seeded the first Freedman's Bank in New York City in 1865. The Freedman's Bank was the third bank chartered by the federal government after the First and Second Banks of the United States. The initial charter set up a board of all-white trustees to oversee the bank's operations, and it restricted uses of the funds deposited there to relatively safe, government-backed securities; it did not allow investment in speculative ventures. The bank's charter also restricted the eligible depositors so that only "persons heretofore held in slavery in the United States, or their descendants" could open accounts.[30] The Freedman's Bank aggressively solicited black patrons. Frederick Douglass recalled that "circulars, tracts, and other papers [promoting the bank] were scattered like snowflakes in winter by this benevolent institution among the sable millions, and they were told to 'look' to the Freedman's Bank and 'live.'"[31] Despite the language in the charter, the bank welcomed customers regardless of race, though formerly enslaved people made up the vast majority of bank customers.[32]

The Freedman's Bank and Freedmen's Bureau, both approved by Congress on the same day, were separate agencies with different goals and objectives, but they were strongly linked in the minds and lived realities of freedpeople. Dozens of Freedman's Bank branches opened, mostly in the South, and freedpeople expected that the Freedman's Bank, like the Freedmen's Bureau, would help protect their economic rights, though they would be sorely disappointed by both. Many customers—and most of the public, for that matter—believed that the federal government protected and guaranteed deposits, and images of Abraham Lincoln and other Republican leaders adorned bank passbooks, reinforcing the connection between the bank and the government in the minds of most depositors, but the fact is that it did not. In its early years, the bank's all-white trustees restricted investments to conservative products such as government securities, but in 1870, Congress made the fateful decision to allow speculative uses of the freedpeople's deposits.[33]

Mismanagement at every level led to the Freedman's Bank's failure in less than a decade. More than $57 million (about $1.2 billion in 2017 dollars) passed through the bank between 1865 and 1874. Despite the demeaning dialect, the title of a pamphlet that circulated a few years after the Freedman's Bank closed expressed the sentiments of many blacks about not only the Freedman's Bank but also their general experiences with emancipation: "White man bery unsartin. Nigger haint got no friends, no how."[34] In *Freaks of Fortune*, historian Jonathan Levy explores the Freedman's Bank as a laboratory for white philanthropists and financiers who experimented with ways to create black citizens. Bank organizers believed that through saving money, black account holders created social and political identities as free agents within a market economy. How much personal risk people assumed for themselves and their dependents marked their identities as liberal subjects in an industrializing society.

The decidedly masculinist vision of citizenship misses the ways that gender marked not only citizenship but also economic practices. For black women in particular, the Freedman's Bank, like the Freedmen's Fund and free labor banks before it, represented a federal version of racial paternalism and economic exploitation that undermined much of the economic autonomy that free black women had forged in the antebellum and earlier periods and that formerly enslaved women struggled to carve out in the postemancipation South. Levy asserts, "Piddling in their individual amounts, Freedman's Bank deposits, premised upon the Yankee ideals of self-ownership and personal responsibility, created a distinct new form of social dependence residing in the opaque sinews of financial intermediation."[35] Black women might disagree slightly: their deposits expressed rather than created their independence—as citizens and as economic actors. And they used their economic influence to force bureaucrats, reformers, and politicians to reckon with their demands for equal citizenship and economic justice.

The Freedman's Bank represented the apogee of economic and social experiments begun during the war, and it expanded free labor banks on a national scale. Although reformers abandoned the notion of a centralized fund, they still saw themselves as stewards of blacks' economic lives. The bank thus institutionalized a model of white paternalism: the all-white trustee board made decisions about blacks' capacity to make investments, handle credit, and take risks with their money because the trustees decided that blacks could not make such high-level economic decisions. In the early years, trustees policed blacks' use of their funds, not allowing them to borrow money but insisting that they save for large purchases. The trustees also required cashiers and tellers to make inquiries into the reasons that blacks withdrew money and to send reports to headquarters.[36]

Whatever its shortcomings, the national network of thirty-seven Freedman's Bank branches did allow black people unfettered access to bank services and helped increase their financial literacy. However, Freedman's Bank accounts complemented rather than replaced women's networks of collective and individual efforts to control their economic lives. Black women ranked higher among depositors in urban branches. In Richmond, for example, women made up 20 percent of depositors. This figure, however, obscures the actual numbers of women depositors. For example, the biggest institutional account holders were societies: mutual aid, church, workingmen, benevolent, and secret societies, many of which were headed by women or had women as officers. Women also often served on banking committees that managed the societies' accounts. Further, male account holders granted wives and female relatives access to their accounts, and women were often the direct beneficiaries in the event of the depositor's death.[37]

Women could build significant accounts of their own, particularly if they were successful businesswomen, property owners, custodians of the funds of mutual aid societies, or the recipients of deceased veterans' benefits. For instance, Milly Chapman of Yazoo City, Mississippi, saved more than $300 in nearly three years. Widowed with a son, Chapman did well enough as a farmer that by 1871, she listed her employment as "Works for Self."[38] Cassandra McGavock, treasurer of the Ladies Beneficial Society No. 1 in Nashville, had full control of the society's $528 in deposits.[39] However, McGavock's solitary control over the Ladies Beneficial's funds was unusual; most societies authorized withdrawals only under two or three other signatures as added assurance against theft or embezzlement. In bylaws and constitutions, they outlined who had access to the funds, created banking or finance committees, and kept detailed financial records. They generally took careful steps to secure collective resources. Unfortunately, despite the most careful planning, hard-won funds were sometimes lost. Private William Moore listed his mother, Martha Moore, as beneficiary for his Freedman's Bank account, and when he died in 1866, his $270 bounty and unspent wages passed to his mother. However, a Freedmen's Bureau clerk in Richmond wrote to General Oliver O. Howard that he and his staff had made "every effort" to locate Martha Moore but to no avail.[40]

Accounts of more than $100 were the exception rather than the rule.[41] A review of a handful of passbooks from Virginia bank accounts owned by black women reveals that, for many, the amounts of their deposits were very small and inconsistent. For instance, Louisa Wood deposited a grand total of $1.50 in all the years she held her account, Susan Ackes made only four deposits in three years, and Sarah Brickhouse made two deposits in as many years. Frances Carey, however, made a rather large opening deposit of $39.71 in 1867, and her money earned nearly seven dollars of interest in more than two years. Likely encouraged by the rate of growth on her small deposit, Carey made one deposit of $1.50 in 1869 and several more throughout 1870, but then no others in the few years before the bank shuttered its doors in 1874.[42]

These women's small, inconsistent deposits in the Freedman's Bank certainly reflect the difficulties that many women faced in providing for themselves and their families with low wages, but they also reflect black women's economic strategies. These strategies sometimes dovetailed with the Freedman's Bank organizers' goals and other times ran contrary to their vision. For example, Frances Carey, like other depositors, may have seen it as an effective savings strategy to accumulate interest rather than make consistent deposits. Historian Marcus Allen observes that free and enslaved blacks in Baltimore took advantage of banks' interest policies to mitigate unstable job markets and unpredictable fluctuations in rates for other types of financial investments. Framers had developed the Freedman's Bank's liberal interest policy to encourage consistent deposits, which they saw as the best path to security. This policy was especially effective in the early years of the bank, when it maintained conservative assets that increased in value steadily rather than dramatically. The consistent interest income worked to the advantage of small depositors who chose to keep small amounts on deposit for extended periods.[43]

The small deposits also reveal other savings strategies. Though their organizers considered banks to be the ultimate security for formerly enslaved people's money, blacks continued to rely on their own institutions for certain savings goals. They insisted on saving money in societies to meet their critical needs, making small payments in mutual aid, secret, and benefit societies. Their investments of a few cents up to a few dollars each month to one or various societies ensured adequate burial and some financial assistance if they were hurt at work or suffering from an illness. Self-confident bank organizers and reformers would have argued that banks better served these needs. Blacks, however, rejected the emphasis on individualistic accumulation that was promoted by the Freedman's Bank. More important, investment in societies represented an investment in institutions that black people controlled. Particularly for women, these societies represented extensions of societies that they had built and nurtured during slavery, and they would prove to be critical institutions for promoting their own vision of economic security and freedom during and after Reconstruction.[44]

Spending money rather than saving it was another way to build—and to share—wealth. While philanthropists and politicians saw savings as the way forward for black men and women, blacks had their own ideas about how to best use their money. In the bank's early years, trustees required local tellers to ask customers the purpose for withdrawing money; the tellers sent reports to the central bank in New York and then, when it was relocated, to Washington, D.C. Such questions infringed on customers' privacy, and some customers probably told the tellers what they thought the tellers wanted to hear. Nonetheless, the surveys and contemporary observations provide some idea of how black depositors used and planned to use their money. They paid off debts and sent money around the country to help relatives. They withdrew money to pay expenses related to farming the land, such as buying seed, tools, and livestock. They also bought land. While land ownership was not a goal that was promoted for women, by pooling together resources in the bank and other places, women were able to participate in collectively investing in land for their families. Black depositors also engaged in activities that the trustees considered to be risky uses of funds, such as speculating and opening businesses.[45]

Women's small deposits may also reflect impediments that discouraged women's active participation as bank customers. Freedman's Bank officials aggressively targeted black men, stressing men's roles as the primary providers and protectors of vulnerable women and children. Banks sought to serve a civilizing role by promoting male breadwinners as the legitimate heads of household. Bank accounts, officials argued, allowed men to support families and become responsible taxpayers and, through careful management, property holders. The market-oriented male-breadwinning head-of-household model embraced an idealized white bourgeois standard that not only delegitimized the relative equity that existed between black men and women in families, forged in large part from the conditions of slavery, but also created economic and status distinctions that obscured black women's critical financial roles in black families.[46]

Such masculinist sentiments ramped up as the bank limped on in the year or so before it finally collapsed in 1874. Trustees appointed Frederick Douglass president of the faltering bank after the panic of 1873. They also added a number of black trustees and local board members to shore up support for the bank in its waning months. In an almost-unanimous chorus, black bank leaders and other enthusiastic bank supporters stressed that saving had only been the first step for the determined black man. As one African Methodist Episcopal minister opined, enterprise was the manly extension of savings to "demonstrate with equal success that we can employ a share of the Capital saved in business enterprises, commercial, manufacturing etc. and so multiply manyfold [*sic*] the accumulating power of our saved capital."[47] On one hand, these sentiments acknowledged thrift as a racial marker of black men's capacity for citizenship. On the other hand, the same sentiments underlined the limitations of savings in gendered terms. The ability to make decisions about the kinds of risks to take with money elevated a mere deposit to the realm of capital. It alternately expressed and proved black men's manhood and essential equality with white men.

On June 29, 1874, the Freedman's Bank closed its doors, undone by unscrupulous speculation among its trustees and politicians—much of it orchestrated by Jay and Henry Cooke. Henry used his connections within the Republican Party machine in Washington to help convince legislators to change the Freedman's Bank charter. In 1870, Congress changed the investment strategy of the bank from its conservative reliance on government-backed securities to aggressive speculation in railroads, real estate, and other private securities. Henry Cooke and the trustees shepherded much of the freedpeople's money to the Jay Cooke & Company brokerage firm, using the justification that they could earn greater returns on investment and pass on the profits to black depositors. The change in those few lines in the charter exposed the millions of dollars of blacks' deposits to incredible risk. The firm's and trustees' speculation in railroads, property, and other assets failed to produce expected returns. Their investments hemorrhaged money and quickly lost value. The panic of 1873 further crippled the bank. By the time the Office of the Comptroller of the Currency inspected the Freedman's Bank, it was teetering perilously close to failure. The inspection made public the bank leaders' abuse and mismanagement but not in time to save it.[48]

In response to public outcry, Congress set up a system to refund a percentage of the Freedman's Bank accounts. Congress authorized five disbursements that amounted—at least in official reports—to refunds of nearly two-thirds (62 percent) of the millions lost when the bank closed. When the bank shut its doors in 1874, 16,131 depositors lost $2.9 million, which was the amount on the books but not necessarily in its coffers. The government sold real estate, called loans due, and sold the bank's holdings—many for mere cents on the dollar—to recover money to pay refunds. The government declared the first refund of 20 percent in 1876 and the last refund in 1883, it but continued to authorize refunds until 1914.

While the Cooke brothers and others may have, as Jonathan Levy argues, "dragged the freedpeople headlong into the Gilded Age," blacks did not remain silent or helpless.[49] Whites did exert pervasive social power over blacks' economic choices, but that power was not absolute. The limits to it are revealed by blacks' resistance. Far into the twentieth century, blacks bitterly complained about unpaid or incomplete refunds. Congressional reports claim that the commissioner issued $1.7 million in refunds, but other sources cast doubt on that figure. After all, the government spent a few hundred thousand dollars of blacks' deposits to pay the salaries and expenses of commissioners, clerks, lawyers, and others working on behalf of the government. Most important, the voices of thousands of account holders and their descendants assert that they never received adequate compensation—and in some cases no compensation at all. Letters to the Freedman's Bank commissioners highlight blacks' political agency in their claims for economic justice, and black women's voices were some of the most insistent.

"ANSER AT ONCE": DEMANDS FOR ECONOMIC JUSTICE FROM THE FREEDMAN'S BANK, 1874–1900

Matilda Scott's letter to Commissioner Williams closes with the demand, "anser at once"; she demanded that he not only address her request for information but also take action regarding her mother's small bank refund. Like thousands of others, Scott's encounter with the federal government began with a claim for lost funds. To make a claim, an individual account holder mailed the passbook to the commissioners. If the account holder was deceased, designated heirs or the closest living relative could send in the original passbook. The commissioners' staff then verified the final balance in the account and sent the approved refund, usually 10 percent of the balance in the account. In practice, however, the process was hardly so straightforward.[50]

For one thing, account holders had trouble locating old passbooks; some had been destroyed by fires and other calamities. For instance, Lucy Seymour implored Commissioner John Knox for help in getting her relative's refund, and relatives of Beverly Diggs provided legal evidence of Diggs's identity because both women's passbooks had been lost in fires. People moved around and lost their passbooks, and account holders or their heirs sometimes gave their passbooks to others for safekeeping but could no longer locate the caretakers.[51]

Even when heirs located the caretakers, they sometimes faced serious impediments to obtaining the passbooks. Pauline Garland took precautions to safeguard her passbook, depositing it at the National Exchange Bank of Lynchburg, Mississippi. When she was alive, Garland told her son Frank Green that she had deposited a few hundred dollars in her account, but when her son made a claim, the commissioners only sent a refund of $15.79. Green insisted that there had to be more but could not prove it without Garland's passbook, so he went to National Exchange Bank for help with his claim. Employees admitted that the bank had lost Garland's passbook. Letters from the bank's bookkeeper and an employee to the commissioners in 1882 verified Green's claim: "old woman Pauline Garland" had deposited between $200 and $300 dollars in her Freedman's Bank account.[52] The bank employees had been kind in using Garland's last name; even well-meaning bank employees often disparaged black women account holders by calling them "Auntie" or refusing the honorifics of "Miss" or "Mrs." Other bank employees impugned the character of account holders and refused to help claimants, telling investigators that they believed the account holders were "ignorant" and intent on defrauding the commissioners.[53]

It was also no simple matter proving heirship by either blood or marriage. Few people had birth records, and many of those who had been born enslaved did not know their own or their loved ones' dates of birth. Many had been sold away so that it was sometimes extremely difficult to prove marriages and family relationships in ways that satisfied the formal requirements of bureaucrats. Thus, heirs could not easily prove their relationships to the deceased or lost account holder. Even when account holders went through the trouble to produce valid documentation, they met challenges. Solomon Howard had a neighbor draw up a will designating that his wife would inherit all his effects, and she presented the will to claim the $7.78 refund, but a clerk wrote to the commissioners questioning whether the will was a legally binding document. It is not known whether the person who drew up the will had much legal experience or even whether Howard's husband had actually directed the creation of a will, but absent any other claims, Mrs. Howard would have been considered the obvious beneficiary of her husband's account. Bank employees who considered themselves de facto agents of the Freedman's Bank Commission and who invested themselves with enormous powers to police blacks seeking refunds created serious impediments to blacks' ability to recoup their refunds if the employees mishandled documents or cast doubt on their veracity.[54]

The commissioner's office sometimes failed to respond even to legitimate claimants and heirs. Lucy Houston of Savannah sought help claiming her cousin Eliza Talbot's deposits and enlisted notary public John H. Deveaux, a man of high standing in Savannah's black community. Deveaux helped Houston prepare an affidavit and submitted a claim on her behalf, but unfortunately for Houston, two men claiming to be Talbot's half-brothers also claimed the money. Deveaux wrote to the commissioner, stating that Houston was a woman of impeachable moral character and that she would not say she was Talbot's closest legal heir unless it was true. A federal employee returned the passbook and suggested that Houston pursue other legal means to establish the legitimacy of her claim to the $2.83 refund. Deveaux appealed to the commissioners' pragmatism and sympathies, suggesting that they issue a check payable to "Lucy Houston in trust" that would cover any other heirs so that the family could at least have what little Talbot left. "Unless you can do this," he insisted, "it will probably end the case forever."[55] Faced with the expensive and lengthy legal recourse of establishing heirship, Houston probably had little choice but to allow the matter to die.[56]

The seriousness with which Freedman's Bank commissioners insisted on establishing the identities of account holders and their beneficiaries posed hardships on account holders and their heirs. Many must surely have wondered whether the bank's closure might have been avoided if the bank had been as fastidious in its dispersal of funds to white speculators as it was with claimants' refunds. Those who still had their passbooks had to pay postage to send them to Washington, and they had to pay for legal documents such as affidavits and for notaries' services to verify their identities. The expenses to establish heirship often outstripped the anticipated refunds.

One positive benefit of the claims process was that many black women were able to establish their legal identities, creating legal paperwork that they could use for other claims for benefits, such as widows' pensions, burial benefits, and life insurance. The legal documents and testimonies that women gathered and the skills they developed mutually reinforced collective and individual demands for control over the black wealth that was held in trust by the federal government. Petitioners seeking refunds of Freedman's Bank deposits are linked with movements for reparative justice that included fights for Civil War widows' pensions and recompense for wealth that was appropriated from enslaved labor.[57]

If an heir was fortunate enough to receive a refund check, she sometimes still had difficulty accessing the funds. In August 1884, Lucy Barber presented her refund check to a bank in Winchester, Virginia, and bank clerk Joseph Jackson refused to cash it. This was a new check replacing one issued previously to Kate Barber, Lucy's deceased sister and owner of the account. Although another clerk at the bank had helped Lucy Barber secure a new check made payable in her own name, Jackson demanded that she also present a power of attorney. Barber had reason to feel confused and angry: confused because her sister Kate had formally named her the heir years before and angry that this new clerk refused to honor her request after she had gone through considerable trouble, including getting an affidavit and making multiple visits to the bank, to prove her right to recover her sister's $8.27 deposit.[58]

Given the administrative hurdles presented by federal bureaucrats and local bank employees, many claimants enlisted the assistance of attorneys and claims agents to help them recover their money, which created a veritable industry around helping depositors and their heirs make claims. It also represented another level of exploitation and extraction. A claims agent could handle one or several individuals' claims. Richmond claims agent Charles Spencer sent the commissioners six passbooks, asking rather cavalierly that they send "whatever dividends may be due."[59] One firm, Lehman and Hartigan, Commission Merchants and Commercial Brokers of Vicksburg, Mississippi, presented an astounding sixty passbooks for refund. Other attorneys and claims agents may have sold these books to Charles Lehman and John Hartigan for a fraction of what the two lawyers hoped to make by collecting commissions on the refunds or on the refunds themselves. The large number of passbooks presented at one time was unusual enough to prompt one commissioner to ask Mississippi representative James Chalmers whether the firm warranted further investigation into whether it was legitimately collecting on behalf of its sixty clients. The sixty accounts represented a total of $4,192 in deposits, with most of the accounts holding less than fifty dollars, about ten holding between fifty and one hundred dollars, and six holding more than one hundred dollars. The smallest account held $0.68 and the largest $758.13. Half the passbooks belonged to women.[60]

Some claims attorneys assisted clients in exchange for a percentage of the amount recovered. Others drew up necessary legal papers, like heirship affidavits and powers of attorney, for a straight fee. Many attorneys failed to follow up with clients and may have even stolen their money. Harriett Mitchell and her husband hired a lawyer in Greenville, Mississippi, to help secure their refund, but she heard nothing from the lawyer, nor did he return the Mitchells' passbook. While waiting for action on their claim, Mitchell's husband passed away, and perhaps without funds to hire a new lawyer or convinced of the futility of relying on legal help, she wrote to the commissioners directly for help in securing her refund.[61]

The claims industry, as one can imagine, was ripe for abuse. Claims agents did help secure refunds but often on onerous terms: sometimes charging as much as half the amount refunded. Some agents speculated in passbooks, buying them for ten cents on the dollar and then collecting the full refunds from the federal government.[62] A clerk at a local bank in New Orleans, outraged with the fleecing of black claimants, begged the commissioners to arrest unscrupulous claims agents and force them to give back account holders' money and passbooks.[63]

One white claims agent proved to be quite unscrupulous. In the spring of 1875, John Baird traveled around Vicksburg offering to help recover refunds and worked on behalf of Hart Naylor and Jefferson Warren, who felt they needed help to get the $1,000 they had each lost when the bank closed. Baird did what he promised; the commissioner issued each man a check for $200, representing the first 20 percent refund. Baird, however, forged the names of the two men, neither of whom could read or write, and cashed the $400 himself. The men tracked Baird down and took him back to First National Bank, the local bank on which the checks were drawn. In the presence of the town's mayor, who also happened to be president of First National, Naylor and Warren exacted a promise from Baird to return their money. When the men demanded that Baird return their passbooks, he told them he did not have the them but that an attorney in Memphis held them. This statement was actually true; Baird worked as a clerk in the law office of Gilbert Moyers, who had a reputation for swindling clients out of federal benefits. Naylor and Warren received only partial justice: they secured new attorneys who were able to retrieve their passbooks but not their stolen refunds.[64]

It is important to remember that a single name on an account may have represented many others. Among freedpeople, bank accounts were not individual but shared, representing collective possessions, efforts, and rights, much like the franchise was shared. That is, women and even children debated issues and discussed candidates, and when men cast their ballots, they cast them not only for themselves but in the interests of women in their immediate and extended families. Similarly, the labor contracts that Union officers and Freedmen's Bureau agents demanded of freedpeople—more accurately, demanded of freed*men* for their entire household—rendered labor and wages that were really mutual household efforts to seem individualistic. Naylor's name was on the account, but the $1,000 may have been the combined funds of his immediate family: his wife, Nancy Ann, and their five children. Or it may have included his extended family, whose names he also listed in his passbook. In 1873, Naylor, Warren, and their families lived on plantations in Warren County. They may have still lived and worked the land on which they had been enslaved. The collective funds represented freedom in many ways: the freedom to buy and farm their own land, even to leave Mississippi if they chose. The loss of their funds in the Freedman's Bank debacle, then, had wider repercussions for families seeking to extricate themselves from the stranglehold of crop liens, peonage, and other exploitative forms of credit and financial relationships that returned many blacks to conditions of quasi-slavery in the late nineteenth century.[65]

Black claims agents could be just as unscrupulous. James Hancock and his live-in partner, Louisiana Cabell, ran a small claims office in Lynchburg, Virginia, that charged clients a 50 percent commission. At least one client, Madison Frazier, complained to the commissioner that Hancock had stolen his entire dividend check of $13.26. A federal investigator dispatched by the commissioner's office acknowledged a string of clients whom Hancock and Cabell had defrauded but concluded that it was doubtful whether any charges that would stick could be made against the pair in court.[66]

One reason for the investigator's doubt lay in the poor likelihood of assembling a jury of the claimants' peers; despite federal laws that reiterated their civil rights, blacks were seldom allowed to sit on juries. The investigator held little faith that a jury of white citizens would care much for what they judged to be the trivial claims of Negroes. The investigator himself, though, also threw derision and suspicion on the motives and legitimacy of the offended parties' claims. In one instance, his suspicions bore fruit. Under the investigator's examination, for example, Frazier, the original complainant, admitted that Hancock had paid him six dollars in cash, but Frazier denied making his mark on the check or going to the bank to cash it. From what might have proven to be an isolated or infrequent occurrence, the investigator determined that most of the defrauded claimants had either colluded with Cabell and Hancock to somehow defraud the federal government or were stupid enough to rely on the couple in the first place and hence deserved their fate. The investigator noted in his official record that Louisiana Cabell was a woman of low morals. His attitude epitomized that of people in some quarters who empathized with the losses of "these poor colored people" but also blamed them as culpable and therefore undeserving of further recompense. In addition, for the investigator, an indictment of black women's morality further legitimated the unsavory and fraudulent status of black claimants in general.[67]

Another black claims agent named Louis Carter, an attorney in New Orleans, defrauded at least three freedpeople out of their refunds. He was arrested and charged with five counts of forgery and two of embezzlement. Witnesses reported that they had seen Carter offer passbooks as collateral for loans and had heard him admit that he had cashed other people's refund checks. Carter would present the endorsed checks to local bank tellers, claiming the payees had made their mark in the presence of witnesses, but in actuality, Carter forged both the clients' marks and the witnesses' signatures. He raised considerable suspicion among bank employees in 1882 when he presented a bill for five dollars along with Louisa Smith's endorsed refund check in exactly the same amount. Smith had, unknown to Carter, passed away seven years prior. Disreputable attorneys and claims agents made a business of traveling to freedpeople's towns and plantations and rounding up their books with promises to help them secure refunds. They trafficked in stolen dreams.[68]

The Freedman's Bank failed because of real estate and stock market speculation and corruption among trustees and officers—people in the highest echelons of the bank's leadership. Local citizens and bank employees, however, could put them to shame in many respects. Some bank employees used their local branches as personal piggy banks for themselves and their associates. An examiner reviewing the accounts of the Lynchburg, Virginia, branch in the final months leading up to the Freedman's Bank closure felt at a loss to express adequately "what neglect and confusion" he found in the branch's records. Among one of the most egregious cases of financial mismanagement involved the bank's cashier, W. F. Bronaugh. In what must have been an exasperated tone, national bank examiner Anson Sperry pondered, "What shall I say about Bronaugh?" Not only were the cashier's records incomplete and his office messy and disorderly, he was also deeply in debt and had used the bank's funds to pay his personal bills, including doctor bills and household expenses. Nor was he above taking a dollar or two from the cash drawer to buy "petty purchases" like lunch or tobacco.[69]

One cannot help but wonder whether Bronaugh ever lifted a dollar or two from Sophia Johnson's small deposits. Johnson, who lived in Yazoo City, Mississippi, a small town fifty miles upriver from Vicksburg, dictated a letter to Albert T. Morgan, Yazoo City's carpetbagger sheriff, for the bank commissioners.[70] In her letter on the sheriff's office letterhead, Johnson stressed that she did "not wish to annoy or harass" Freedman's Bank commissioner Robert Leipold, then she proceeded to do both. She stressed her right as a widow to information about her deposits and insisted that is was "an act of simple justice" that he answer her questions about how much the government owed her.[71] Not relying on the commissioner's moral sensibilities, she shrewdly capitalized on her relationship to a powerful local white man to help make a plea on her behalf, which she clearly calculated might be more effective than a letter in her own hand. The widow Johnson's demands for her refund echoed other appeals to federal agencies for other forms of assistance, particularly Civil War widows' pensions.

The economic experiments of the mid- to late nineteenth century failed many black women and their families. The experiments signified a belief that black women's proper place lay in others' fields, kitchens, and factories. Reformers accepted as gospel beliefs that black women had to work but that they would not do so willingly. Labor contracts, for example, ensured that women would earn money to save but also assumed that black women responded best to strict supervision and, in some instances, coercion. Emancipation-era economic experiments assumed that they were incapable of directing their wages on their own. Whatever wages women earned needed administration, a responsibility that fell variously on military officials, philanthropists, and the federal government. These reformers and their experiments placed black women in a tight gender bind. They elevated the liberal ideal of a male breadwinner and protector even as they actively destabilized black families by ignoring the actual circumstances, realities, and preferences of black women. They cared very little about what black women truly wanted: autonomy and control over their lives.

The Freedmen's Funds reinforced in the minds of military and aid society officials whites' paternalistic role as judge and jury regarding freedpeople's economic futures. The handful of banks created exclusively for free laborers and black soldiers responded in some ways to blacks' demands for control over their money. Created specifically for male workers and soldiers, they foreshadowed the continued veneration of the male head-of-household and breadwinner role in black families. The Freedman's Bank built on these economic experiments. Despite some limitations placed on depositors, black account holders capitalized on financial literacy skills that they had gained under enslavement and through these postbellum economic experiments. Blacks also developed and practiced their own individual and collective wealth-building strategies within and sometimes in contradiction to reformers' narrowed possibilities. The bank's failure highlighted the deception and corruption behind the bank's organizers' and leaders' high-minded rhetoric. Black women used various strategies to secure refunds, writing letters directly to the Freedman's Bank commissioners, hiring lawyers, engaging the services of claims agents, and enlisting help from people in their communities.

It is not known whether Matilda Scott, the insistent daughter of a formerly enslaved woman mentioned at the beginning of this chapter, ever received her mother's eighteen dollars. Indeed, it is not always clear from the extant sources whether claimants were successful in getting any part of their money back, but the women who used and made demands on the Freedman's Bank reveal how black women's elaborated political sensibilities sometimes forced the hands of state actors—even if the women failed to achieve restitution. In the decades after the bank closed, heirs and beneficiaries refused to allow the matter to rest. The fight for bank refunds existed alongside other demands for economic justice that reached into the early twentieth century, including Civil War widows' and ex-slaves' pensions, washerwomen's strikes, and streetcar boycotts. Black women's insistent claims for economic independence fulfilled bureaucrats', reformers', and philanthropists' desires that black women be financially self-sufficient and prudent with money but troubled their expectations that these same women remain compliant, meek, and dependent.

2

"Who Is So Helpless as the Negro Woman?"

THE INDEPENDENT ORDER OF ST. LUKE AND THE QUEST FOR ECONOMIC SECURITY, 1856–1902

Everyone will see. Everyone will know. Lizzie Draper could no longer hide the dark-brown belly growing under her skirts. Only fourteen years old, she had not understood when the Irish Confederate soldier who was boarding with her mistress had forced himself inside her, but she understood now that she was pregnant, that a life was growing inside her. Her thoughts turned to her own mother. She did not know her mother's name. Had she ever known it? Had she forgotten it? She shook her head at the last thought, not wanting to believe that she could ever have let it slip from her memory. Now she wrung her mind for any recollection, any scrap of memory, hoping that the woman whose name she did not know might show her what to do now. Had her mother tried to hide her, too, knowing the kind of life that lay ahead for her daughter? Had she chosen to love her daughter, or had she kept her distance, knowing that either of them might be sold away from the other at a moment's notice? Lizzie's mistress, Elizabeth Van Lew, was kind enough, but an enslaved woman could never know what a white slaveholder might do.

Lizzie's worlds—inside and out—had been turned upside down. It was a difficult, hard time in Richmond that summer of 1864. The dead haunted the city; soldiers' bodies lay in rough-hewn coffins that lined the streets.

White women begged on nearly every corner for a peck of meal. Miss Van Lew had money—she was one of the richest women in the city—but Lizzie wondered how long it could last when a barrel of meal sold for more than $200. Perhaps Miss Van Lew would sell Lizzie or her baby. Lizzie had little choice, no choice at all, really. She gave birth on July 15, 1864, to a little girl the color of curdled milk. She called her Maggie Lena, named for a woman she had heard some call a prostitute, but Lizzie knew she walked with Jesus. Everyone would see. Everyone would know.

Everyone will see. Everyone will know. William M. T. Forrester had gotten used to lying on the tattered, rolled up linen flag, with its thirty-three fading white stars, but he could never shake the fear that someone might find it. Some of his neighbors grudgingly accepted the presence of a colored family in the affluent Shockoe Hill section of Richmond, only a block from the Confederate capitol, but what would people do if they knew about the U.S. flag? It had been three years since his brother Richard, working as a page at the Virginia Capitol, had picked the flag out of a pile of rubble that the Confederates planned to burn after they hoisted their own flag and transformed the capitol from the symbolic to the actual headquarters of the Confederacy. In the heady excitement of May 1861, the men celebrating what they felt would be a short assertion of southern honor and way of life did not pay much attention to a thirteen-year-old colored boy running in the crowd. Richard had hidden the flag under the bed he shared with his two brothers. Now, on April 3, 1865, almost four years later, William watched Richmond burn. He worried that the flag, even more than the city, might be destroyed, too.

Thankfully, the Forresters' home escaped damage. The city quickly recovered—physically, at least, if not psychologically—from its traumatic losses: the fire, the war, slavery. William had always been free and had lived a relatively privileged life as the grandson of an enslaved cook and a Jewish lawyer in Richmond on his father's side and a free woman of color and a wealthy Jewish merchant in New Orleans on his mother's. His Jewish family in Richmond had accepted his parents as part of their family and had left his parents a home and some money. At the war's end, however, people who had been both free and enslaved now sought refuge and opportunity in whatever quarter they could. The Freedmen's Bureau represented one refuge. Richard carefully gathered up the flag, hidden away for four years, and took it to the Freedmen's Union Industrial School, which his sister attended. The women there, those formerly enslaved and those who had always been free, cried and sung and clapped their hands at the sight of the worn flag. They hung it on the wall of the school so that they could see it every day of their new free lives. Everyone would see. Everyone would know.[1]

The fates of Elizabeth Draper, an illiterate, formerly enslaved woman, and Richard and William Forrester, educated, privileged men of Richmond's colored elite, might never have converged if not for the Independent Order of St. Luke (IOSL), a secret society that the former joined for a measure of security and the latter for a taste of power. Their lives would entwine through Draper's daughter, Maggie Lena Draper Mitchell Walker, who devoted more than fifty years of her life to the IOSL. Walker's life and service in the IOSL reflect the challenges and opportunities that freedom presented to the first generations of African Americans born in freedom. She lived a life of both poverty and privilege, which shaped her vision of economic security and development for African American women in particular and for African Americans in general. Walker would come to wield incredible economic, social, and cultural power within Richmond's black community and beyond.

In 1901, as the new grand secretary of the IOSL, Maggie Lena Walker wondered aloud to an audience of several hundred IOSL delegates, "Who is so helpless as the Negro woman? Who is so circumscribed and hemmed in, in the race of life, in the struggle for bread, meat, and clothing as the Negro woman?" She had saved the IOSL from near collapse only a few years before, and she saw the so-called helpless Negro woman as the key to the IOSL's future strength and prosperity. She saw them as "so many good women, willing women, noble women, *whose money is here*."[2] The IOSL would turn that money into capital, collecting and mobilizing it to create businesses and jobs. Walker envisioned the IOSL as a financial institution, not merely a social one. Buildings and halls were the showplaces of a fraternal order's popularity and strength, but alongside manufacturing and industrial concerns, banks, stores, and other businesses, they represented important investments in black communities.

This chapter explores the development of the Independent Order of St. Luke and its efforts to provide economic security for black women and their families. Fraternal societies like the IOSL brought workers and capitalists into relationships in unexpected ways. The IOSL turned workers' small savings and investments into capital, creating businesses that offered services, created jobs, and provided security for working people. It also revealed the important roles that gender and race played in shaping broader economic processes and practices by creating and maintaining important financial institutions: a bank and an insurance company. In the decades after emancipation, however, the IOSL's success was hardly a foregone conclusion. It struggled to create viable and affordable long-term financial products in which black communities were willing to trust and invest. As major stakeholders in their communities and institutions, black women struggled against conflicting narratives of their dependency and inadequacy, narratives that undermined the financial autonomy they struggled to carve out in the mid-nineteenth and early twentieth century.

"LIKE DOVES TO THEIR WINDOWS": THE BIRTH OF THE GRAND UNITED ORDER OF ST. LUKE, 1856–1869

Mary Ann Prout (see fig. 2.1) organized the St. Luke Society, a mutual benefit society that provided modest sickness and death benefits for women and children, in 1856. The group met in her beloved Bethel African Methodist Episcopal (AME) Church in Baltimore.[3] Prout had joined Bethel before the church was formally organized, when black Methodists knew the congregation as the Bethel Free African Society.[4] When the church formally organized in April 1816, Bethel AME grew into the largest church in Baltimore and the second-largest AME church in the country. In a sermon calling for the congregation's formal incorporation, Rev. Daniel Coker declared, "We shall see our brethren come flocking to us like doves to their windows. And we as a band of brethren, shall sit down under our own vine to worship, and none to make us afraid."[5] Prout, who remained an active and devoted member her entire life, used the church as a platform and the St. Luke Society as a tool to open up opportunities for black women.[6]

Prout had been born a free woman in South River, Maryland, on February 14, 1800 or 1801, and her family moved to Baltimore when she was a small child.[7] As a young woman, Prout and her family were actively involved in

FIGURE 2.1 Mary Ann Prout, date unknown.
Source: 99-0228.02, courtesy of National Park Service, Maggie L. Walker National Historic Site.

the Liberian emigration movement. Though Prout's brothers, William and Jacob, emigrated to Liberia and became prominent leaders there, Prout remained in Baltimore. Although she embodied many of the ideas that emigration supporters promoted regarding black political and economic independence, she felt that blacks could achieve significant change at home in the United States. Prout and other members of Bethel melded religious zeal with public service, social activism, and economic development. Her experiences as a free black woman in the Upper South undergirded her commitment to providing services and institutions for black women and families. The St. Luke Society and other self-help societies like it reflect her need to protect her freedom and to provide for the material needs of black communities.[8]

When Prout formed the St. Luke Society in the mid-1850s, she was breaking the law: Baltimore's laws forbade free blacks from organizing any type of secret society. The law reflected whites' fears of slave rebellion, but they also revealed their efforts to undermine black self-help efforts. The city made an exception for charitable societies, but even then, city officials placed burdensome restrictions on such societies. They allowed only blacks whom the officials judged to be of good character to form a society, and then those blacks had to pay a five-dollar tax, procure written permission from the mayor, and allow police access to their meetings. Because it was ensconced within the church, the society was able to flout the ordinance, escape white surveillance, and protect its members from state intimidation. By the early 1850s, Bethel AME was the largest black church in Baltimore, a city with the largest free black population in the country. The St. Luke Society, then, was likely among the city's largest, most active, and important societies providing a measure of economic security to black women and their families.[9]

Prout imagined St. Luke as an organization created by women for women.[10] From the beginning, the order challenged many of the gender expectations of the times, though Prout would have believed that her work reflected the power of women's traditional feminine influence in the home and society. Like other AME women, Prout did not openly question women's exclusion from the pulpit and formal church leadership. Instead, she and others focused on building religious and social organizations with strong moral foundations to serve fellow congregants and their communities. They operated within the church's imprimatur but not necessarily under its strictures. As head of the St. Luke Society, Prout led prayer meetings and held funeral processions for deceased children who had been members of the order, sometimes conducting graveside services in the absence of a male pastor or elder. She justified and perhaps even had to defend her right to do so. In 1830, she had opened a day school on Rubourgh Street, which operated until 1867, when the city established public schools. After the school closed, Prout helped open the Gregory Aged Women's Home, "a Widow's Home, for aged and infirm old women."[11] Her administrative, fundraising, and ecclesiastical work under the auspices of St. Luke implicitly challenged notions that women were not equipped to lead. In this way, women leveraged their essential roles in the church's growth and success to press for their ad hoc inclusion in influential positions so they could sustain important community outreach missions and services, especially for the most vulnerable. Rather than argue that women should be in such roles, she merely posed the question: If not wives and mothers, who else was better equipped to care for widows and orphans?[12]

Prout herself contravened gender norms. She never married or had children. "Private" and "public" could be arbitrary distinctions in nineteenth-century society, but they nonetheless possessed the power to shape expectations and place limits on women's participation in public life. Because Prout devoted considerable resources and attention to issues such as the education of children and the care of the elderly, she fulfilled expected gender norms in which women in an industrializing society were expected to temper the harsher edges of capitalism. She, like so many other antebellum reformers, practiced a public-oriented domesticity to create and sustain women-centered institutions. Yet she also demonstrated a capacity for the ambitious, producerist, and self-interested orientation—typically ascribed to the male body—that was increasingly valued in capitalist society. In most cultural ledgers of the period, she is illegible: reading as neither wife nor mother, cultured nor erudite. In the early-postbellum Upper South, where traditional notions were being disrupted and remade, where family and work were being transformed, and where black women challenged who held what rights and on what terms, Prout was both unique and well suited to the times.[13]

It certainly took more than virtue to make the St. Luke Society effective; it took money. Teaching children, preparing food, and providing nursing care required constant funds. Women in church societies and other groups around the country raised significant funds to run schools, purchase supplies for the needy and sick, and build and maintain orphanages, hospitals, and elderly homes. More than merely philanthropic enterprises, these efforts were entrepreneurial. Prout set a standard and example for other women in the St. Luke Society through not only her leadership but also her fundraising. In addition to the small amounts she raised from selling cakes and preserves, she was able to raise tens of thousands of dollars through fairs and festivals that attracted thousands of attendees and lasted several days. She also planned excursions and was not averse to walking door to door in Baltimore neighborhoods asking for donations.[14]

While fundraising events and donations were important sources of funding, the critical role of members' small, consistent financial pledges cannot be overstated. For example, members of societies like the African Female Union and the Sisters of Dorcas paid twelve cents per month to support their societies' activities. As examples of women's informal investment and saving, these small, regular donations underscore the critical strategies and activities that encouraged participation, maintained members' commitment to the societies' goals and activities, and ensured a steady stream of funding and support.[15]

The services offered by societies like the St. Luke could not have come at a more important time. As the Civil War ravaged the country, Bethel AME in Baltimore continued to play a role in the struggle for freedom in the Upper South. Lying at the crossroads of the free North, the slave South, and the nation's capital, Baltimore had been a hotbed of abolitionist sentiment. Bethel, particularly under the leadership of popular but controversial pastor Daniel Coker, had hosted and raised money for abolitionists, and its members had assisted fugitives in the Underground Railroad. During the war, Baltimore drew tens of thousands of self-emancipated and displaced blacks, many making their way to the District of Columbia, Virginia, or other parts of Maryland.[16]

A significant proportion of the migrants included thousands of women, many of whom were war widows, and children. They certainly needed every kind of assistance imaginable—from basics like food, clothing, and shelter to more ambitious services like education and jobs. The Freedmen's Bureau, white-led charitable associations, northern and southern plantation lessees, and industrialists tended to shuttle black women back into the same kind of work they had typically performed as slaves. In cities and towns, women worked as low-paid laundresses, cooks, and domestic help and also provided other kinds of unskilled labor, such as working in local canneries and other industries. In rural areas, black women and children worked on abandoned plantations. What the sting of the lash could not accomplish in keeping them productive and bound to the land, exploitative sharecropping contracts and coercive apprenticeship arrangements tried to achieve.[17]

It was not only in fields and factories, however, but also in whites' homes that black women resisted exploitative, low-paying contracts; separation from their families and communities; physical violence at the hands of employer-mistresses; and sexual harassment from men connected to those households. They relied on their marriages, families, and institutions to truly transform their labor. Given such circumstances, Prout understood that she needed to do even more to meet the growing challenges facing black women and families. In 1867, the elderly Prout formally organized the Grand United Order of St. Luke (GUOSL), establishing it as a free-standing organization.[18]

Prout's decision to move St. Luke out of the church was a response to the complex realities of life in the postemancipation Upper South and larger changes in the U.S. economy and labor. The exigencies of war served as one powerful motivator: veterans and families displaced by the war needed health and other financial benefits, and Prout could not ignore this potential market. Other societies certainly did not; scores of them organized and formally incorporated in Baltimore in the mid-1860s, no longer constrained by antebellum ordinances outlawing black secret societies. To remain competitive and useful, the GUOSL created a more formal structure that allowed for the creation of branches beyond the church and beyond Baltimore.

Economic change provided another motivation for enlarging Prout's vision. As an industrialized port city, postemancipation Baltimore represented a complex and uneasy amalgam of modernizing industry and traditional prejudices against black striving. On one hand, the city represented promise for enterprising and hardworking blacks who were attracted to opportunities in skilled trades that were dependent on shipping and construction and in low-skill and unskilled work in manufacturing, canning, and other industries. On the other hand, long-standing problems of discrimination and conflicts with white, Irish, German, and other ethnic laborers on docks, factory floors, and construction sites limited blacks' economic prospects.[19]

A small but determined labor movement thrived in Baltimore. The city birthed one of the earliest black trade unions in the country: the Association of Black Caulkers, which traced its roots to the 1830s and formally organized in 1858. Unions and workingmen's associations spread apace, spurred along by ambitious associations such as the Colored National Labor Union, a labor organization and movement that started in Baltimore in 1869. Other groups like the First Laborers' Beneficial Association, the First Baltimore Colored Barbers' Beneficial Society, and the Musicians Social and Beneficial Association reflected associational, self-help impulses in the black community. They were also part of the nationwide growth of labor-related benefit societies after the war. John Jordan Upchurch epitomized the associational movement occurring throughout U.S. society when in 1868 he helped organize the Ancient Order of United Workmen (AOUW) in Meadville, Pennsylvania. The AOUW became one of the earliest formal fraternal insurance societies in the country. Members paid one dollar per month and received $500 upon death.[20]

Black women's labor organizing is often left out of consideration of early unions and workingmen's associations.[21] Women turned their own ploughshares into swords, and they used secret societies like the GUOSL as an important mechanism for wielding and exercising economic power. For example, after the Civil War, black women leveraged secret societies against exploitative white employers. Mrs. George Ward, a former slaveholder who contracted black women to perform domestic work in her home, ridiculed the black women's societies with their "funny" names, though her criticism bore witness that the societies that were "organized among them to look after and provide for the wants of those that are out of a job" allowed black women to feel "perfectly independent." These women, Ward claimed, had no "fear of being discharged, because when they are discharged they go right straight to some of these 'sisters.'"[22] Though Ward meant to denigrate the "sisters," black women's secret societies helped mitigate the exploitative aspects of their formal economic relations with whites during and after Reconstruction.[23]

The Grand United Order of St. Luke, then, reflected the deep interconnections between social activism, mutual aid societies, and inchoate labor unions in the black community. Though Prout created the St. Luke Society for women, she admitted men into its fold and set her sights on new levels of achievement. She strove to meet the needs of those sistren and brethren, drawn from all parts of the region, who flocked "like doves to their windows" in search of security and respect. Forced, on one hand, by the fading embers of Reconstruction's fiery promise and encouraged, on the other, by blacks' achievements and tenacity despite the failures of freedom, the GUOSL endeavored to open those windows further for an even larger community. If Prout ever suspected that the presence of men could be disruptive to her beloved order, her worst fears were soon realized.

"TO STAY THE HURTFUL TIDE": THE INDEPENDENT ORDER OF ST. LUKE

William M. T. Forrester had always been free, but the freedom that emerged after the Civil War was in many ways new even for those who had never been enslaved. Within months of the Confederate surrender, Richmond instituted a pass system to control blacks' movements. In a collective letter, self-described prominent colored men criticized the new pass system. A group of black artisans drafted another letter that made distinctions between themselves and "the unskilled majority," coded language for the larger masses of blacks. They marked themselves as liberators rather than the liberated. Freedpeople pressed the prominent blacks to be more assertive in their protests and for greater inclusion in decision-making. Freedpeople also took matters into their own hands and tested the bounds of white supremacy. For example, in early June 1865, police arrested eight hundred men, women, and children for violating the pass system. Although Richmond was a hotbed of resistance, various protests such as this also revealed and reinforced hierarchies based on former slave status.[24]

Richmond was also the cradle of black capitalism. It was no coincidence that Afro-Richmonders organized the first black-owned bank and insurance company during the 1880s. Both risk and opportunity shaped the lives of blacks in the postemancipation Upper South, a reality that uniquely positioned Richmond at the forefront of movements for black economic, political, and cultural autonomy. Antebellum Richmond had been one of the few Southern cities where industrial slavery had flourished, and it had boasted one of the most diverse slave labor systems in the country. Free and enslaved blacks had toiled in tobacco factories, flour mills, iron and coal mines, and stone quarries, and they had worked in the construction trades on buildings and public works projects like canals and railroads. They made up the majority of workers in shipyards, drayage, and warehousing.[25]

The character of black labor, both enslaved and free, in antebellum Richmond engendered not only a sense of independence but also a need for economic security. Afro-Richmonders' sense of independence shaped and was shaped by the communities and institutions that flourished in all-black neighborhoods, through shared experiences on factory floors, and in the shipyards, kitchens, and alleys of the city where they worked and lived. These communities only grew in their commitment to protecting their freedoms and economic opportunities after the Civil War.

Blacks' activism and the economic transformations taking place in the city after the Civil War spurred the creation of a Richmond-based contingent of the Order of St. Luke. In 1869, William Forrester and his father, who were the leaders of St. Luke Lodge No. 9, splintered from the GUOSL to form the Independent Order of the Sons and Daughters of St. Luke (later shortened to the Independent Order of St. Luke, or IOSL) (see fig. 2.2), headquartered in Richmond.[26] The charter members elected William Forrester right worthy grand (RWG) secretary of the infant order, a position he would hold for thirty years.[27] The next year, 1870, Forrester's father, Richard, and two other men, all listed as trustees, opened an account for St. Luke's Lodge No. 9, comprising mostly men, at the Freedman's Bank in Richmond. The move placed the young order on firmer footing in Virginia and further attested to its separation from the GUOSL.[28]

Forrester created a separate ritual, or works, for the IOSL in the mid-1870s that he modeled on the GUOSL's works. One of Forrester's initiation odes began,

> Come, brothers, let us all unite
> (Or sisters, as the case may be)
> To stay the hurtful tide;
> Against the world we'll bravely fight,
> And spread our Order wide.[29]

FIGURE 2.2 William M. T. Forrester, date unknown.
Source: 99-0228.03, courtesy of National Park Service, Maggie L. Walker National Historic Site.

For Lizzie Draper, the simple words of that ode held profound meaning. By the mid-1870s, she had been a wife, a new mother to a son, and a widow. She had married William Mitchell, a fellow former slave in the Van Lew household, in 1868, and they moved with Maggie Lena to a modest clapboard house in College Alley. In 1870, Elizabeth Draper Mitchell gave birth to a son, Johnnie. But then, in 1876, the police fished William's bloodied body out of the James River. The coroner ruled his death a suicide, but Elizabeth believed her husband had been robbed and then murdered.[30] Recalling the words of the IOSL ode, she would have appreciated some small solace "to stay the hateful tide" that threatened to swallow up her life and the lives of her two small children.

That small solace would have included a small burial benefit to lay William to rest. Working as headwaiter at a prestigious hotel in Richmond, William would have been attracted to, perhaps even recruited into, groups like the IOSL. Men with families to protect and provide for were just the kind of members that Forrester hoped to attract. In this way, the IOSL affirmed the role of black men as protectors and providers. It was a message that attracted black women as well. IOSL councils included both men and women, but a number of them had all-men or all-women memberships. As a society started for women by women, despite the decidedly muscular divisions on the part of the Forrester faction, a number of women poured into the new IOSL.

The "conversion" of formerly enslaved and free women's secret, mutual aid, and church societies into IOSL councils after emancipation is certainly one reason the IOSL grew in Virginia. These societies chose to federate with the fledgling IOSL largely through the work of organizers like Martha Carter. It is Carter, not the Forresters, who deserves much of the credit for grounding the IOSL in Virginia. She established one of the earliest St. Luke councils in 1867 or 1868, the Prout Council No. 2 in Norfolk, along with other councils in Portsmouth, Petersburg, and Richmond. Nothing is known of Carter's life—it is not known whether she had been a former slave or a free woman of color—but in either status, given the speed with which she organized IOSL councils, she had probably been intimately involved in antebellum secret and church benevolent societies.[31]

Carter's contemporary Eliza Allen offers a model of the connections forged between antebellum and postbellum societies organized for mutual benefit and protection. Allen joined the Grand Fountain of the United Order of True Reformers when William W. Browne moved the virtually moribund order to Richmond in 1880. She organized one of the first three fountains (as the Reformers' local groups were called) in the state. Shiloh

Fountain in Petersburg, organized by Allen, boasted ninety charter members. Most of the more than one hundred members of the Rahabs (a burial society that also collected money to care for the sick) became Silver Link Fountain No. 17. She also organized Richmond's first four fountains.[32]

Allen's success in organizing such large fountains for a small, relatively unknown organization attests to her long history of organizing and running secret societies as an enslaved woman. Allen had organized several secret societies among her fellow enslaved women, including the Consolation Sisters, Tabitha, and the Sisters of Usefulness. After the war, Allen and her family moved to Petersburg where she came to occupy an elite stratum of women who filled high-ranking, influential positions in numerous organizations. For example, the True Reformers elected her grand worthy governess at its first convention in 1881. In 1888, she was the only woman on the charter of the True Reformers Savings Bank, one of the earliest black-owned banks in the United States. In addition to leadership positions in other societies, she served as right worthy grand vice chief of the IOSL in 1896. Her reputation as a successful recruiter and organizer attracted many new men and women to the IOSL and to other societies in which she was involved.[33]

Without the tireless efforts of women like Allen and Carter, who embodied the Forresters' call "to spread our Order wide," the IOSL would not have been able to build on the foundation of mutual aid, benevolence, and burial societies that had been laid during slavery. Nor would these societies have been able to adapt to new conditions. The immense challenges of the postemancipation Upper South forced freedpeople to not only rely on their established networks but also transform them. These societies popularized new forms of financial products among black working classes.

CREATING SECURITY IN THE POST-RECONSTRUCTION ERA

In 1881, the IOSL took the big leap into the life insurance industry. In some ways, they entered the fray late. During the late 1860s and 1870s, John J. Upchurch of the Ancient Order of United Workmen demonstrated that workers would pay more for larger payouts beyond burial and sickness benefits, and John F. Dryden's experiment with the Prudential Friendly Society, which would become the Prudential Insurance Company, bore profitable fruit. Around the same time, pioneers like William Browne of the True Reformers, who failed in Alabama and then succeeded in Virginia; John E. Bush of the Mosaic Templars in Arkansas; and Thomas Stringer of the Colored Masons and the Colored Knights of Pythias in Mississippi created and promoted new models of insurance within black secret societies. Their models borrowed elements from workingmen's societies like Upchurch's and benevolent societies like Dryden's, such as establishing classes of risk based on age, though they met with many challenges in striking the right balance between price point and age. Pioneers Browne, Bush, and Stringer also capitalized on long-standing features of secret societies, such as their conviviality, orientation toward self-help, and secrecy. These visionaries saw the need for more robust insurance plans to provide security for workers. They also believed that harnessing the nickels and dimes collected to care for the sick, bury the dead, and provide funds after death could also form the economic foundation for strong, independent black institutions and a viable business community.[34]

Initially, however, it proved easier to persuade members to join the societies than to join the new insurance plans that were so enthusiastically endorsed by fraternal leaders. Most antebellum societies had provided money for burials and funds for days missed from work because of injury, sickness, or childbirth, but larger sums of money beyond the cost of a casket, a nice suit of clothes, or a few weeks' rent and food sat uneasily with some. Some recently emancipated black workers pouring into the southern economy were suspicious of the whole concept of insurance, believing it was a self-fulfilling prophecy: as soon as you insured your life, you would die. In addition, others felt uneasy about promoting their "selfish," individual interests above communal ones.[35]

The IOSL struggled alongside other Virginia secret societies to work out a successful insurance feature. In the second year of the True Reformers' endowment, for example, it paid a mere $477 in death policies. An 1882 newspaper article noted that the new program needed "time, care, and patience to make it one of the best."[36] The Grand United Order of Odd Fellows (GUOOF) of Virginia instituted an insurance plan in 1879, a few years before either the IOSL or the Reformers, but according to an early GUOOF historian and officer, it "struggled along for a few years and died from want of support."[37] A similar fate nearly befell the IOSL.

In 1881, Forrester crafted an endowment insurance plan for the Right Worthy Grand (RWG) Council, the IOSL's national-level governing body.[38] The IOSL collected a twenty-five-cent entrance fee and assessed a nickel from all subordinate council members to replenish the treasury when a member died. The entrance and assessment fees were very small—indeed, too small to cover council expenses at the local and state levels and still provide an adequate insurance benefit for the beneficiaries. The IOSL record does not specify the benefit amount, but it was probably between twenty-five and fifty dollars, or about one to two months' salary for many black workers.[39] As RWG secretary, Forrester controlled all aspects of the endowment plan he created. When a member passed away, Forrester verified whether the member had been "financial," or paid up to date. He verified the death through multiple sources, including local council members, the attending physician (if any), and the undertaker. Then he sent notices to the deceased member's local council, ensured that it collected the additional nickel assessments, and finally distributed the funds. Such a labyrinthine system was doomed to fail considering that the IOSL had grown to more than seventy councils and 2,500 members by the early 1880s.[40]

Anthropologist Gertrude Marlowe suggests that this system of centralizing all the endowment activities in one person resulted from the social networks forged between Forrester and the members. Locals had to be persuaded to entrust one of their most important functions, providing for the families of the deceased, in the hands of the RWG Council, outside their local council. The personal relationships and bonds they shared with the IOSL's founders supposedly helped motivate councils to participate in the new insurance feature. Other scholars of early insurance organizations have also stressed the importance of trust among members, especially in the context of dramatic social and cultural changes wrought by economic transformations, labor instability, urbanization, and migration. The absence of well-developed actuarial and credit standards also left ample room for other mechanisms like social bonds and trust to dictate financial practices, such as insurance and even banking.[41]

Virtually all the councils, however, refused to participate in the new insurance scheme. Given such abysmal rates of participation, factors beyond trust figured in members' decisions not to participate. Some may have resented Forrester's near-exclusive control over the new insurance feature. Even if he sought help administering the program, few would have volunteered to perform so many duties. The RWG treasurer-secretary remained the IOSL's only paid leadership position. Forrester earned $300 per year, and he conducted all RWG Council business out of his home.[42] He also operated a regalia-manufacturing business, and he earned a very good living from his society-related businesses. It is unlikely, though, that Forrester would have sought help, either paid or volunteer: he wanted to centralize authority for potentially the most lucrative and powerful feature of the order in his own hands. Trust was important, but profit and power figured as dominant motivations as well. His control over the works, the regalia, and the insurance plan gave him ideological, sartorial, and financial dominion over the order.

His dominion, though, had limits. In the mid-1880s, the RWG Council officers struck a pleading tone with local councils, imploring them to participate in the insurance plan: "New life would spring up in the whole Order, and it would be the cause of rapid growth of interest and spread of our Order."[43] The councils jealously guarded their control over the collection and administration of burial benefits, the lifeblood of their local influence. Some secret societies made a great ceremony of awarding beneficiary checks, including processions to the beneficiaries' homes. The RWG Council reworked the insurance plan in 1887, making participation for all members compulsory; any council that refused to pay the new entrance fees and administer the benefit could face suspension.[44]

The threat had little effect; few councils complied. Members expressed their dissatisfaction by closing their pocketbooks, and they likely complained about paying entrance fees, higher weekly fees for the new benefit, and the tax that was required to replenish the insurance fund after the council paid each death claim. A year after the launch of the new 1887 plan, the RWG Council collected only $26.30 from its more than two thousand members. Payment requests came in for six deceased members, and the endowment committee voted to divide equally the proceeds they had received, paying out a paltry $4.38 for each claim.[45]

The fees, with the exception of the entrance fee, were small, ranging from around a nickel to twenty-five cents. Grumbling about costs masked a deeper source of frustration: dissatisfaction with Forrester's leadership. Forrester's fraternal affections shifted toward the Grand United Order of Odd Fellows in the early 1870s as he became actively involved as a member of the Lone Star Lodge No. 1340 in Richmond. Forrester helped organize Virginia's women's auxiliary of GUOOF, the Household of Ruth. In 1883, he served as a delegate at the first session of the Grand Household, the state-level meeting of the auxiliary held in Richmond. The GUOOF in Virginia tended toward a membership of the educated, skilled, and aspiring classes.[46]

Aside from class, the gendered message of larger, all-male societies like the Masons, the GUOOF, and the Knights of Pythias spoke to male members' claims on sources of power in society at large. Fraternal values expressed larger social, economic, and cultural values. Historian Martin Summers's observations about the Colored Masons are equally appropriate to other exclusively male societies like the GUOOF: men like Forrester linked their understandings of what made a good Odd Fellow, Mason, or Pythian to notions of what made a good man, that is, "economic prosperity, national belonging, and, for many, their position within racial, ethnic, and class hierarchies."[47] The increasingly competitive capitalist reconfigurations of the economy threw into even sharper relief black men's struggles in the period to hold on to the franchise, escape economic exploitation and physical violence, and keep their families together. Male-dominated societies that had women's auxiliaries reinforced and helped construct, through ritual and practices in spaces beyond white surveillance and control, identities that reserved for black men positions of power and authority both inside and outside the fraternal meeting halls.

As bastions of male influence and leadership, male fraternalists took a paternalistic attitude toward both their relationship to the black community and their societies' entrepreneurial activities. Collectively, male-segregated societies imagined women and children as beneficiaries, the objects of their largess rather than partners or active agents. Individually, fraternalists could enrich themselves economically from the works, administration functions, and insurance business. Forrester and other black male fraternal leaders determined that black men were the proper producers, consumers, and managers of financial products designed to provide security and long-term investment.[48]

In the fraternal ethos, women worked within narrow gender expectations—and expanded them. Faced with many of the same incursions to their economic and social autonomy as men, black women faced a uniquely gendered set of challenges as well, especially low wages, limited employment options, lack of formal political power, and the persistent threat of racial sexual violence. In the increasingly capitalist ethos of the last decades of the nineteenth century, they insisted on communal and collective responses to the need for security. It was in the areas of insurance and finance, in financial protection and savings, that the most enthusiastic voices for independent black institutions—and the uniquely qualified group of women to lead it—emerged. One of the most sustained and insistent voices came from Maggie Lena Draper Mitchell Walker.

THE HAND THAT ROCKS THE CRADLE RULES THE WORLD: THE RISE OF MAGGIE LENA WALKER

Much about Maggie Lena's life had changed by the early 1880s. After her stepfather's suspicious death, her family had plunged into poverty and insecurity. Elizabeth Mitchell worked as a washerwoman, earning perhaps four or five dollars a month. Eccles "Max" Cuthbert, Maggie Lena's biological father, learned of William Mitchell's death and the family's destitute status. Instead of leaving Richmond after the war, he had begun working as the southern correspondent for the *New York Herald* shortly after the war ended, and he stayed apprised of his only daughter's life as much as he could, though he understood how much Elizabeth despised him. Perhaps Cuthbert learned of William's death from the Van Lews or their servants. Perhaps he tried to visit Maggie Lena. Regardless of how he learned about Elizabeth's misfortune, he determined to do something about it. He offered to send Maggie Lena to a Catholic school in Baltimore. He may have even expected that she could pass for white and live openly as his daughter. Elizabeth, however, refused to be separated from her daughter.[49]

The Mitchells struggled for many years. Elizabeth (see fig. 2.3) worked as a laundress, one of the few jobs available for black women. Young Maggie

FIGURE 2.3 Elizabeth Draper Mitchell, later in her life, date unknown.
Source: MAWA 158, courtesy of National Park Service, Maggie L. Walker National Historic Site.

Lena helped her mother by picking up and delivering loads of laundry for customers and carrying buckets of water for the wash and coal for the fires. She played barefoot in the alleys and streets near her home. Years later she would say of her early life, "I was not born with a silver spoon in my mouth but a laundry basket practically on my head."[50] Education was important to Elizabeth. She had been a school-age young woman when the war ended, but she never learned to read or write. She made sure her children did, however. Maggie Lena excelled academically and hoped to become a schoolteacher to provide a better life for her family. When Maggie Lena graduated from Armstrong Colored Normal School in 1883, Cuthbert sent her a dress for her graduation. Elizabeth immediately burned it. After graduation, she secured a position as a schoolteacher at the Valley School for a wage of thirty-five dollars a month.[51]

In 1883, IOSL council Good Idea No. 16 elected Maggie Lena Mitchell (see fig. 2.4) secretary and sent her as its delegate to the annual session of the RWG Council. Her mother was also a member of Good Idea. Though still a young woman, Maggie Lena must have inspired great confidence among Good Idea members. It was during the IOSL convention in 1883 that she drew the attention of the RWG secretary William M. T. Forrester. Soon after, the IOSL hired Maggie Lena as a clerk for eight dollars a month. She was also active in the United Order of Tents J. R. Giddings and Jolliffe Union, an order exclusively for women, and in the early 1880s, she worked as a clerk with the True Reformers.[52]

In 1886, Maggie Lena married Armstead Walker Jr., a man fifteen years her senior whose family owned a brick contracting company. Virginia law prohibited married women from teaching, so Walker was forced to quit teaching. Walker and Armstead had three children: Russell Eccles Talmadge in 1890; Armstead Mitchell in 1893, who died before turning one year old; and Melvin DeWitt in 1897. Walker could have enjoyed a life of relative ease, married to a scion of one of Richmond's solidly upper-middle-class families and part of an elite generation of Afro-Richmonders. Like other educated, middle-class women of her day, Walker could have filled her time with her focus exclusively on homemaking and entertaining. She could have joined any number of women's clubs and even been socially active in reform- and uplift-oriented activities directed at poor and working-class women and children. Instead she chose a life of work and activism because she saw business as the way to create opportunities for women.[53]

The young Walker poured her great energy and ambition into communal organizations that were focused not only on women of the aspiring classes like herself but also on women like her mother who worked tirelessly at low-paying jobs to support their families. She was not immediately

FIGURE 2.4 Maggie Lena Mitchell, c. 1885.
Source: 99-0694, courtesy of National Park Service, Maggie L. Walker National Historic Site.

attracted to social reform and club work, though IOSL councils addressed serious social issues affecting black women. For example, the Good Idea Council donated money for the legal defense of Pokey and Mary Barnes in 1895, two women accused of the brutal ax murder of a white woman. Walker wanted to put into action her beliefs about providing real economic solutions for working women. While working as a teacher at Valley School, she had worked as a part-time insurance agent with the beneficial department of the Woman's Union (WU), a cooperative society, and she had earned far more from sales commissions than from her teacher's salary.[54] Insurance was not only an acceptable professional pursuit for women but also a way for Walker to remain active and connected to other women who shared her commitment to economic empowerment. She continued her involvement in the WU for many years after her marriage. Unlike teaching, Walker's work at the WU allowed her to discover unimagined possibilities for developing her own skills and talents as well as those of other women. Convinced that she wanted to rise higher in the world of business, she took night classes in accounting, which was an advanced business field that included very few women.[55]

The WU was a cooperative society composed entirely of women who were engaged in businesses that met the practical needs of Richmond's black community. The benefit, or insurance, department grew out of a split in the Woman's Corner-Stone Beneficial Association, which incorporated in early 1897. Louisa E. Williams served as president and Walker served as vice president at Woman's Corner-Stone, which offered sickness and death benefits for as low as a nickel per week. Walker may have had personal differences with Williams, or the women may have split over their ambitions for the business. Walker and some of her close women associates, most of whom were also part of the IOSL, formally incorporated the Woman's Union in July 1898. The impressive list of women in the WU shared a commitment to collective economic development and issues that lay at the heart of women's concerns that were not adequately met by the club movement: financial protection and opportunities for women and their families. The first WU board elected Rosa Kinckle Jones president and Walker vice president. Jones was a private music teacher and taught music at Hartshorn Memorial College. Other officers included treasurer Fannie Coles Thompson, who owned a significant amount of real estate in Jackson Ward, and secretary-manager Patsie Keiley Anderson, a teacher at Navy Hill School. Other powerful women who were Walker's allies in the IOSL served on the WU's board of directors, including Lillian H. Payne, Julia Harris Hayes, and Rosa Watson.[56]

The WU's motto was "The hand that rocks the cradle, rules the world," and the officers and board were exclusively female as were the staff and sales agents. They provided benefits regardless of gender or fraternal association; men, women, and children, ages two to sixty, were welcome to take out policies. In addition, the WU provided jobs, leadership opportunities, and training for women. For example, in 1900, it began operating the Woman's Union Rooms, a boarding house, and in 1902, the Woman's Union School, and Anderson served as manager for the Woman's Union Grocery Company.[57]

In addition to the WU, Walker devoted a great deal of time and energy to the IOSL. She climbed the ranks in the IOSL, rising from a clerk in 1883 to an organizer and lecturer in the 1890s. In the 1880s, as a member of the endowment board, which oversaw the insurance feature, she worked in earnest to improve the program. Walker was committee chair and the driving force of the juvenile department, which she created in 1895, drafting the constitution and creating the ritual for it. Walker wholeheartedly supported the endowment feature, believing it was "absolutely necessary" to compete with the myriad other fraternal organizations that were finding success with the endowment.[58]

She instituted a small (thirty-dollar) insurance plan within the circles, as the local juvenile groups were called. Walker streamlined the process for paying death claims: the matrons (or presidents) of each juvenile circle documented deaths. An executive board comprising Richmond-area matrons and grand (state-level) juvenile officers met twice a month to review claims. The grand matron signed and sent checks to beneficiaries and verified receipt of payment. The juvenile plan was an immediate success, quickly outpacing the IOSL's adult plan. Like Prout's, Walker's efforts were not mere altruism or charity; they were entrepreneurial—and profitably so. Organizers received four dollars of the eleven-dollar charter fee and twenty-five cents for each youth joining the charter council. Walker personally organized more than one hundred councils in the first year alone, earning her several hundred dollars of additional income, and the juvenile department reported a surplus in its bank account at the 1896 convention.[59]

Even as Walker's plan prospered, the IOSL's old guard ignored it. Struggling to work out a plan for the entire order, the mostly male leadership of the IOSL did not see anything of value in a program designed by a woman for women and children. Walker struggled over the years to institute new reforms and initiatives in the IOSL's adult insurance plan. She served on the committee created in 1887 to update the endowment plan, and the IOSL elected Walker secretary of the endowment fund's new board of directors created in 1898.[60]

In a city boasting more than a few popular and successful fraternal organizations, including the True Reformers and the Knights of Pythias, the IOSL leadership desired to stake a claim as well. A formal headquarters and meeting hall would signal a significant step forward. Forrester remained satisfied drawing a salary from the order, operating an exclusive regalia business, and conducting the order's affairs out of his home on West Leigh Street. It is doubtful that he had much time to devote to the IOSL considering his involvement in other societies, including his tenure as the national grand master of the Colored Odd Fellows. Forrester's primary interest in the IOSL was financial. He earned money from his regalia business and the fees remitted by the councils for using the works (or ritual) he had created in the 1870s.[61]

In 1897, the state-level RWG Council (comprising mostly Richmond-area officers) and Richmond councils made a bold and aggressive move. Many in the council had grown weary of operating out of Forrester's parlor for nearly thirty years. They held enough sway on the board to form the St. Luke Association, which sold shares for ten dollars each, to purchase a headquarters for the order. Leaders from each of the twenty-five local Richmond councils, current and past officers of the RWG Council, and top-ranking matrons in the juvenile department made up the St. Luke Association's board of directors, which included Walker. The association bought a property at 900 St. James Street for $4,000, paying $500 down (see fig. 2.5). Walker orchestrated fundraising efforts to pay the mortgage, including a two-week bazaar. She also planned to lease offices and rent meeting space in the new hall to create revenue.[62]

The same year, RWG Chief R. Bruce Evans gave voice to members' growing dissatisfaction with Forrester. Evans told delegates at the 1897 convention that he felt it vitally important that "the outside world might know that we are not asleep, nor in the dark, but standing out in the broad open light of day, having as grand a mission as any other organization under the sun."[63]

FIGURE 2.5 Original St. Luke Hall, c. 1903.
Source: 99-0228.05, courtesy of National Park Service, Maggie L. Walker National Historic Site.

To add heft to these words, the RWG Council altered its charter in 1898, acknowledging its continued commitment to pay sickness and death benefits and to assist with burials but stressing its desire that the endowment become the centerpiece of the order. The St. Luke Association and the IOSL's parliamentary actions represented a tacit indictment of Forrester's increasingly ineffective leadership.

Trouble sprouted from other sources as well. The rift created in the late 1860s by the Forresters' defection from the Grand United Order of St. Luke in Maryland had never properly healed. When Prout died in 1884, her niece and successor, Lucy A. Vincent, continued Prout's outright rejection of any insurance feature beyond traditional death and sickness benefits. Though no extant letters or reports exist to offer an explanation, the motherhead may have privileged other forms of collective response to caring for the needy. Prout and Vincent may have seen collective investment in social institutions, such as schools, aged homes, and possibly hospitals, as the proper function of a mutual aid society in keeping with the long tradition of the original St. Luke Society. In addition, for the very devout, insurance resembled gambling: people effectively placed a wager on the likelihood of death. Finally, with only three councils in Maryland, the GUOSL may have felt overwhelmed by the notion of administering a state or regional insurance program.

In 1895, Forrester attempted to create a National Grand Council comprising the Virginia and New York councils. Such a union would give him a monopoly on sales of the works, regalia, and supplies. But instead of strengthening the IOSL, his efforts threw the various councils into rebellion. In 1897, a rival faction of IOSL councils in Maryland elected Rosa Bowser RWG grand chief. Gertrude Marlowe describes Bowser as "the undisputed representative of Richmond's elite African American clubwomen."[64] While Walker saw providing financial services as the path toward economic security, Bowser believed that social service institutions and programs were key. In the vacuum created by Forrester's inattentive and lackluster leadership, Bowser succeeded in creating a rival state-level council in 1898. Delegates from disaffected IOSL councils in Maryland and Virginia met in Urbanna, Virginia, and created the Supreme Grand Council of the IOSL, an obvious rival to the Right Worthy Grand Council. The Supreme Grand Council never approached the success, either in money or members, of the RWG Council under Walker's leadership, but its very existence underscored William Forrester's neglect and ineffective leadership of the order.[65]

The IOSL's 1899 report is cryptic in its announcement that Forrester refused to serve further as RWG secretary, with only a few observations by Forrester. He was deeply critical of the order that he and his father had helped plant in Virginia thirty years earlier, saying he felt that it could sink no lower; he carped that it was bankrupt and was "not spreading as it should."

He also complained about the "lack of co-operation" within the RWG Council and between it and the local councils.[66] The struggle over the insurance feature and efforts to modernize the order tapped the last bit of his resolve.

Things did indeed look bleak for the IOSL. It had lost one-third of its councils and two-thirds of its members. The order had less than thirty-two dollars in the bank, and its debts surpassed $400. A little more than one thousand active members still clung on in fifty-seven councils. Delegates elected Maggie Lena Walker the new RWG secretary, a position Walker accepted for a salary of one hundred dollars a year, one-third of Forester's salary. Walker saw opportunity where Forrester saw defeat.[67]

"THE WELL AND THE SICK, THE LIVING AND THE DEAD": WALKER TAKES OVER THE IOSL

Walker saw great promise in a group of mostly women, "helpless" women who threw their lots in together and entrusted their money and future prosperity to each other. Walker relied on not only women working in middle-class professions like teachers, stenographers, and nurses but also working-class women. Indeed, it would be washerwomen, low-skilled factory workers, seamstresses, hucksters, and agricultural workers who combined their modest resources to resurrect the IOSL, and it would be their care and advancement that animated the new IOSL. One significant sign of the changed perspective of the IOSL was its choice of leader. Delegates elected Ella Onley RWG chief. Onley was a thirty-four-year-old washerwoman who lived in Jackson Ward and was described in the record as "diligent" in her work with the IOSL. In just one year, the IOSL added thirty new councils and nearly quadrupled its adult membership.[68]

Walker believed the future strength and longevity of the IOSL lay in its financial services: "The well and the sick, the living and the dead must be our care in the future."[69] It was only through a successful and profitable insurance feature that the order could accumulate the capital needed to fulfill the IOSL leadership's other ambitious economic development goals. Walker and a cadre of ambitious women saw their vision sprout roots in Corner-Stone Beneficial and the Woman's Union. They believed it could bear real fruit in a nationwide society that addressed the practical needs of black communities in general and black women in particular.

The women in charge of the IOSL had to get tough, but they chose to exercise power in a way that respected the realities and experiences of the members they hoped to draw back into the IOSL. The sixty or so remaining councils were given fifteen days to either begin participating in the insurance program or, for those already nominally participating, begin consistently collecting and reporting premiums. Those who did not participate or who failed to collect assessments and send in the required monthly and quarterly reports would be not only suspended but also fined until they complied. Walker and her close associate Lillian Payne, however, worked closely with local councils, listening to complaints and smoothing over resistance to the insurance feature.[70]

The IOSL made it clear that its focus lay in helping members rather than profiting from them. Under Forrester's financial stewardship, the order had lost sight of Prout's original vision and the larger implications of the IOSL's work. Parliamentary procedure, elections, selling and buying degrees, and later, improving the endowment had consumed much of the order's time and effort. These remained important activities in the councils, but engagement with the community through service, education, and conviviality received far more attention under Onley and Walker. The pages of the *Richmond Planet* highlighted IOSL activities: initiating new councils, juvenile circles, Christmas programs with local schoolchildren, Easter exercises, and mass meetings. Walker, Onley, and other IOSL officers and deputies traveled throughout Virginia planting new councils.[71]

Afro-Richmonders from various backgrounds joined the IOSL. Working women from all income levels recommitted themselves to collective goals of protection and security, and they revived the IOSL. The "new" IOSL would struggle to accommodate differences among its members, especially differences in gender, class, generation, and ideology, but women took full advantage of their power in the organization to develop their skills and address the unique challenges that black women continued to face. Walker and the women in the IOSL executive leadership had a commitment to their constituency and its challenges, and it quickly bore fruit. By the end of 1899, after only a few months under Walker's leadership, virtually all the subordinate councils complied with the insurance program and reporting requirements.[72]

In 1900, in her first report as RWG secretary, Walker mentioned some of the difficulties that she, Onley, and the executive leadership faced in the wake of the near demise of the IOSL. For instance, Forrester had torn several pages out of the order's ledgers, and he had not turned over any of the check registers from before August 1898. It was only many years later that she openly criticized the men who stood in the way of the IOSL's progress. In 1907, she told the membership, "Some of the strongest and brainiest men dropped from the ranks of the Order and waited patiently for the grand old Order to drop in pieces."[73] In 1900, however, Walker chose to look forward rather than backward. She recommended that every council organize at least one juvenile circle, and she instituted new revenue sources, such as an additional tax on members based on their longevity in the IOSL and new fees for entering members and convention delegates. She also increased the insurance benefit.[74]

Walker instituted a number of leadership reforms that gave a nod to local councils' autonomy but left little doubt of the supremacy of the RWG Council and executive board. She reiterated that individual councils would retain full control over paying sickness and burial benefits. In 1901, Walker also established a new executive board with members from not only local Richmond councils but also other parts of Virginia. Patsie K. Anderson, Ella Onley, and Lillian Payne joined Walker and four men to form the new IOSL executive board. The move helped her consolidate her power and influence. She also encouraged building up and planting councils outside of Virginia. She relied on women and men associates in the District of Columbia, New Jersey, New York, and Pennsylvania to build the IOSL beyond Virginia.[75]

Like Moses, Walker held the staff, but she needed help to part the waters. She hired a small staff of four women for the IOSL headquarters: Maggie Macklin, Lillian Payne, Emeline Johnson, and Estella Bagby. These women would take on the momentous task of administering the order's new financial savings programs and Walker's vision for the order. Unlike Rosa Bowser and the Maryland IOSL councils, Walker would not make social reform the IOSL's focus. Walker wholeheartedly embraced financial services as the foundation of the order's prosperity. In 1902, the IOSL established a second, noncompulsory insurance program for the general public. Walker advertised the new benefit in the new IOSL organ the *St. Luke Herald*, which began publication in March of that year. She was determined that the IOSL play a significant role in the economic lives of black communities throughout Virginia and beyond.[76]

The IOSL changed dramatically over the years, from its roots in Mary Ann Prout's 1850s St. Luke Society at Bethel AME in Maryland to the Forresters' defection in the late 1860s to Walker's ascension to leadership in 1899. Walker assembled a trusted group of talented and ambitious women to shepherd the order into new business pursuits in a supportive though competitive environment. Walker promoted a vision of service, fraternalism, and activism that she saw as key to helping women cultivate thrift, gain a measure of autonomy, and create collective empowerment. The women of the IOSL shaped and inspired that vision. In the wake of Jim Crow, Afro-Richmonders would not readjust to their place but wrest freedom, however imperfect, from the ways they performed their labor, spent their time and money, and cared for their families and communities. At the turn of the twentieth century, Walker certainly felt confident about how far the IOSL had come from the brink of disaster. New opportunities and challenges awaited.

Everyone would see. Everyone would know.

3

"Let Us Have a Bank"

ST. LUKE PENNY SAVINGS BANK, ECONOMIC ACTIVISM, AND STATE REGULATION, 1903 TO WORLD WAR I

Sarah tried hard to forget the tight new shoes that were pinching her toes. Her skin gleamed like a polished stone after her mother's insistent scrubbing. Her mother had put extra starch in her dress, and the wide sailor collar scratched her neck. Sarah carefully switched her basket full of crisp white envelopes from one hand to the other. She knocked gently on the door, taking a quick look back at her mother, who was standing near the gate. As the door swung open, Sarah straightened her back, smiled, and forgot all about her pinching toes and scratchy collar. She handed the woman who opened the door an invitation to the opening of the St. Luke Penny Savings Bank scheduled for November 3, 1903.[1]

It had been two long years since Maggie Lena Walker had first announced her intention to open a bank. "Let us have a bank," Walker had told an excited audience of mostly women Independent Order of St. Luke members. She spoke specifically to them, the "many good women, willing women, noble women, whose money is here." Together, they could create businesses and job opportunities for women. "First we need a savings bank," she continued. "Let us have a bank that will take the nickels and turn them into dollars."[2] Planning and then building a new hall for the IOSL headquarters, however, had consumed most of her attention since 1901, when she first shared publicly her vision for the order. Within only a few short years under her leadership, the near-moribund order sprouted new life. The IOSL quickly outgrew the St. James Street property that the St. Luke Association had purchased in 1897, but Walker waited to move until the IOSL paid off the mortgage on the St. James Street property, which it did in 1902. Construction on the new headquarters began in the spring of 1903. It was not until late summer that the IOSL's attorney drew up the bank's charter. By August, the bank did not even have a vault. But Walker was not the type of woman to make empty, even if earnest, promises; the St. Luke Bank would come into being, and it would be something different.

Walker's declaration that the bank would turn nickels into dollars did not apply only to accumulating savings. Walker fully expected to grow black women's and other customers' money through investment in profit-making—and job-creating—business and property holdings. The St. Luke Penny Savings Bank board certainly shared some of the paternalistic concerns of white elites who created savings institutions for the poor and working classes in northern and midwestern cities beginning in the early 1800s. They saw savings as a way to instill values and shape morals; however, the St. Luke board's vision was far more expansive. They wanted to encourage individual savings for collective wealth building. The bank would invest in and extend credit to for-profit, capital-intensive projects that built up black communities.[3]

This chapter explores the early years of the St. Luke Penny Savings Bank and Walker's tenacious efforts to align her vision of economic empowerment with the bank's practices. Black women stood at the center of Walker's vision for the St. Luke Bank. Girls and working-class women—washerwomen, tobacco factory laborers, sharecroppers, and domestics—would be more than just the bank's target customers. The gendered economic practices and values of the bank's primary customer and shareholder base—women and girls—shaped the bank's business operations and lending priorities. That vision faced a number of threats, including division among board members, the erosion of blacks' civil rights, extralegal harassment from the white business community, a lack of support from the black middle class, and aggressive state oversight. But the bank's agenda of empowerment possessed a broad enough appeal across race, gender, and class to assure its survival through its first critical years.

OPENING THE BANK

The St. Luke Bank, like all early black banks, struggled against a steep learning curve, and the IOSL had few options for learning the banking business. The Freedman's Bank had provided training for a small number of blacks who worked in different branches. Some served as trustees, but did so primarily in its waning years after it fell into deep financial straits. Employees from local white banks sometimes offered assistance, with cashiers and other employees spending a few days with bank staff, teaching basic operations. J. O. Ross, president of the Atlanta State Savings Bank in Atlanta, Georgia, however, recalled that white bankers were not helpful at all and merely waited for his bank to fail. Early black bankers also relied on industry books and on correspondence courses in bookkeeping and accounting; Henry William Wolff's *Co-operative Banking, Its Principles and Practice* and Charles Arthur Conant's two-volume *The Principles of Money and Banking* were popular titles in the early twentieth century. Bankers relied on each other as well. William R. Pettiford, who founded the Alabama Penny Savings Bank in Birmingham in 1890, traveled around the country, offering training and assistance with bank operations. Most black banks, however, learned the banking business through trial and error.[4]

Walker took some business and accounting correspondence courses in the 1890s, but she knew that she needed a more thorough banking education if the St. Luke Bank stood any chance of success. Before the bank's opening, Walker spent several hours a week for as many months closely observing bank operations at the Merchants National Bank of Richmond. To be sure, in her capacity as secretary-treasurer of the IOSL, Walker had forged her own professional relationships with well-placed whites in Richmond, but her biological father Eccles "Max" Cuthbert may have played a crucial role here. Cuthbert may have tapped into his network of highly placed businessmen, like banker John P. Branch, to help his only daughter gain coveted access to the inner workings of one of the city's oldest and largest banks.[5]

John Patteson Branch, cofounder and president of the Merchants National Bank, authorized Walker's visits and allowed her unfettered access to all aspects of the bank's operations. Firmly ensconced as one of Richmond's civic-business elite, Branch served as trustee of the Negro Reformatory Association and donated generously to some charitable initiatives for Richmond's black community. One scholar described Branch as "an elderly Virginia gentleman" who "felt an old-fashioned concern for the black race." At the loss of his family's mammy, Aunt Critty Williams, Branch reportedly "mourn[ed] as if she had indeed been his aunt."[6] Branch could hardly confuse Walker with his beloved mammy; the imagined devotion that had endeared Aunt Critty to six generations of Branches was not part of Walker's character or demeanor. Rather, Branch supported Walker's practical lessons in banking in part because it polished the "veneer of civility" that signified civic-minded white Richmonders' approach to managing and controlling the race problem without mob violence or overt racial harassment.[7]

Walker's light complexion and finely tailored dress minimized stares from customers who would have been puzzled about the continuous presence of an African American in the bank, but her gender probably raised more than a few brows. Women were more the exception than the norm in many banks in the period. Larger banks created separate women's departments that catered to their female clientele. Beginning in the first decade of the twentieth century, banks also hired women tellers who assisted women customers exclusively. In the South, however, some banks created ladies' rooms rather than full-fledged departments. Few of these special dedicated banking rooms provided women direct teller access. Many did, however, feature private booths for viewing the contents of safety deposit boxes, writing desks for personal and business correspondence, lounge areas for visiting with friends or sewing, and maid service. Banks reserved their ladies' room services for affluent clients. Thus, women of a certain race and class, specifically white and affluent, were welcomed in banks but largely in domesticated spaces separated from the main activities of the bank. Walker defied racial and gender conventions in the financial industry. She stood squarely in the midst of the bank's main hustle and bustle, and she observed the bank's back-office operations. Over several months, her patient observations and notes helped her prepare to run the St. Luke Bank.[8]

The board of directors of the St. Luke Penny Savings Bank, consisting of eight men and five women, held its first meeting on August 19, 1903. The male directors included Rev. Zachariah D. Lewis, pastor of Second Baptist Church; Walden Banks, an undertaker and fraternal leader in Boston; Charles F. Norman of the Workingmen's Aid and Beneficial Society; and IOSL district deputy Alexander F. Angel. The board resembled, in some ways, the boards of other black financial institutions. It included prominent civic, educational, religious, and business leaders from the local community. The logic of such choices included the obvious advantages: having trusted leaders in leadership positions lent the institution some built-in legitimacy. The bank's board also reflected Walker's skill at compromise and consensus building. Walker included among the directors men from large cities like Boston and Philadelphia, where the bank might be assured strong IOSL support outside Virginia. The presence of labor and fraternal leaders encouraged support among a broad class base: artisans and skilled and unskilled workers as well as middle-class and professional working people.[9]

The bank's board was unusual given the number of women directors. Some of the women directors were prominent church and society leaders, educators, and business owners, but all came from modest backgrounds and had long experience working in Richmond's black community. The women Walker drew around her included women who had worked with her in the Woman's Union and who had helped her rebuild the IOSL, including Patsie Keiley Anderson, who managed the Woman's Union enterprises and served on the IOSL endowment board; Ella Onley Waller, a former washerwoman, active fraternalist, and prolific IOSL organizer; Frances Cox, a stemmer in a tobacco factory; and Lillian H. Payne, who also worked as a clerk with the IOSL (see fig. 3.1).

The new board quickly set about planning for the bank's opening. In quick succession, it purchased a vault and hired a watchman. It set the bank's operating hours at nine in the morning until ten at night during the week and nine in the morning to noon and five to eight in the evening on Saturday. The evening and weekend hours reflected hours that were convenient for domestic and industrial workers, who often worked late into the evenings on weekdays and Saturdays.[10]

The impending opening date, however, also meant that frayed nerves, inflated egos, and concerns about stock subscriptions erupted into bickering and conflict among some board members. During the first board meeting in

FIGURE 3.1 St. Luke Penny Savings Bank officers, c. 1917. The two women pictured are Maggie Lena Walker (*top center*) and Ella Onley Waller (*bottom*).
Source: 99-0228.21, courtesy of National Park Service, Maggie L. Walker National Historic Site.

August, Armstead Washington, vice president of the Richmond Hospital and Training School for Nurses, walked out because he felt ignored. At its second meeting, the board voted to invite Washington back, a move that signaled its willingness to compromise but also its concern about public perceptions that the bank's leadership was coming apart even before the bank could get off the ground.[11]

Concerns about stock subscriptions also placed a significant amount of stress on the board. Some board members could not afford to purchase the required minimum ten shares, or $100 worth, of stock. Walker called out William W. Fields, a postal carrier, and Walden Banks for failing to pay for their stock by the deadline. It was not enough to flaunt fancy titles like "board member"; Walker demanded that board members demonstrate their commitment by taking the risk to make a significant investment in the bank. The board required Fields and Banks to either pay at least fifty dollars by the end of 1903 or step down from the board. The board removed Fields in January 1904 when he failed to pay. Banks borrowed $100 from the bank to purchase his shares but had trouble paying back the loan. The board had little choice but to remove him. Two other male board members did not wait for Walker's admonishment. They resigned, writing that they could not pay their subscriptions.[12]

The women board members also had difficulty paying their stock subscriptions, which was perhaps even more of a financial hardship for them given women's lower wages. Of the original five female directors, only Walker, Payne, and Anderson fulfilled their subscriptions. The board members, male and female, reflected the economic realities of most black Richmonders who found it difficult to save large sums. For women in particular, low-paying jobs, even professional ones, meant that they experienced an even harder time saving large sums. Even if they did manage to save a nice nest egg, it would have been difficult to part with substantial savings for what was, despite the ebullient rhetoric, a speculative enterprise.[13]

In the months between the bank's charter and opening, Walker traveled extensively, drumming up interest in and excitement for the bank. In September 1903 in Newark, New Jersey, she promised audiences "capital furnished by Southern Negroes" to help start businesses in the northeast.[14] Such promises belied the modest "Penny Savings" in the bank's name and revealed Walker's thinly veiled intention to put depositors' savings to work. Walker planned for the St. Luke Bank to take an active role in creating and directing black women's wealth.

The St. Luke Penny Savings Bank opened its doors at nine o'clock on the morning of Tuesday, November 3, 1903. The bank held opening-day festivities, which included a parade, music, and a full dais of speakers and lasted until close to midnight. IOSL representatives from throughout Virginia and other states, including Delaware, New York, New Jersey, Pennsylvania, and West Virginia, came on opening day to make deposits and enjoy the festivities. The bank also distributed five hundred coin banks to help people save money at home. When bearers saved at least a dollar, they could bring their change to the bank and open an account or deposit it into an existing account. Cash deposits totaled $9,430.44 the first day, which exceeded the $7,500 the board had projected.[15]

Scores of IOSL councils and circles met the board's challenge for each council to deposit at least ten dollars and for each juvenile circle, at least five dollars. Walker's council, Good Idea, was the first local council to make a deposit, placing $100 in the bank. The IOSL's RWG Council deposited $800, and the juvenile department deposited $858. Other women's societies and auxiliaries deposited money, such as Julia's Tent of the United Order of Tents of the J. R. Giddings and Jolliffe Union and Naomi Lodge of the Household of Ruth, the women's auxiliary of the Grand United Order of Odd Fellows. Local businesses such as the Richmond Beneficial Insurance Company also opened accounts on the first day.

The first person to make a deposit was James H. Chiles, a grocer in Richmond, who deposited fifty dollars. Walker made the second deposit for $160. Rosa Watson made one of the largest single deposits, $441. Most of the nearly three hundred other accounts opened that day were much more modest. Hundreds of women and men deposited small amounts, including some deposits for less than a dollar, and a number of children deposited money. Walker's sons, Russell and Melvin, each deposited a dollar. Brothers Robert and Lovic Thomas deposited twenty cents and thirty-one cents respectively. Coin banks for juveniles to use at home helped scores of children save money to deposit in their St. Luke Bank accounts.[16]

Women demonstrated their overwhelming support of the bank and made up the largest number of depositors. Perhaps they recognized that the bank considered the economic realities of its women's depositors. For example, the bank allowed extremely small deposits, even those of a few cents, because the large deposits of women like Walker and Watson were the exception rather than the rule. Most of the St. Luke's female depositors had small incomes and could only afford to save small amounts. Some deposited a few dollars, but most deposited a dollar or less. The bank also solicited accounts from a variety of women's societies and groups. These associational accounts reinforced the economic import of women's community-building activities. The bank safeguarded the money that women's societies and groups raised for nurseries, homes for the elderly, schools, and other essential institutions.

The bank sold $1,400 worth of shares on its opening day. Even more important than the board's stock subscription, the public sale of stock proved critical. IOSL members from as far away as New York, the District of Columbia, West Virginia, and other states purchased stock. These members, overwhelmingly washerwomen, domestics, tobacco factory workers, sharecroppers, seamstresses, teachers, and nurses—women from every occupation and station—became shareholders in the bank. Most of them purchased a single ten-dollar share, and then by putting only a dollar down. Alongside their insurance policies, these shares represented their active efforts to build wealth through investment in the things that mattered most to them: their families and each other. Walker had relied on these working women and their commitment to the collective goals of protection and security to revive the moribund order four years earlier, and she relied on them now to turn her dream of the bank into a reality.[17]

Another key for the bank's future success lay in securing a competent staff to run it. The board chose wisely for the bank's cashier: Emmett C. Burke. He had begun working as a clerk for the True Reformers in 1894 and rose through the ranks, advancing to the position of assistant paying and receiving teller for the True Reformers Savings Bank before applying for the head cashier position at the St. Luke Bank. Beyond his experience, business intuition, and work ethic, Burke was willing to stand up to and even go against Walker. For example, when Walker hired a young woman in whom she saw some promise for the teller's cage but the young lady proved to be inadequate to Burke's standards, Walker realized she had to step back and allow the board fill the position. She also wished her eldest son, Russell, still a teenager when the bank opened, to work as a cashier at the bank, but Burke made it clear that nepotism held little sway in his calculus of the bank's needs.[18]

Walker and Burke put their full energies into growing the bank so that it could meet the needs of its customers. Like other small banks, the St. Luke Bank established relationships with larger banks to act as its clearinghouses. Smaller banks could not afford the steep fees and capital requirements to become members in the clearinghouse association but needed the ability to accept and cash checks from other banks. The local banks in Richmond advocated for the St. Luke, threatening to withdraw their funds from the national banks if the national banks did not allow the St. Luke Bank to use them as clearinghouses. They were not simply being magnanimous: banks that acted as clearinghouses for smaller banks charged fees and a percentage of the accounts handled. In addition to providing convenience to the customer, the arrangement earned money. American National Bank of Richmond acted as the St. Luke Bank's primary clearinghouse agent, and they also used the Richmond Bank and the Merchants National Bank.

Through their New York correspondent bank, the St. Luke Bank could also draw on foreign correspondents if needed.[19]

In 1904, Walker began work on another prong of her economic vision for the order when the IOSL opened the St. Luke Emporium in the heart of Richmond's white central business district on Broad Street. Three board members suggested—likely with Walker's encouragement—that the bank purchase five hundred shares of emporium stock. The St. Luke Bank's investment in an outside business expanded the bounds of its savings mission. By investing the bank's deposits and capital in such an enterprise. The emporium provided jobs and services to black women. The bank moved its offices to the emporium's building in late 1905 and operated there until 1911, when the IOSL completed construction on a new bank building at the corner of First and Marshall Streets.[20]

The bank held its first annual stockholders' meeting at St. Luke Hall in January 1905. The meeting represented an important milestone for the bank. The vast majority of the bank's stockholders were women. Most owned only one share, but it was small shareholders such as these who capitalized the bank. Walker swelled with pride at the sight of a room filled largely with women. No text of her remarks survives, but she likely reminded each of the women in the audience that even one share in the bank represented a stake in the IOSL's collective vision and future success. She proudly reported that the bank had handled $222,000 (about $6.1 million in 2017 dollars) in 1904.[21] The board decided against declaring dividends because profits were so small. The sixteen people who held at least ten shares were nominated and approved to join the board.[22]

The bank's activity in its first year reflected the tension between its ideals and its economic reality. In the bank's first six months, it had sold about $4,500 of its stock to two hundred individuals and groups—less than 10 percent of the $50,000 total stock. In the same period, it loaned out nearly twice that amount: $8,424. These disparate figures highlight one of the great challenges that the bank had to overcome. In relying on working-class people to capitalize the bank, raising significant funds would always be a challenge. The bank already offered easy terms for buying stock on an installment plan, wherein stockholders put some money down and then made monthly payments over one year to pay for their shares, but selling sufficient stock would remain a long-standing problem. For example, in 1906, when attorney James Hayes stressed the dire need to sell more stock, the board initiated a plan to pay 10 percent commission on sales of stock. By 1913, the bank allowed customers to take out loans to buy stock. Beyond stock sales, the bank's profits remained small. It depended on financial assistance from the Right Worthy Grand Council to help it meet the challenges of staying profitable with low capitalization, small deposits, and large loan portfolios. Aside from being the largest stockholder and depositor, the RWG Council helped the bank by subsidizing the salary of at least one bank employee.[23]

In addition, providing white collar jobs for women in the bank remained a difficult hurdle. One reason Walker focused so much attention on advocating for a woman in the assistant cashier position was that, besides herself, she was the only female employee of the bank. To remain true to her vision of creating skilled white-collar jobs for women, the bank had to hire actual women. Beyond female tellers who served female clients in larger northeastern banks, very few women worked in the public areas of early twentieth-century banks. There was at least one black woman who held the position of head cashier at a bank: Mabel Z. Mollison at the Knights of Honor Bank in Vicksburg, Mississippi.[24]

The gender makeup of the teller's cage held import to other members of the board as well, but for different reasons than Walker's. Some board members felt that men working in the bank's front office projected a sense of security, power, and prestige. For instance, Rev. Zachariah Lewis insisted on "the necessity" of having men in the bank, and in 1906, he nominated Clifford Winfree of Manchester, Virginia, for the assistant cashier position.[25] Winfree's qualifications, besides his gender, included his experience as a business owner, Sunday school teacher, and devoted church worker. Lewis noted that Winfree had also "opened and closed a bank" and had a good reputation "on both sides of the river," which meant that he was well respected among both blacks and whites. The motion to offer the position to Winfree carried, and the new assistant cashier was hired with a salary of thirty-five dollars a month, twenty-five to be paid by the Right Worthy Grand Council and ten by the bank. Winfree had to secure a $3,000 bond, which required a third-party agency to conduct a background and credit check.[26]

Winfree passed muster and accepted the position, but he quickly grew disillusioned given his myriad responsibilities. He saw the position as a part-time one, subordinate to his responsibilities as a member of the school board in his hometown of Manchester. He also felt that he added value to the position, considering his efforts to recruit new depositors, especially other businesses. Thus, he felt justified in demanding that he split his time at the bank, earn a salary of sixty-five dollars, and receive a two-year guarantee. He did not think it "an unreasonable proposition" because "the hours are unusually long and [the] responsibilities are great," and he made it clear that the salary was not negotiable.[27] Unwilling to concede, the board rejected his offer and declared that the assistant cashier position would remain vacant until a suitable candidate was found. Soon thereafter, the board interviewed and hired Mary Hoyt Dawson (see fig. 3.2). The board set her salary at forty-five dollars per month. Walker must have been delighted with the choice, especially since Dawson, an experienced IOSL organizer, had also worked in the IOSL's juvenile division.[28]

While Dawson's presence in the cage gave Walker some sense of accomplishment, the dwindling number of women on the board must have given her some pause. Walker, of course, served as president of the bank, but women made up less than half of the bank's board of directors and officers. They did, however, occupy key positions in the bank's operations. Walker served as the representative of the RWG Council, which was the largest shareholder, and women controlled key committees, such as the auditing committee, which oversaw day-to-day bank operations, and the finance committee, which made loan decisions.[29]

As the bank continued to grow, relations between it and the three other black-owned banks in Richmond remained cordial but competitive. Each bank depended primarily on the residents of Jackson Ward and other black communities in and around Richmond. Walker relished the fact that the first day's deposits at the St. Luke Bank's dwarfed those of the True Reformers, the Mechanics Savings, and the Nickel Savings Banks combined. But it required work to maintain the depositors' early enthusiasm. When the Mechanics Savings Bank took the unusual step of canvassing door to door in early 1906, the St. Luke Bank board decided to "appoint someone to canvass and drum up business for the bank."[30] Walker distributed blank

FIGURE 3.2 Staff of the St. Luke Penny Savings Bank, c. 1910s–1920s. Mary Hoyt Dawson and Emmett C. Burke stand to the left. The other three people's names are not known. *Source*: 99-0677, courtesy of National Park Service, Maggie L. Walker National Historic Site.

deposit slips at stockholders meetings, hoping to "bring results"—that is, additional cash deposits—with the aggressive gesture.[31] Like other savings banks, the St. Luke Bank distributed small metal coin banks to children so that they could save their small change until they had a dollar or more to open or add to their St. Luke Bank accounts. All of the black banks in Richmond solicited the business of black companies, and they cooperated in many ways rather than undercut each other. The Improved Benevolent Order of Elks, headquartered in Philadelphia, deposited its significant funds at both the St. Luke Penny Savings Bank and Mechanics Savings Bank in Richmond.[32]

The bank did a brisk enough business in its early years to consider opening a branch bank. A few other black banks had branches; the Alabama Penny Savings Bank in Birmingham operated three branches in Selma, Anniston, and Montgomery, and the Nickel Savings Bank in Richmond operated a branch office in the *Richmond Planet* building. When Walker discussed opening a branch with the board, Rev. Lewis said he disliked the idea. Other board members, however, immediately saw the benefit of opening a bank in other areas where strong concentrations of St. Luke members lived, such as Washington, D.C., and parts of Virginia. A branch bank in the District of Columbia would have been a potent symbol, especially given the failure of the central Freedman's Bank in the mid-1870s. Branch banks would also have benefitted the hundreds of depositors in New York, Philadelphia, and other states. Out-of-town depositors—individuals, councils, circles, and businesses—had to mail their deposits, payments, and passbooks to the bank for reconciliation, risking loss or mishandling through the mail. And there were borrowers who wanted to support the bank and its mission but did not because the costs and delays associated with banking through the mail represented a major impediment. The stockholders discussed the branch option at a special meeting in September 1906. The board actually filed an application to open a branch in the District of Columbia in August 1909. For unknown reasons, a branch was never opened.[33]

The early years of the St. Luke Penny Savings Bank reflected a period of growth and prosperity. Walker and other key women in the IOSL along with male members of the board of directors helped build legitimacy for the bank. Walker's unconventional approaches to capitalizing and learning the banking business helped make the bank a success. The bank did have to reckon with tensions between its ideals and economic realities with regard to stock, profits, and women's roles in the bank. Over the years, the bank grew in popularity, competing and cooperating with other black banks, fueled in equal parts by Walker's community-focused ethos and by her competitive, driven nature. The bank met many of its challenges, even if it did not fully resolve them. However, Walker's vision and the bank's very existence were challenged when they became entangled with the state and local white merchants.

"WHAT THINK YOU OF THIS?": ECONOMIC JUSTICE ACTIVISM AND JIM CROW FINANCIAL REGULATION

In 1907, North Carolina's Department of Insurance returned a report that the IOSL had submitted to the department to comply with the state's regulations. The state insurance commission claimed the IOSL had failed to demonstrate that it had an adequate "Reserved Fund." Increasingly, regulators required fraternal organizations to create reserve funds to protect their consumers.[34] Walker, a few IOSL executives, and the IOSL's attorney visited Raleigh to meet with North Carolina's insurance commissioner, James R. Young, who questioned Walker extensively about IOSL's assets, mortality rates, and reserve funds. He told her, "I expect to sit here in my office and know every dollar you have."[35] Walker took his statement as a provocation rather than an offer of assistance, likely aware that Young had helped orchestrate the demise of one of the oldest black-owned insurance companies in that state.[36]

North Carolina was not the only state making increased demands on black financial institutions. In 1907, the Georgia legislature instituted new regulations on financial industries—the same year it enacted a new disenfranchisement amendment and other legislation designed to keep blacks in a subordinate status. Whites expressed jealousy and suspicion about black secret societies and fraternal orders, and as subterfuge for their anxieties about blacks' financial success, white legislators and their constituents claimed that members of the societies were planning subversive activities against whites, especially in rural areas. Citing an unnamed lodge that had helped black farm workers boycott a local white planter, Georgia representative Edward H. McMichael wrote a bill requiring that no society could meet for any purpose, meet behind closed doors, post a guard, or bar nonmembers unless it posted a bond of between $5,000 and $20,000 (or $133,000 and $534,000 in 2017 dollars). Although the bill would fail to pass, Walker (see fig. 3.3) feared that it would when she spoke at the IOSL's annual

FIGURE 3.3 Maggie Lena Walker, 1905.
Source: MAWA 822, courtesy of National Park Service, Maggie L. Walker National Historic Site.

convention in 1907. At the same time, Virginia regulators ramped up pressures on financial services companies just as their counterparts had in North Carolina, Georgia, Texas, and other states where the IOSL did business.[37]

Walker believed that the southern state legislators' zealous oversight was motivated by the desire to cudgel successful black businesses rather than to protect consumers. Walker wondered aloud: "Why has each State an Insurance Commission now? Why are we compelled to disclose even to the smallest particular, our membership, our money, and our methods of obtaining and disbursing the same? *What think you of this?*"[38]

She believed that she had the answer: The financial success and growing strength of black-controlled insurance companies and banks had drawn the attention and rancor of the state. "Are we so blind that we do not see?" she asked. "So dull that we can not understand?. . . This bank book tells the tale."[39] She also understood that the close relationship between the IOSL's insurance feature and its bank made it a particularly vulnerable target.

The state's regulation of business and industry from the early 1900s to the early 1920s is one very tangible example of how racism and sexism intersected in the Progressive Era to undermine black financial initiative. Bureaucrats and regulatory commissions balanced competing motives and constituencies as they grappled with regulating financial industries, but the new state regulations in that period were hardly neutral in their application. They worked in tandem with disenfranchisement, segregation of public accommodations and business spaces, economic exploitation of workers, and extralegal intimidation and violence. Reform-minded politicians and regulators narrowly defined legitimate institutions and policed participation in the economy and polity based on race, gender, and class. They construed black economic autonomy and civic involvement as threats to democratic capitalism and the existing social order. But the IOSL succeeded in meeting the demands of state regulators, even as other black-controlled financial institutions failed, in part because of the visionary leadership of Walker and the board, who stayed focused on providing economic opportunities for working women and kept the organization grounded in meeting the social and economic needs of black women and their families.[40]

Understanding the wave of regulations in Virginia near the end of the first decade of the twentieth century requires revisiting the early years of that century. The turn of the century proved particularly stormy as Afro-Richmonders faced assaults on their political, civic, and economic rights. At conventions in 1901 and 1902, the state of Virginia rewrote its constitution. The new 1902 constitution and its cornerstone agency, the new State Corporation Commission (SCC), signaled a bold step into Virginia's modern future. The legislature placed all business-related charters under the SCC's authority. Centralizing into one agency the functions of registering and formalizing businesses would help attract new capital, build up existing capital, and keep that capital in the state.

The SCC also assumed some of the functions of other state departments. For example, insurance companies and banks operating in the state were now required to submit annual reports to the SCC rather than to the state auditor. The required reporting feature, however, represented only nominal regulatory power. The SCC, like the auditor, supplied the form that the banks and insurance companies used but had no power to designate what data to require or punitive powers against companies that neglected to fill out the forms. One delegate stressed the SCC's power as "practically ministerial only."[41] Crusading bureaucrats, however, took only a few years to realize the full potential of the SCC.

The future-forward vision of business and industrial growth glanced backward as well: the 1902 constitution passed the most restrictive voting and segregation laws in Virginia's history to date. In debates on the suffrage provisions of the constitution, Lynchburg delegate Carter Glass, a committed reformer and future secretary of the treasury under President Woodrow Wilson, used election fraud as the pretense for checking "Negro rule." Glass praised the constitution's suffrage restrictions as an important step toward "eliminat[ing] the darkey as a political factor."[42] Reform meant that protecting certain citizens also narrowed and excluded others.

The effect on those targeted by the new constitution was immediate. Within a year, legislators succeeded in purging for the voter rolls nearly 90 percent of black registered voters in Richmond. Jackson Ward, which boasted a healthy and active black electorate, went from 2,983 registered black voters in the late 1890s to only thirty-three in 1903. In addition to constitutional provisions, the legislature gerrymandered Jackson Ward into oblivion, assuring that its record of having twenty blacks elected from the ward since 1865 would never be repeated. The creative gerrymandering dashed any hopes of electing even an alderman to office.[43]

Blacks did not remain silent or passive in the face of these assaults on their civil and economic rights. They formed coalitions, such as the Negro Industrial and Agricultural League (NIAL) and the Virginia Educational and Industrial Association. At a NIAL meeting in 1905, Walker and other members of the St. Luke Bank board of directors spoke, vowing to fight "till the very foundation of the republic trembles."[44] These organizations lobbied white legislators, funded and launched legal challenges, and ran slates of independent political candidates. That protestors appended "industrial" to the names of their associations is telling. They linked the assaults on their political and social status to their paycheck and pocketbook. It was clear that, alongside the franchise and civic involvement, Virginia's political and economic elite imagined black economic autonomy as a threat to the state's modern image of itself. It sought to force blacks into a subordinate status through a combination of regulations to control their access not just to public spaces but also to private sources of jobs and basic financial benefits like insurance policies and bank accounts.[45]

Walker attacked racial segregation and sexism through gendered appeals to black economic self-sufficiency. She tried to stay a step ahead of regulators and even openly resisted regulations that would leave already-vulnerable widows and orphans without much-needed insurance benefits and bank customers without access to credit. To detractors who were critical of black women's encroachment on the sources of male authority, she subverted questions about women's capacity for business to ask the question (reminiscent of IOSL founder Mary Ann Prout): If not wives and mothers, who else was better positioned to provide for widows and orphans? The St. Luke Bank lay at the center of a series of conflicts that tested Walker's deep wells of resolve. An ongoing streetcar boycott in Richmond, public attacks on black women's character, discriminatory actions of local white merchants, a recalcitrant black middle class, and predatory state regulators reveal attacks on black women's economic autonomy at the legal, physical, and ideological levels.

In 1904, the Virginia legislature constructed a carefully worded statute that allowed public transport companies to choose whether to segregate their streetcars and railcars. The Virginia Passenger and Power Company (VPPC), which operated streetcars in Richmond, chose to segregate its cars. Particularly outraged by the affront to their social status and concerned about further incursions on their fragile political and social rights, the black professional and business classes sprang immediately into action. Business and civic leaders such as John Mitchell, editor of the *Richmond Planet* and founder and president of the Mechanics Savings Bank in Richmond, rhetorically protested encroaching discrimination on streetcars, in politics, and in society through bold editorials published in his newspaper. Attorney Giles Jackson, who had successfully fought a similar 1900 ordinance, also protested the VPPC's new segregation policies.[46]

The protests of middle-class, professional men like Mitchell and Jackson drew on discourses that marked distinctions between the "low-lived and unclean" Negroes who rode the cars and "Genteel Negro[es]" like themselves. Mitchell appealed to class interests that cut across racial lines; he argued that he shared the same disdain for bad Negroes as whites felt toward the "white jail-birds, penitentiary convicts, dive keepers, [and] white women of questionable character" who vexed proper white society.[47] But Maggie Lena Walker took a different tack. She understood that the IOSL was a democratic organization representing women and men from various socioeconomic backgrounds: laborers, maids, waitresses, farmers, merchants, teachers, college professors, white-collar clerks, doctors, and civil servants. She did not rely on appeals to middle-class sensibilities that demeaned the working-class people who relied on the public streetcars—and who made up the IOSL's membership and customer base.

Walker's concern for working- and lower-class blacks may have been self-serving; it would not be profitable to disparage one's client base. Even Mitchell toned down some of his comments about lower-class blacks in the pages of the *Planet* to maintain sales of his paper and encourage support for the boycott of Richmond streetcars, which lasted from 1903 to 1907. However, Walker had always demonstrated a commitment to working-class issues. Working-class men and women relied on public transportation, especially women who had to travel around the city to reach their workplaces, particularly whites' homes.

IOSL women did not stop at rhetoric but mobilized for action. When the VPPC appealed to and won support for the segregated conditions from

Richmond's black ministers, six hundred Afro-Richmonders participated in a mass meeting at the True Reformers Hall in mid-April 1904. The speakers urged a mass boycott. The only woman speaker on the dais, Patsie Keiley Anderson, demanded rather than asked, "We, the women, urge you to walk."[48] The audience met her statement with thunderous applause. Walker, along with the presidents of the three other black-owned banks in Richmond, pledged the St. Luke Penny Savings Bank's financial support to start a black-owned transit company. The Richmond Negro Business League, in which Walker served as an executive officer, emptied its treasury to pay legal fees to fight the Jim Crow streetcar ordinance. In addition, Lillian Payne, editor of the new *St. Luke Herald*, used the *Herald*'s pages to urge IOSL members, who had grown to more than ten thousand by 1904, and other readers not to stand still for Jim Crow insults. Walker then tried to build a broad-based coalition to attack segregation and disenfranchisement that cut across class.[49]

Walker, women on the St. Luke Bank's board, and women in the IOSL managed other difficult terrain in the midst of the streetcar boycott. In late 1905, the St. Luke Penny Savings Bank moved out of the space it leased from John Mitchell Jr. and into the St. Luke Emporium (see fig. 3.4). Twenty-two women had signed the charter of the St. Luke Emporium, and the store opened in spring 1905 on 112 East Broad Street to great fanfare. Walker certainly calculated the impact of the sight of black women conducting business, both banking and shopping, along the city's main business thoroughfare as a visual cue of their economic importance to and influence in their communities.[50]

Walker kept a weather eye on the white merchants on and near Broad Street, but even she could not anticipate their apoplectic reaction. Before the emporium opened, a cabal of white merchants offered the IOSL $4,000 above the sales price to sell the emporium building. Walker told St. Luke Bank board members, "If it is worth that much to them, it is as valuable to us."[51] The merchants' offer represented the first salvo in what would become a protracted battle over the material and symbolic meaning of black women conducting business in the white central business district anchored by Broad Street. Walker was always intentional. She meant to test segregation's invisible boundaries. She saw Jim Crow lines as a provocation, a boundary to cross rather than respect. Other board members may not have shared

FIGURE 3.4 St. Luke Emporium and St. Luke Penny Savings Bank on 112 East Broad Street, c. 1904–1910. The image also shows the emporium workers, most of whom were women.

Source: 99-0228.22, courtesy of National Park Service, Maggie L. Walker National Historic Site.

Walker's brazen disregard of the white merchants' attempted rout, but the official record does not note any doubts expressed by other directors or efforts to dissuade Walker.

By August 1905, however, when she proposed moving the St. Luke Bank out of a space leased from John Mitchell and into the emporium, some board members did speak out. The minutes cryptically note a discussion among the board members. Some may have mentioned practical considerations, such as the expense already incurred fitting Mitchell's offices for the bank, or more serious concerns about reprisals. Walker likely countered that the emporium's location on Broad Street could also attract greater traffic. She may even have argued the strategic, competitive merits of moving the bank out of a space that was owned by a rival banker. In addition, a number of other black businesses had purchased properties and planned to open near the emporium. The board decided unanimously, in the end, to move the bank to the emporium property.[52]

For the white civic elite, the St. Luke Bank and the emporium together made corporeal the specter of black women's illegitimate presence in the sphere of commerce. It was not long before the white merchants made the emporium a flashpoint. A rapprochement remained untenable as long as blacks moved outside of Jackson Ward. The merchants formed an all-white retailers' organization. It threatened to suspend business with any vendor that sold goods to the emporium. Some of the emporium's vendors called bills immediately due and payable for goods that they had previously sold on credit. At least one wholesaler called its bills due sooner than customary and then brought a civil suit against the emporium. Other wholesalers that had sold store merchandise to the emporium when it first opened suddenly refused to sell more goods to restock its shelves.[53]

White merchants' reactions proved Walker's point about the importance of black women's symbolic and practical economic power. The black women customers at the emporium and bank were no longer invisible as whites could pretend black women were in kitchens, laundries, and other service work. For the black community, too, the association of the bank and the emporium made public the private and domestic dimensions of black women's economic influence in the marketplace. To be sure, black women displayed their economic influence in public culture; black community institutions like clubhouses, orphanages, and settlement houses evinced black women's formidable fundraising prowess and charitable support. Clubs, pageants, and other social and cultural events reveal their roles as not merely participants in but committed patrons of black public culture.[54]

The links between the bank and the emporium made those associations more manifest, highlighting women's role in what one might imagine as a public commercial culture. Scholars have done much work elaborating the importance of women in the marketplace, and black women did the majority of the shopping for their families. Their treatment by employees and managers at stores, the cost and quality of goods, and their access to a variety brands represented not only a cultural terrain of style and taste but also political and even intellectual terrains as well.[55]

By operating the bank out of the store, Walker linked areas in which women were already powerful and influential, namely labor and consumption, with ones in which they were less frequently associated: banking and finance. More than their presence along an artery of commercial Richmond, their control and ownership of property and capital contended for a reconfiguration of black women to the market. In this public commercial culture, black women as consumers and capitalists attenuated the tenets of a Jim Crow marketplace that preferred to imagine blacks in general and black women in particular as foolish spendthrifts with little inclination or capacity for thrift or economic foresight. The St. Luke Emporium and the St. Luke Bank proved discursive spaces: they articulated and mutually constituted in powerful ways black women's economic roles, not only as consumers and workers but also as builders, savers, and investors. The spaces rived and then reconfigured links between black women's cultural and economic practices and market relationships.[56]

In early February 1906, a saloon planned to open next door to the emporium. Rubbing salt in the wound, the white real estate broker, J. Thompson Brown, invited Walker to bid on the property. Board member Rev. Zachariah Lewis proposed that the bank purchase the 114 Broad Street building to avoid the "calamity" of having a saloon next door, but the board did not second Lewis's motion. What seemed an easy solution could just as easily have become a perilous one. The young bank was doing well, but it was hardly in a position to take on the added burden of a second major outlay of capital. The order could, perhaps, find a use for another commercial building—Walker's economic development vision did call for a factory—but the location, timing, and planning were not quite right for such a major undertaking. In addition, white intimidation could not be ignored. One could never rule out the possibility of violence directed against employees and customers or vandalism and arson against the store. Whites made it clear that racial boundaries were not imaginary. Not only would they draw the lines, they would control, defend, and police them.[57]

The implication of having the saloon next to the store was obvious: its proximity attenuated the respectable image that both the emporium and the bank sought to cultivate. The oblique association with a barroom was enough to sully the reputations of both concerns. Theoretically, no respectable black person would frequent a store so close to a barroom. The particular affront to women could not have been lost on Walker, her fellow bank board members, or the twenty-two women who chartered the emporium. Beyond the association with a red light district business, women customers and employees would be exposed to drunken, rowdy men and would be vulnerable to various levels of sexual violence, from lewd comments and stares to groping and even assault. Opening a saloon endangered the emporium's and the bank's women workers and customers. It made them all vulnerable, a feat accomplished not with extralegal mob violence, which would have tarnished the veneer of civility that the white civic elite imagined governed racial relations in Richmond. The means were more insidious: economic extortion and reprisal. The goals, though, were the same: to undermine black economic autonomy.

White machinations against the emporium combined with a national affront to black women and rapacious state regulation fueled Walker's most vehement public responses against Jim Crow and in support of black economic initiative. Derisive comments by writer Thomas Dixon Jr. about black women's morality fueled Walker's already-simmering rage. At a 1906 meeting in New York City's Carnegie Hall, a meeting whose attendees included Booker T. Washington, businessman and philanthropist Robert Ogden, and writer Mark Twain, Dixon stated that Negro women "do not know what virtue means," and as such, no white man ever raped or took sexual advantage of a Negro woman.[58] Walker commented on the streetcar boycott in conjunction with both Dixon's affront to black womanhood and the threat to the IOSL's businesses in particular and black enterprise in general.

In a public speech in 1906 entitled "Benaiah's Honor—For Men Only," Walker thundered, "We are being oppressed by the passage of laws which not only have for their object the degradation of Negro manhood and Negro womanhood, but also the destruction of all kinds of Negro enterprises."[59] She linked the symbolic, political, and economic outrages together as mutually reinforcing depredations, and she bitterly criticized the " 'jim crow' car" and "degrading 'jim-crow' signs," lamenting that Negroes pay "first class price for second and third class accommodation."[60] She then called attention to active and pending state regulations threatening black-owned financial institutions: "The white man doesn't intend to wait until the Negro becomes a financial giant, he intends to attack him and fetter him now, while he is an infant in his swaddling clothes, helpless in his cradle."[61] The encroachment of Jim Crow did not limit itself to public humiliations on public conveyances but insidiously targeted black ambition and initiative.

Walker had little patience for appeals based on alleged cultural differences among the black socioeconomic classes, such as had been suggested by Mitchell and some others during the streetcar boycott. Indeed, she saw the black middle class as complicit in some ways. She compared aspiring and professional-class blacks to the Pharisees and Jews who scorned Jesus: "But some of our 'best' people, some of the most refined and best educated—the teachers, priests, and lawyers, were much disgusted at the noise and the cries of the multitudes as they sang Hosanna and praised the Lord, and they said to Jesus—'Master, rebuke thy disciples. Stop them. Make them cease their noise and clamor.' . . . As in the days of Jesus so today; . . . our men [must not] forget to do their duty, . . . our women [must not] remain silent."[62]

The St. Luke Emporium suffered poor sales and struggled to make a profit because it endured attacks from both sides: the machinations of jealous white merchants determined to close it down and the recalcitrant black aspiring and professional classes who seldom shopped at the emporium. Both threatened to bankrupt it. Walker mentioned white merchants' efforts to close down the store in her speech, but she used the occasion to directly address concerns about black patronage and its effect on not only the future of the black separate economy but also the economic future and development of black women. Walker pointed the accusatory finger at this segment of blacks and their lack of support for black business, linking that problem with white attacks on black initiative and showing them to be as serious as Jim Crow and state regulation. She skillfully directed her appeals to both sexes, admonishing men to act and challenging women to speak up.

Walker singled out black men in the audience. Throughout her address, Walker's tone shifted between harsh admonishment and plaintive appeals. She reproved the men in attendance: "ARE WE NOT AS MUCH TO YOU AS THE WHITE WOMEN YOU ARE SO LOYALLY SUPPORTING by the nickels, dimes, and dollars you are spending with them each week?"[63] Walker then implored them, "Is there one single colored man in here that will now deliberately go and carry his dollars to the white merchant so that he can fight us? Are you really going to feed the lion of prejudice and make him stronger and stronger so that he can all the more easily devour us?"[64] Walker inverted the politics of respectability, indicting middle-class blacks in particular and daring to define the paradigm of respectability beyond its treacherous cultural teleology. If black men and women failed to support women who were engaged in respectable enterprises, the effect was more than symbolic. They undercut the black community in ways that had far-reaching real-world consequences. If the emporium closed due to lack of community support, its largely female staff, some of them the primary wage earners in their families, would lose their jobs and be forced into less respectable—and lower paying—jobs. The men and women who did frequent the emporium would have to spend their money in other places, perhaps outside the black community. The store's failure would also communicate the implicit message that blacks could not handle large-scale commercial enterprises like department stores and that blacks would fold under a barrage of extralegal and legal intimidation without even a fight.

THE BLACK FINANCIAL INDUSTRY AND STATE REGULATION IN VIRGINIA

Walker clearly understood the ways in which racism and sexism each eroded the progressive sensibility in U.S. society but, when taken together, cleaved it completely. If the progressive mood reflected a vision of the state's expanded commitment to its citizens, bureaucratic activism zealously embraced a commitment to protect certain citizens and marginalize others. Race and gender muddled the categories of the worthy citizen and the unruly other, the line between them dividing those most in need of state protections from those who posed a threat to the polity. In this way, poor, uneducated, and landless whites; immigrants; and blacks often merged to pose a constant threat to the freedom and security of worthy citizens, threats that needed both policing and defending against.

On October 15, 1908, Walker's portents about the machinations of state commissioners against black financial organizations took on flesh and bone. Examiners with the Virginia Department of Insurance made an unexpected and unannounced visit to the IOSL headquarters to conduct a full audit. The IOSL passed the surprise audit, which was no mean feat considering that the IOSL staff had done so without Walker's constant guidance and reassuring presence. In March 1908, Walker had suffered a serious fall at her residence that had broken her kneecap and left her bedridden for some months. The injury would cause her chronic pain for the rest of her life, crippling her in her last decade. The confinement was difficult for Walker, and it was made more difficult when she saw that her IOSL was under assault and that she could do little from her sickbed. Many of her friends and associates stressed that it was important to get as much rest as possible and trust in the training and guidance she had invested in her staff. With this audit, the commissioner of the Virginia insurance department, Joseph Button, planted a seed of enmity between himself and Walker. When state agencies pushed, the IOSL pushed back.[65]

In 1909, Commissioner Button advised the IOSL of a new law that no longer allowed children under sixteen to take out life insurance policies. He ordered Walker to end juvenile policies, but Walker flagrantly disregarded Button. She probably asked her own legal advisers' opinions of the new law, but she likely felt that Button's orders were arbitrary. To be sure, Walker would have been resistant to any adulteration of the juvenile plan, which held special importance to her. Prout had worked closely with children and young adults in the St. Luke Society, and Walker had built on that legacy, almost singlehandedly creating the IOSL juvenile circles. In its early years,

Walker's juvenile insurance plan had prospered when the IOSL's floundered. The juvenile circles and juvenile insurance policies also created an important pipeline of new members into the adult IOSL order and insurance plan. They had nurtured a generation of women organizers. More important, Walker asserted the IOSL's right, in the face of bureaucratic and legal harassment, to provide not only distinct and special protections for children and teenagers but also a pathway out of poverty for young people.[66]

Button demanded Walker's compliance and threatened to suspend the IOSL. Walker toyed with Button, telling him that, to her knowledge, the IOSL was not in violation. However, he produced evidence from the IOSL's home office records showing that it had issued new policies to youths under sixteen. One of the state's examiners wrote in his report that the IOSL "persistently violated" the new rules.[67] The commissioner called Walker to his office, and he must have been very displeased with their interaction because he directed the local police to issue a warrant for Walker's arrest. Button alleged that Walker had been made aware of the new restrictions early in the year, but she had still encouraged IOSL councils and circles to continue enrolling youths younger than sixteen. It was inconceivable that Walker would spend any actual time behind bars. Beyond her impeccable public renown, it was not clear that Button had the power to arrest anyone. She did go to the courthouse and pay a small fine. The IOSL worked around the restriction by requiring parents, rather than the adolescents, take out policies on children under sixteen.[68]

The regulatory hurdles only continued. In 1910, new statutes endowed the State Corporation Commission with sharper legislative teeth. The legislature also created a new regulatory body to complement the insurance department: the banking division. The division's new chief examiner, Charles C. Barksdale, approached his new position with a tenacity that rivaled many state bureaucrats. Barksdale clearly wanted to project the power of his new office while at the same time setting it on firm, professional grounding. From the moment he first sat in his office on July 1, 1910, he fired off letters to Virginia's 243 banks requesting reports of their financial conditions. When banks returned their reports, he demanded explanations for inconsistencies, names of customers who consistently overdrafted their accounts, and details about the security offered for loans.[69]

Barksdale especially targeted abuses by bank directors. His comments to the State Bank of Columbia in Columbia, Virginia, sum up his philosophy: "Your bank will not be permitted to continue practices that have prevailed in the past."[70] He demanded that directors bring overdrafted accounts to a positive balance immediately, ordered banks to dispose of the compromised assets, and refused extensions when banks pled that they needed more time. Even when the banks had broken no laws or codes, Barksdale still wanted explanations and compliance with best practices in the absence of actual statutes.[71]

The banks fought back. Some argued that the new laws did not apply retroactively. Others quibbled over semantics and the finer details of the new code, such as the meaning of terms like "total liability." Still others complained that even when they made changes to comply, Barksdale judged their efforts to be insufficient. Some banks resorted to legal tactics, such as seeking injunctions to force the SCC to stop examining banks. The bankers could also be petty: after nearly two weeks without having the trash emptied at the banking division, clerks learned that the janitor had been ordered by unknown sources to pass over Barksdale's office.[72]

Banks were local institutions, shaped by and responsive to local rhythms. They set their own priorities. Many relied on "gentlemen's agreements," arrangements based on custom and mutual trust. Some were, in fact, rather mismanaged. For example, Barksdale wrote to the president of the Bank of Elba, stating that the state of affairs in his bank "exceed[ed] all bounds of conservative banking."[73] Of the L. E. Mumford Banking Company, Barksdale wryly conceded, "The Banking Division is forcibly impressed with the very bad management of this institution."[74] Many bankers, however, bristled under what they saw as a barrage of regulations and demands that interfered with their local practices. They considered the new scrutiny to be a serious and intrusive impediment to business as usual.[75]

Thus, the St. Luke Bank was not alone in feeling angst against the new chief examiner, but it should not have had to worry. The new statutes did not include specific provisions for savings banks but only applied to commercial banks. Thus, technically, savings banks were not subject to the new banking division's authority. Barksdale expanded his authority to savings banks, however, by arguing that a good portion of commercial banks in the state under his control, about 20 percent, took savings deposits. He also likely figured that by holding up some savings banks as particularly egregious examples of mismanagement and fraud, he could sidestep questions about his authority to review them. Unlike many of the commercial banks, savings banks were typically smaller and capitalized for less, which meant that they had fewer resources to challenge the banking division. The True Reformers Savings Bank, for instance, lay squarely in Barksdale crosshairs.[76]

On one hand, it made sense that Barksdale would include the True Reformers among his savings bank targets; it was the first-chartered and largest black bank in the country, and the bank did have serious problems. For nearly two years, customers had complained that the bank would not honor the order's insurance claims checks. The insurance commissioner suggested separating the bank and other concerns from the order, but the True Reformers' leadership refused to do so. On the other hand, the bank's very visible success, illustrated by the money in its vaults and its offshoot businesses, made the True Reformers a veritable franchise. The True Reformers Bank held $300,000 in its vaults (about $8 million in 2017 dollars), and its offshoot businesses included a newspaper, a real estate company, a hotel, and a general store. Its success challenged the logic of Jim Crow, undergirded by stereotypes of blacks as inept, lazy wastrels.

Regulators calling for more stringent regulations held up the True Reformers as a special case and even requested permission to take early action against the organization, which Insurance Commissioner Button said "had been long suspected . . . [of] mismanagement and corruption."[77] In 1910, Button succeeded in forcing the president of the True Reformers out of office. On October 18, 1910, Barksdale personally conducted an audit of the True Reformers Bank, and two days later, he declared the bank and insurance divisions insolvent and placed the bank under receivership. The loss of True Reformers struck a deep blow, not just in lost deposits but also in spirit. Some described the closure as "the downfall of Africa."[78]

Flush with new legislative powers and copious amounts of progressive zeal, Barksdale audited every one of the state's fourteen black banks (see table 3.1). By comparison, he audited only about half of all the banks in the state. The black banks held combined assets of at least $886,000, or about

TABLE 3.1 Black Banks Operating in Virginia, 1910

Bank	Location	Year Opened
Brickhouse Savings Bank	Hare Valley	1910
Brown Savings Bank	Norfolk	1909
Crown Savings Bank	Newport News	1908
Galilean Fishermen's Bank	Hampton	1901
Knights of Gideon Savings	Norfolk	1905
Mechanics Savings Bank	Richmond	1902
Nickel Savings Bank	Richmond	1896
People's Savings Bank	Petersburg	1908
People's Dime Savings Bank and Trust Association	Staunton	1908
St. Luke Penny Savings Bank	Richmond	1903
Sons and Daughters of Peace Penny, Nickel, and Dime Savings Bank	Newport News	1904
Southern One Cent Savings Bank	Waynesboro	1905
Sussex-Surrey-Southampton Savings Bank–American Home and Missionary Banking Association	Courtland	1903
True Reformers Savings Bank	Richmond	1888

$23 million in today's dollars. This impressive number, however, represented only 1 percent of the total assets of the state's 230 other banks.[79]

Almost all the black banks were formally or informally connected to fraternal orders or insurance companies. The deep interconnections between fraternal orders, their insurance and banking divisions, and their spin-off business inadvertently granted Barksdale incredible power to strike a blow against these potent symbols of black economic achievement. For example, Barksdale placed the People's Southern One Cent Savings Bank in Basic City under receivership. That bank was the depository for the Imperial Grand United Order of Abraham, and the closure meant not only that the order's claims would go unpaid but also that mortgages held by both the order and bank could be called due immediately. The bank customers' and insurance company's property could be sold for cents on the dollar.[80] Barksdale saw black banks' shortcomings as particularly threatening. For example, he described the state of affairs at the Grand United Order of Galilean Fisherman's Consolidated Bank in Hampton as "dangerous."[81]

Indeed, the quick succession of black bank closures and the chief examiner's aggressive posturing justifiably appeared to Walker and other black bankers to take on the proportions of a vendetta. Barksdale told reporters that he considered the surprise audit essential to the effectiveness of the new banking division. In his first six months as chief examiner, Barksdale's office audited 110 banks, and ten banks were placed in the hands of receivers, liquidated, or dissolved completely; six of the ten were black banks. Bureaucrats often framed discrimination as fairness and worked hard to represent publicly that their actions under the color of law did not reflect personal biases. Expertise and public good, not prejudice or caprice, motivated their actions. Privately, Barksdale seemed to gloat about his success in closing black banks. In October, he wrote to Lawrence Murray, the U.S. comptroller of the currency, about his success in closing colored banks since taking office in July. The cordial exchange between Barksdale and other bureaucrats suggests the social and professional pressure exerted to target black financial institutions.[82]

Barksdale wielded the surprise audit as a weapon with great effect against black banks. The banks did have minor and some even serious problems, but they were not necessarily guilty of the criminal misbehavior of the True Reformers. Some minor issues included incomplete forms, small overdrafted accounts, and missing signatures.[83] Their major problems reflected deeper structural issues, particularly lack of access to modern business methods, depressed property values in racially segregated areas, and customers' difficulties obtaining credit elsewhere. For example, in the examiner's report for People's Dime Savings Bank and Trust Association in Staunton, examiner Charles Hunter complained that he could not get a true financial picture of the bank because it utilized "the old debit and credit ledgers of long ago" and its books were "in disarray."[84] Hunter advised a full review, from customer passbooks to every ledger in the files, and then a complete overhaul of the bank. It is doubtful that any of the bank's management had any formal education in the financial field; the vice president of People's Dime Savings was a former laborer, and the cashier, who earned only fifteen dollars a month, was a former schoolteacher. [85]

Walker and the St. Luke staff kept abreast of the latest business methods by reading industry publications. Walker also continued to observe operations of successful financial institutions. For example, she occasionally visited the Port Huron, Michigan, offices of the Women's Benefit Association (WBA), one of the largest fraternal insurance organizations in the country. The WBA helped Walker develop a reserve fund, and it allowed her to observe new accounting and management methods. Based on what she saw there, she sent clippings of state-of-the-art office equipment and systems to Emmett Burke to order and implement in the bank. Professionals and sympathetic bureaucrats sometimes proved helpful, too, offering invaluable advice to Walker and the IOSL staff. For example, an actuary advised the order to adopt a new bookkeeping system and to audit its books every month rather than every quarter. A state examiner suggested that the RWG Council purchase its headquarters building from the St. Luke Association rather than continue leasing it. Walker instituted the suggestions.[86]

Examiners consistently lowered the value of real estate held by black banks. For example, examiner Hunter wrote to the president of the People's Dime Savings that his staff had obtained from "reliable sources" that the bank had overvalued its banking house by $1,100, more than a quarter of its estimated value.[87] Black banks typically held various properties, some that banks acquired through foreclosure but also residential and commercial properties that they rented for profit. The St. Luke Bank owned commercial and residential property, some of which it managed through IOSL-related businesses such as the East End Association. On top of being forced outside of the central business districts and residential areas into black enclaves, real estate was affected by the number of black residences and property holders in an area, which lowered its value in the perception of public assessors and private appraisers. Indeed, racial hierarchies inured to place. With few options for buying property in other parts of the city and little control over the perceived inferiority of black spaces, black banks collectively fought a Sisyphean battle with regard to the value of their real estate holdings.[88]

In addition, sections of the new banking laws that limited loan amounts also made black banks particularly vulnerable to sanction. Most black banks struggled with low or undercapitalization. At least one bank, Crown Savings Bank in Newport News, had not raised its minimum $10,000 capital after two years of operation. However, the St. Luke Bank boasted a surplus of more than twice its paid-in capital. While it was the largest black bank in Virginia, it was still a small savings bank compared to other banks in Virginia. Under the 1910 law, a bank could not issue any single loan or hold a combination of loans that exceeded 25 percent of its paid-in capital and surplus. Given the low capitalization of black banks, this restriction meant that black banks were formally limited to loan portfolios between about $1,250 and $6,000—figures that made it impossible to provide sufficient numbers of loans for provisioning a farm, continuing a child's or one's own education, investing in a business, or buying a home for the banks' thousands of customers. Banks could exceed these loan thresholds with the written consent of the board of directors, but even with board consent, examiners exercised their discretion to require banks to curtail or call loans due and payable if, in the examiners' estimation, the bank's loans were too numerous or large.

Overextended loan portfolios were hardly a problem limited to black banks, but black bank customers had fewer options for credit and loans. Black banks felt obliged and indeed privileged to lend money when few other banks would. As one might expect, their loan portfolios sometimes outpaced their assets and deposit accounts (see table 3.2), certainly exceeding the 25 percent limit on the ratio of loans to capital and surplus. Such large loan-to-asset ratios left black banks vulnerable.

Examiners admonished banks for excessive single-name paper, which were loans endorsed by the lien holders. Since the strength of the borrowers' character, social standing, and economic worth buttressed their creditworthiness, for certain borrowers, banks sometimes required little or no collateral as security or accepted the value of the borrowers' assets with little to no vetting. These loans were important for individuals with immense social capital but limited or tight economic resources. For example, Nickel Savings had $9,600 in single-name paper, nearly half its outstanding loans. Admittedly, highly placed bank officers and directors could easily abuse single-name loans for their personal gain.[89]

Barksdale reproached the St. Luke Bank for single-name paper by its subsidiary businesses: $9,222 in loans to the St. Luke Emporium (in addition to the $5,050 in stock held by the bank) and an $820 loan to the IOSL Press, which published the *St. Luke Herald*. Easy access to working capital was

TABLE 3.2 Loans to Asset Ratios of Black Banks Operating in Virginia, 1910

Bank	Capital	Surplus and Undivided Profits	Deposits	Loans and Discounts	Loans and Discounts as Percentage‡
Brickhouse Savings Bank	$10,000	$360	$3,912	$8,417	81.25%
Brown Savings Bank	$10,000	$1,142	$9,073	$6,516	58.48%
Crown Savings Bank	$10,000	($1,777)	$16,212	$10,407	126.56%
Galilean Fishermen's Bank*	$5,000	$3,988	—	—	—
Knights of Gideon Savings*	$1,500	$5,945	—	—	—
Mechanics Savings Bank	$10,000	$21,917	$173,868	$25,936	81.26%
Nickel Savings Bank	$2,000	$9,356	$30,121	$19,507	171.78%
People's Savings Bank	$10,000	$1,941	$17,902	$23,115	193.58%
People's Dime Savings Bank and Trust Association	$500**	$1,442	$4,889	$2,104	108.34%
St. Luke Penny Savings Bank	$10,000	$25,630	$85,183	$38,410	107.80%
Sons and Daughters of Peace Penny, Nickel, and Dime Savings Bank	$5,000	$2,984	$12,790	$9,507	119.08%
Southern One Cent Savings Bank*	$10,000	$149	—	—	—
Sussex-Surrey-Southampton Savings Bank–American Home and Missionary Banking Association*	$5,000	$12,615	—	—	—
True Reformers Savings Bank*	$10,000	$215,459	$232,003	$470,566	208.71%

Note: Amounts are in 1910 dollars.

Source: Annual Reports of the Secretary of Virginia, 1909 and 1910.

‡ Loans and discounts as a percentage of capital paid in, surplus, and undivided profits.

* 1909 figures.

** It is unclear why the People's Dime had such a low amount for required capital, but it must have gotten special permission from the legislature. No other bank in the state had a capital requirement this low.

essential for any business, but it was difficult for black-owned businesses to acquire. Without St. Luke Bank loans, the IOSL businesses could not operate effectively. Walker met with Barksdale to discuss stock the bank owned and loans it made to IOSL concerns. She argued that the stock was valuable and could be easily sold without loss to the bank. In addition, the businesses could pay back the loans. The truth was that by 1910, the St. Luke board had resorted to paying commissions to encourage stock sales, and the emporium consistently failed to make a profit. Barksdale called Walker's bluff: he ordered her to sell off the emporium stock in the bank's portfolio and collect the emporium's loan. He also insisted that the bank "dis-connect itself from the St. Luke insurance order as rapidly as possible."[90] Faced with poor sales, the machinations of white merchants, and state pressure, the emporium shut its doors in 1910. The bank also ended its formal connection to the IOSL and IOSL businesses.

Walker was not one to retreat from a fight without a plan. As one of the two surviving banks in Richmond, Walker wanted to protect the bank's shareholders and the IOSL membership. She also wanted to remain competitive. To mark a new era in the bank's history, the board authorized the construction of a new bank building, which would increase public confidence and, she hoped, in short order, increase deposits, shareholders, and profits. The St. Luke Penny Savings Bank moved into a newly constructed, three-story bank building in the heart of the black community of Jackson Ward in the fall of 1911 (see fig. 3.5).[91]

In 1909, Walker probably took it as both a personal and a collective attack when insurance commissioner Button's examiners invaded her beloved IOSL offices. After passing the surprise audit, Walker praised the IOSL as passing "from an old-fashioned, old-timed secret benevolent society . . . to a fraternal endowment association."[92] No doubt Walker intended her statement to stress the IOSL's modernity and competitiveness in the marketplace and to indict capitalist values that stressed individualism and rivalry as ends in themselves. The phrase "fraternal endowment association" retained the cherished, traditional secret ritual and ceremony that bound members together and accentuated the character of its members, but it also stressed the modernity, professionalism, and institutionalized business

FIGURE 3.5 St. Luke Penny Savings Bank building, First and Marshall Streets, c. 1911. *Source*: 99-0228.19, courtesy of National Park Service, Maggie L. Walker National Historic Site.

practices and standards that would help it more effectively compete with the banking and insurance behemoths of the white—and black—business world.

Wrangling with regulators had the unintended consequence of making the St. Luke's board more politically astute, economically self-reliant, and culturally distinctive. It worked with lawyers to avoid fines and other litigation and created public relations strategies to attract borrowers and detract from regulators' criticism. It also refined its banking practices and methods. In working with bureaucrats and politicians, the bank did not lobby in the formal sense but did promote its special interests. More important, contests with regulators and the civic-business elite helped the bank construct its own practices and values, which the industry would test as the bank grew.[93]

Reforms and updated business practices not only kept the bank beyond the reproach of regulators but also reinforced Walker's belief in the critical necessity of doing business on the bank's own terms. The St. Luke Bank would rely on its own cultural referents, using the IOSL as a model for its organizational structure and underwriting practices. While it became more difficult over time for the bank to preserve its internal processes, the bank's success and steady growth did prove that it could preserve a woman-centered vision that could adapt in the face of increasing state requirements and the growing complexities of the U.S. financial industry.

4

Rituals of Risk and Respectability

GENDERED ECONOMIC PRACTICES, CREDIT, AND DEBT TO WORLD WAR I

Annie J. Evans, a paid IOSL organizing deputy and self-employed stenographer in Attleborough, Massachusetts, apologized to the St. Luke Bank when it rejected her loan application. "I am also sorry," she continued, "that I am looked upon with dishonor by the President and Board of Directors." She simply could not fathom how they could have turned her down for a loan: "[I] spend *all of my time in building up the work* [of the order]." She claimed to have singlehandedly recruited all the New England councils save one and then to have encouraged them all to deposit money in the bank. Evans relied on her work and personal honor, rather than her income or employment, to stand in for her creditworthiness. The work she did for the order, she felt, obligated the bank to her, given what she had contributed to the IOSL's—and, by extension, the bank's—success.[1]

This chapter explores gendered economic practices in order to understand the St. Luke Bank staff's assessment of risk and reliance on respectability in its lending and debt-collection practices. Gendered economic practices encompass multiple sites and both financial and nonfinancial transactions and processes. The social reproduction of meaning around noneconomic processes imbued the economic with cultural value. This production of meaning and values constitutes critical, though sometimes hidden, practices in a market economy. In addition to gendered economic practices, the IOSL's fraternal administrative structure and esoteric ritual shaped the bank's lending programs and guidelines in the early years of the bank. By the mid-1910s, however, the bank also relied on standard industry practices and aggressive debt-collection techniques to appease regulators and to ensure the steady flow of credit to its customers.

Mitigating risk played a crucial role in the extension of credit and the repayment of loans, but race, gender, and class shaped what constituted risk. The growing consumer lending market often reflected stereotypes about race and gender that constructed the bulk of the St. Luke Bank's customers as illegitimate credit risks. The bank helped women negotiate the dialectic between risk and respectability. It acknowledged women's important economic roles in their families and communities and strove to increase women's financial literacy and make borrowing a respectable activity. The bank relied on its own administrative models and cosmology to mitigate and determine acceptable risk. Within a few years of the bank's 1903 opening, increased state oversight as well as the practical experience of lending money led to more systematic and institutionalized records and procedures. The bank, however, never rejected whole cloth its own cultural referents or the gendered economic practices of its members in managing its risks.

Mutuality and obligation proved to be useful and protean resources to negotiate risk, link respectability and borrowing, and promote both individual benefit and collective good. Obligation helped naturalize financial exchanges between the bank and its customers, but it held inherent tensions. The tactics that borrowers relied on to press their cases for loans, the bank's efforts to collect from delinquent debtors, and the limitations that appeals to respectability placed on women borrowers reflect these tensions.

In considering the ways that gender shaped the bank's practices and priorities, it is important to understand the world of quotidian credit that black borrowers confronted before World War I and the interlocking roles of risk, race, and gender in the finance industry. These social realities molded the bank's strategies for mitigating and managing its risks to ensure that it provided adequate credit to meet the needs of its customers. The bank tapped into the IOSL's administrative and symbolic resources to mold those strategies as well. The IOSL ritual, for example, was highly complex but also logical, effective, and malleable enough to provide elements through which to assess specific attributes used as criteria for credit underwriting. It stood on its own authority, an imprimatur against racist and sexist stereotypes that made credit more expensive, difficult to procure, and unequal for marginal economic actors. It drew on similar experiences and cultural referents to endorse mutual obligations and interdependencies in contrast to self-interested, free-market imperatives. Rather than reinforce hierarchical, exploitative relationships of credit, the bank revealed its "productive potential" to open avenues of independent enterprise, homeownership, and (individual and collective) racial uplift.[2]

The ritual diminished but could not completely erase social and class tensions. Standard industry practices correlated social standing and income with creditworthiness. The bank resisted the standards and practices that underlay formal risk assessment with regard to black lives and livelihoods because it could not trust the people, institutions, or standards to be fair. The bank constructed respectability based on racial pride, financial literacy, and other attributes that cut across racial and class differences. It did, however, sometimes by choice and sometimes by force, adopt standard business and accounting practices. It also used high-pressure tactics to shame borrowers into paying their debts. The bank's high rate of lending, though troubling to state regulators, reflected what Nicholas Osborne describes as "one of the tangible ways that the growth of for-profit savings banking helped to reshape the finance economy" in the first decade of the twentieth century.[3] The bank's lending habits reflected, then, a critique and capitulation: they coexisted within crystallizing logics of financial markets that took black people in general and black women in particular as a priori risks.

AFRICAN AMERICANS AND THE WORLD OF EVERYDAY CREDIT BEFORE WORLD WAR I

The options available to poor, working-class, and middle-class borrowers who needed money included a mix of extralegal and legal options. Borrowers of all classes concerned reformers and financiers enough that they moved beyond rhetoric to institutional solutions. They grudgingly acknowledged the necessity, and sometimes wisdom, of poor and working-class people borrowing to meet emergency needs. They rationalized their magnanimity by conjuring images of the profligate spendthrift infected with the "borrowing germ" and the imperiled worker trapped by a series of salary loans who became a "veritable slave" to loan sharks.[4] Reform-minded financiers organized the first remedial-lending organizations in the late nineteenth century. By 1910, a national network crisscrossed parts of the United States. Theoretically, blacks had access to these organizations, but it is unclear how often they used them. None were in Richmond, but it is possible that IOSL members used them in New York, Baltimore, the District of Columbia, and other places where these loosely federated savings banks, workingman's loan associations, and pawners' societies existed. Remedial loans, however, were not the panacea that reformers promised. The savings organizations offered limited services, and they placed some restrictions on borrowers: borrowers had to have verifiable and lengthy employment, some form of acceptable collateral, and income that met minimum limits.[5]

Closer to Richmond, the Virginia Bankers Association considered the problem of poor and working-class borrowers. The association encouraged its member banks to enlarge and devote more attention to their savings departments. The bankers highlighted working-class borrowers as needing special attention, though their rhetoric about discouraging loans and speculation among working-class risks reinforced their own self-important roles as guardians of character. In Norfolk, lawyer Arthur J. Morris promoted his eponymous plan, "a lending method that struck a compromise between the lawlessness of the salary lenders and the paternalistic self-sacrifice promoted by reformers."[6] He opened the first Morris-plan bank, Fidelity Savings and Trust Company, in Norfolk in 1910.[7]

In addition to remedial loans, needy borrowers turned to chattel loans, salary loans, and private lenders to help make ends meet. These options were all legal and vitally important options for quick access to cash, but under certain circumstances, they skirted the law. Chattel loans and pawnbroking provided an accessible, convenient form of everyday credit. Beverly Lemire's observations that pawning clothes, household goods, and jewelry was an adaptive strategy to bridge the inevitable shortfalls in limited, irregular, or seasonal income remain as true for early twentieth-century Afro-Richmonders as it did for her seventeenth-century men and women living on urban side streets and in rural hamlets in England. Black women, as managers of household credit and budgets, figured prominently, if not disproportionately, high among pawners. Women labored in a market that was fragmented by race and gender, which translated into limited employment opportunities and lower wages. They were especially dependent, then, on local, quotidian sources of credit.[8]

The amounts loaned were small, which reflected careful rather than risky considerations of the amounts needed to manage household budgets. As isolated transactions, the amounts borrowed seem trivial, but their consequence multiplied through repeated transactions over time. Women borrowers seeking loans on their personal and household items had to learn which brokers extended generous terms, treated pawners fairly, and acted with discretion. It was in the interest of brokers, at least reputable ones, to know their customers as a strategy to avoid receiving stolen goods and to establish repeat business. In rare instances, a pawnbroker might lend money based solely on the borrower's reputation, but placing some item up as collateral provided greater security for the loan. Thus, pawning broadened women's market for credit in ways that reputation, income, and other conventional markers of creditworthiness did not. If she owned something of value, she could get some money for it. Pawnshops were local institutions, embedded in their neighborhoods (see fig. 4.1). The neighborhood-level credit relationship was in many ways an intimate one. As such, pawnbroking

FIGURE 4.1 Uncle Paul's Pawn Shop, Augusta, Georgia, c. 1899.
Source: LC-USZ62-111067, Library of Congress.

embedded commercial credit relations with social, cultural, and community bonds of sociability and personal relationships.[9]

Pawnbroking also strained those bonds, as subsistence credit and loans subverted patriarchal family and labor structures, destabilized class and racial boundaries, and attracted state surveillance. As women became proficient in securing short-term credit, they gained greater control over their household budgets in spite of limited work opportunities. Women's control over household goods also meant that they did not have to depend on husbands, partners, relatives, or other family members for money to pay for necessities and personal wants. They could pawn household items without others' permission or knowledge. In addition to controlling the nature of the collateral required, women exercised some flexibility and control over the terms and duration of the loan in their negotiations with pawnbrokers. Unfortunately, frequent pawners and cultural arbiters often held different conceptions of pawning as a measure of women's thriftiness. Women customers considered it their right and prerogative to draw on the value of their property when faced with financial strain. Critics believed women's reliance on pawnbroking did not conform to idealized, bourgeois expectations about how women should spend money or manage their household budgets.[10]

Racial stereotypes tainted pawnbroking for black women of every class. Women were sometimes forced to observe humiliating racial etiquette from bigoted storeowners, but a pawnbroker who engaged in repeated racial denigration was likely to drive away potential or repeat customers. Black members of the aspiring and intellectual classes rebuked blacks of the lower classes who frequented pawnbrokers. They sometimes accepted the assumed innate improvidence of black people. W. E. B. Du Bois bemoaned, "Instead then of a struggling people being met by aid in the direction of their greatest weakness [spending], they are surrounded by agencies which tend to make them more wasteful and dependent on chance than they are now."[11] In addition to lottery games and gambling places, he highlighted pawnbrokers and "usurers" among the groups that tested the moral resolve of black communities. Black newspapers published short, satirical stories that denigrated the practice of pawnbroking through humor, but the stories underscore its pervasiveness as a strategy to secure short-term credit. Cultural arbiters also associated pawnbroking with criminality, describing thieves who sold stolen goods to pawnbrokers, thieves who stole goods from pawnbrokers, and people who discounted pawn tickets (i.e., purchased pawn tickets for a fraction of the amount loaned).[12]

In addition to concerns about housing, education, and social services, groups such as the Colored YMCA in Washington, D.C., and the Colored Charity Workers in Birmingham conducted research about credit markets in black communities. Their investigations exposed the exploitation of middle- and working-class borrowers at the hands of salary lenders and pawnshops. More important, although blacks did not have full advantage of the franchise, they still exercised political leverage by challenging local and state officials to regulate the small-scale consumer lending industry. Well-meaning reformers, however, may have done as much harm as good in their efforts to improve local loan options for black borrowers.[13]

Particularly for women who relied on pawning to extend household budgets, the domestic and commercial collided with the state. State responses to reforming the industry considered who borrowed and who lent, often framing the former as the victim and the latter as the perpetrator. Reformers and politicians constructed certain borrowers as victims who needed protection but were not quite ready for or capable of managing credit. Concerned reformers latched on to the image of the poor, victimized woman or extravagant, spendthrift housewife being exploited by burdensome, unmanageable hidden fees and high interest rates. Both images assumed women's relationship to credit, unmediated by a husband or other male, was fraught with the potential for discord. By implication, it was in the state's interest to step in where a leavening male influence was absent or undermined. Reformers and bureaucrats intended the regulation of pawn shops as a way to help poor women avoid charity in particular and to help all women in general to be more efficient, frugal, and prudent housewives.

Abuses by pawnbrokers led authorities to pass laws and regulations governing the industry, but these laws did not always bring relief or protection to borrowers. These regulations, however, had the practical effects of adversely affecting women's control over private property converted to cash and, ironically, leaving them more vulnerable to exploitation. For example, in 1913, in response to state pressure, Richmond passed new local ordinances regulating pawnbrokers. These regulations increased the costs and risks of lending for regulated brokers, expenses they undoubtedly passed on to pawners. For unregulated brokers, these regulations drove many borrowers' transactions underground, forcing them to engage in extralegal and illegal credit markets. Similar legislation that was designed to check the abuses of salary lenders and high-interest, short-term private lenders, who were often lumped under the category of loan sharks, provided relief from some abuses but further constrained borrowers' options and autonomy. None of the regulations addressed the underlying conditions—namely low wages, limited job options, and high costs of living—that led black women especially to continued dependence on expensive, local forms of everyday credit.[14]

Gambling and playing the numbers and other games of chance, represented popular extralegal and illegal forms of everyday credit. An underground world of betting houses, crap shoots, and gambling parlors flourished in and around Richmond. Betting houses took wagers on sports as well as on the outcomes of widely publicized civil and criminal trials in Richmond. As long as the houses conducted games fairly, they escaped strict policing. The houses, however, were sometimes the sites of violent shootings.[15] One indication of gambling's widespread popularity is suggested by the alleged religious conversion of one notorious gambler. During a large Baptist revival in Norfolk in 1911, Big Hughsie, one of the black community's most prolific and well-known gamblers, caught the spirit and repented his sinful ways. He then "urged all those whom he had taught to gamble to raise their hands; at least a hundred hands were raised."[16] Though the number of converts was probably exaggerated for comic effect, the story underscores the fact that many people saw gambling as an acceptable and popular source of funds.

Before playing the numbers gained widespread popularity in the interwar years, people played a variety of games of chance. Missing-letter and missing-word contests were popular enough that the U.S. Postal Service warned that it would report people to authorities if they were caught playing or promoting the games.[17] Games of chance provided entertainment and offered the possibility of turning a tiny investment of a few cents into hundreds of dollars. A veritable informal industry sprang up around these games of chance. Though it was largely male-dominated, women carved out a niche in the gambling industry. Women earned commissions from selling and collecting for the games. They also worked as waitresses in saloons and

FIGURE 4.2 Caroline Dye, known as "Aunt Caroline," was a famous spiritualist based in Arkansas. The white-line drawings and winged figure on this souvenir postcard suggest her connections to the spiritual world. People relied on the counsel of spiritualists to help improve their odds in games of chance, an important activity for raising funds in times of need.
Source: Jackson County Historical Society, Newport, Arkansas.

gambling establishments, as jitney drivers, and as spiritual consultants.[18] Fortunetellers, clairvoyants, and spiritualists—most of whom were women—openly advertised their services in Richmond papers. Some placed discreet classifieds advertising lucky products like charms and dream books as well as other supernatural services. Others relied on large, flashy ads in the black press like those of Madam Eldon, who traveled around the United States providing "scientific palmist" and fortunetelling services. Caroline "Aunt Caroline" Tracy Dye, one of the most famous spiritualists in the South, did not advertise her services, but thousands, including prominent white politicians, sought her services in person and by mail (see fig. 4.2). She did not charge money for her services, but people gave her money so that she became a wealthy woman, owning multiple properties and land in and around her hometown of Newport, Arkansas.[19]

Often roundly condemned as an immoral and corruptible activity, extralegal gambling represented one approach to managing risk—or to managing hard times, as players saw it. Gamblers believed they could cope with, even control, the forces of chance. They were calculating, rational economic actors. Aside from the entertainment aspect, Ivan Light stresses that numbers gambling in particular could be seen "as a rational economic activity" and notes that blacks typically described their lottery ticket purchases as "investments."[20] Even a small windfall helped make ends meet. Gambling provided a vehicle for savings and credit, which working and poor people needed despite reformers' assumptions about their use of that credit. Race and gender, in addition to class, shaped attitudes about lending, credit, and risk at the turn of the twentieth century.[21]

RISK, RACE, AND GENDER IN U.S. FINANCE

The master's pocket, local stores, and installment payments were well-known financial options available to blacks for saving, borrowing, and acquiring credit in antebellum, postemancipation, and early twentieth-century U.S. history.[22] The world of consumer lending at the turn of the twentieth century was a shady, highly exploitative world dominated by pawnbrokers, loan sharks, and salary lenders. The popularity of these sources reveals a great deal about the problems associated with capitalism and the need to establish long-term credit opportunities for working people. Changes in public opinion about working- and middle-class people's saving and borrowing shifted in the period. Banks and other types of consumer-focused financial institutions developed best practices and institutional networks. Through these practices and networks, they were able to gather adequate information about a borrower's collateral; understand various factors in the market; and identify risks through monitoring, screening, and enforcing debt contracts.[23]

What constituted risk, however, was racialized and gendered. Blacks were considered among the worst risks, not just because they made less money and borrowed smaller sums but also because they were seen as inherently criminal, less intelligent, prone to disease, and unable to exercise self-restraint. A growing tide of statistics and science reinforced what many saw as an apparent fact: the Negro Problem was real.[24] Bankers and insurers classed women as being greater risks. A patchwork of legal restrictions, largely affecting white women, further limited women's legal autonomy and made them higher lending risks. For example, although women generally lived longer than men, women faced higher insurance premiums because it was believed they were more likely than men to die. Insurers judged married, middle-class white women to be high risks because insurers believed they were better able to conceal health issues. Ironically, middle-class black women could get insurance policies, but they paid very high rates. Black women's policies were an implicit statement of their devalued femininity and an explicit marker of the impediment of race. To be black and woman, then, was to be an existential risk.[25]

The St. Luke Bank embraced this existential risk. It advanced approaches that were novel in their focus on women and banking but representative of the movement among black communities to create viable alternatives to exploitative and racist financial practices. Racial and gendered economic practices and values shaped the bank's practices and values, which paid close attention to the structural barriers and cultural implications of black women's working lives. Racial and sexual discrimination worked in tandem to exclude women from high-paying, high-skilled industrial and other types of jobs. The bank certainly acknowledged women's important economic roles in their families, but women's low salaries made it harder for them to meet the demands of providing for their families. The banks' gendered economic practices and values helped establish women as providers. Working-class laborers and middle-class professionals alike needed secure places to keep their money and the flexibility to deposit very small amounts. They also relied on credit to supplement low wages and periodic scarcity in work. The bank dignified the work that women performed outside the home. For both working women and homemakers, the bank stressed women's financial literacy and education as being essential to the empowerment of black families and communities.

The bank complemented rather than undercut women's economic networks in churches, secret societies, and clubs by safeguarding their funds. The bank also allowed women shareholders a voice. Even women who owned only a fraction of a share could participate in elections and make decisions about the bank's leadership, administration, and policies. These were roles to which many black women had become accustomed in their associational lives: roles that allowed them to carve out a space in which to enact civil and economic rights that they had been denied in larger society. In addition, a bank largely funded by and dependent on black women's wealth provided economic support and services to black businesses, neighborhoods, and institutions, which reaffirmed women's larger economic influence in creating security and stability in black communities. The bank's black women leaders and customers used the bank to produce and maintain their economic autonomy and authority. Thus, the bank embedded racial and gendered economic practices onto standard banking practices to assert a distinct "black women's way" of banking and managing risk.[26]

The politics of respectability, which emerged in the early twentieth century and was typically associated with black women's activism and social reform, became a strategy to manage risk. In the context of Jim Crow, industrialization, and imperialism, it served as a counternarrative to negative discourses about black women's morality, intellect, and fitness for citizenship. Relying on a predominately middle-class focus on propriety and comportment, the politics of respectability asserted an image of black womanhood that went beyond the prevailing negative, racist stereotypes. These cultural politics constituted a protean discourse that justified black women's risk taking and participation in the public sphere. It defended what Stephanie Shaw, a historian of early twentieth-century black professional women, describes as "socially responsible individualism."[27] A number of enterprising black women felt it important to create opportunities for themselves and others as markers of both individual and collective achievement. Insurance and banking could help women achieve financial security—and, in turn, respectability—in a socially responsible way.[28]

The undercurrents of class, gender, and race that buoyed insurance, black banking, and other forms of communal capitalism, however, roiled beneath the surface and proved treacherous to navigate. Invoking the cultural politics of respectability constituted a double-edged form of resistance and risk management. First, it powerfully reinforced the nascent cultural and economic identities of black men as emblems of authority and merit in a modernizing age. Business, religious, and civic leaders promoted black men's ascendancy and black women's subordination both in the public market and in the private home as the best resolution to the myriad problems affecting the black family and community. Black men became, then, the ideal providers and producers of financial security, as reflected in the promotion of banking and insurance as a manly domain. It was the duty and responsibility of the husband and father to protect and provide for his wife and children. The emphasis on manliness in the home and business extended to efforts to discourage women's participation in the business aspects of the financial industry.

Control over financial resources and opportunities represented important markers of black women's interrelated claims to full citizenship and respectable womanhood despite masculinist rhetoric that excluded women from being agents of economic development in the black community and obscured women's financial roles in their families and communities. Respectability, though, was deeply contested among women as a strategy and practice. As a strategy to manage the logics of antiblackness, respectability politics often contributed to the pathologizing of blackness in general and black womanhood in particular. For example, women policing the boundaries of bourgeois respectability promoted financial products and services like stock, time certificates of deposit, and insurance policies as respectable ways to ensure women's financial security. Alternatively, borrowing from loan sharks, pawning, gambling, and public charity represented economic activities that assailed respectable womanhood.[29]

The St. Luke Bank strove to make savings and, under certain circumstances, borrowing through short-term bank loans respectable for black women. Black women shared risk collectively but also individually: each woman had an individual stake in the perception of the whole. Respectability figured in the bank's assessment of risk. The bank weighed factors beyond income and other standard underwriting measures to determine individual's creditworthiness and to guide its investment decisions.

If, as Rowena Olegario observes in *A Culture of Credit*, determining credit risk in this period involved "more art than science," some might suggest that the St. Luke Bank's finance committee used a broad brush.[30] Considerations of race and gender shaped perceptions of risk, particularly regarding access to credit and distinct approaches to evaluations of creditworthiness and collateral. The St. Luke Penny Savings Bank committed itself to providing inexpensive credit to working-class blacks, a mission that put it in step and in tension with the large number of industrial savings banks and postal banks around the country that were also focused on the needs of working-class people. The finance committee certainly weighed generous elements of cooperative economics, respectability, and uplift in its decisions to provide mortgages and short-term loans.

Black women, the bank's primary consumer market, were often considered risky in every register of the concept: as moral hazard, peril, and risk. Just as the bank shaped its business operations around the needs of women and girls, gendered economic practices also influenced its lending priorities. It allowed loan amounts as small as five dollars; that five dollars represented a week's income for washerwomen and unskilled laborers. The bank instituted a system to make fast loan decisions, typically in a few days but sometimes within twenty-four hours. Small loan amounts and quick loan decisions mirrored quotidian credit practices. Women now had comparable options beyond the expensive credit offered by pawnbrokers and salary lenders.

In the very early days, borrowers wrote letters explaining their needs and stating the amount of time they needed to pay back their loans. Thus, the bank allowed women some latitude in setting the length of their loan terms. Coupled with the ability to extend and renew loan terms on very short notice for a small fee, these features resembled practices associated with pawnbroking. Alongside pawning, black women had also mastered in-kind and cash-based trade in local stores and with street peddlers to secure short-term credit and small loans. The bank offered women a similar type of economic autonomy that complemented their local, quotidian credit market practices.

The St. Luke Bank made individualized financial services, namely lending and credit, an institutional marker of its commitment to individual economic development within a collective ethos. If the bank's priorities were measured in dollars, lending was clearly more important than savings—despite the words "Penny Savings" in the bank's name. The extant board minutes and auditing committee reports provide a snapshot of the bank's increasing commitment to its lending business. Six months after opening, the bank had made $8,400 in loans and held $9,600 in time certificates of deposit. In June 1913, the bank held a total of $119,036 in outstanding loans and $17,004 in cash deposits. Thus, in a decade, savings had grown modestly while lending had grown more than 1,000 percent.[31]

The bank took a broad array of factors into consideration to determine creditworthiness and ability to pay back those loans. A borrower's moral character, work ethic, and community associations rather than income or employment often determined whether to extend a loan. Because racial and sexual exploitation depressed the wages of most working- and middle-class black women, how much a person earned or even whether she had a job was not necessarily an accurate measure of her ability to pay. What looked to outsiders, especially critics and regulators, like risky and careless decisions were often the strategic transfiguration of fraternal rituals and knowledge systems, which helped the bank mitigate its risks.

TO "BECOME USEFUL AND TRUE": USING THE IOSL RITUAL TO MITIGATE CREDIT RISKS

If they chose to, IOSL members could advance in the order through the degree system. The ritual language of the degree ceremonies required members to recite various oaths and vows. Initiates swore fealty to God, the IOSL, and humanity, as expressed in one of the solemn oaths: "So that I may become useful and true to all mankind, but more especially to a brother or sister of the Order wherever found."[32] Those members who did choose to participate in the degree system evinced a commitment to the IOSL's values that the finance committee could consider in its evaluation process.[33]

Even before considering the IOSL ritual as a resource to mitigate risks, the St. Luke Bank could and did draw from the IOSL's fraternal structure to organize its lending. When Walker took over the reins of the IOSL in 1899, she modeled its insurance feature after one she had instituted in the juvenile circles, which prospered even as the IOSL's veered dangerously close to failing. One of her innovations included creating a committee of matrons who met regularly to review claims. In the IOSL, she centralized the life insurance feature but allowed local councils to maintain control over sickness and burial benefits. The bank used a similar structure to vet loan applications. Three members from the board of directors constituted the bank's finance committee. The initial three members were Maggie Lena Walker, Lillian Payne, and Rev. Zachariah D. Lewis. In semiweekly meetings, they vetted application letters and brought their recommendations up for a vote by the entire board.

Lillian Harris Payne was effectively Walker's second in command. She worked with Walker on the board of the Woman's Union, and Payne was one of the women Walker brought on to the IOSL board of directors and as an employee when she assumed the role of RWG secretary for the ailing order. Little is known of Payne's personal life. She was born in Richmond in 1867 to Henry and Henrietta Harris and later taught in Richmond-area schools. She married Winston Payne in the mid-1890s, and they had one son, Winston Jr. In addition to managing the *St. Luke Herald* for several years, Payne managed the minute details of thousands of councils, took to the road several times a year to recruit new members and encourage existing ones, and helped supervise workers at headquarters. She remained active as the financial secretary in her own local council, Heliotrope Council No. 160. Indeed, it was her personal experience with running the financial affairs of a local council that immensely helped in her duties as the equivalent of a chief financial officer in the IOSL and as a member of the critical finance and auditing committees for the St. Luke Bank.[34]

The IOSL councils represented an excellent model of collective financial stewardship. Every local council administered sickness and burial benefits locally and helped the Right Worthy Grand Council, the state-level body, administer funds for death benefits. Many local councils already had banking or finance committees that collected and recorded dues, fees, and taxes and paid tributes. These committees discussed accounting and business matters and administered fundraising drives. Councils that owned their own halls also rented out meeting space for churches and other societies. Some even leased office space to black professionals and businesses. Local council finance or banking committees oversaw small loans to their members. Even the smallest council maintained a charity board, and the more ambitious ones often had a building fund. The councils' financial assistance went beyond Christian charity; it had political implications. Councils donated money to political, social service, and civic groups at the local and national level, such as the Community Chest, the NAACP, and later the Urban League. To be sure, financial concerns dominated local council meetings.[35]

The St. Luke bank tapped into the financial administrative strengths of the IOSL. Some local council committees vetted people seeking loans before they contacted the bank, and they sometimes stepped in as endorsers for members who applied to the bank for loans. The finance committee relied on local councils to help it parse applicants and answer the bank's requests for additional clarification and documentation. Applicants for loans mentioned their timely records of paying taxes and dues, their tenure, and their records of attendance in local councils to vouchsafe their dependability: elements that the finance committee verified and took into consideration alongside traditional indices of creditworthiness.[36]

For example, borrowers welcomed the bank's inquiries to their councils for references about their character or financial habits but worried that their financial difficulties would be made the stuff of gossip, particularly among other IOSL members. S. A. Bright of Gainesville, Virginia, worried that the circumstances leading her to seek a loan might become public knowledge: "[I] also hope the RWG Council will not publish anything but what it must." However, she encouraged Burke to contact her local council in Washington, D.C., regarding whether she was up to date with her dues, whether she attended meetings regularly, and how far she had advanced in the mysteries of the order.[37]

Councils applied for loans from the bank as well. These loans were typically for larger sums to start or complete building projects or to conduct large events. Local council committees met and discussed collectively with their members the details of loans requested on behalf of the entire council. As the bank positioned itself as a crucial source of credit for IOSL members, the bank's experiences with IOSL councils helped it become more efficient in making loan decisions. The bank sometimes represented a last and only resort for funding. For example, the Pride of Louisa Council No. 314 needed a quick answer to its request for a $300 loan. A local black man had agreed to sell them a lot in downtown Louisa, Virginia, but local whites had maneuvered to buy the lot out from under the council. The sense of urgency expressed by the chair of the council's banking committee indicated that he believed the new owners might inflate the price to resell the land to the council—or not sell it to them at all. He made it clear that the council had few options for getting a loan from local white banks in the town.[38]

Councils sometimes sought special consideration. Through its positive and negative experiences accommodating those considerations, the bank refined its techniques for vetting risks—and councils refined their risk profiles. The bank loaned the Union Prospect Council No. 93 of Richmond $4,500 to build a new hall. When a fire destroyed the partially constructed hall, the bank learned that the council had neglected to buy fire insurance. The contractor had a $1,000 policy of his own that covered his losses, but the council—and the bank—suffered serious losses. The council promised to get fire insurance "to show that you and ourselves are to be protected in a business way."[39] A couple of years later, Union Prospect needed another loan, and it presented its fire insurance policy, but the finance committee declined to extend further credit. The council had to borrow $3,000 from another financial institution.[40]

The St. Luke finance committee denied Ham's Council No. 175 of Rio Vista, Virginia, a $300 loan to build a new hall. The council's finance committee wrote to the bank, expressing a mix of disappointment and surprise: "We was sure that we could do business with the Bank on conditions being one of our race." The council had already secured a builder and bought lumber but lacked the funds to start construction, so the finance committee met again and submitted a revised funding application to the bank. It requested a total of $800 for a one-year term, and various individual members of the council were willing to "give security" for the council's loan. The bank loaned the council the money for one year at 6 percent interest. A few months into the project, the council sought another $250, and in its third application, Ham's Council referenced its past good payment history, pledged its completed hall as security, and agreed to make quarterly payments on all its notes.[41]

Thus, by centralizing underwriting within the bank's finance committee, relying on local committees' assistance to collect information, and allowing local committees some autonomy over their own members and projects, the bank increased its efficiency and encouraged support from members and councils. Experiences in lending to councils and their performance in repaying loans also helped institutionalize, though not necessarily standardize, the bank's underwriting and reference processes. The bank also learned actuarial practices from the IOSL by paying attention to loan amounts, reasons for borrowing money, and who paid back loans and when. Those observations helped shape the finance committee's credit decisions. After 1910, state oversight led the bank to maintain some records on borrowers that examiners could evaluate. Based on examiners' evaluations of these records, they suggested that the bank conduct more frequent audits. Bank employees relied on these borrowers' records along with other records of transactions as part of its internal quality control and rudimentary risk-mitigation processes.[42]

Indeed, new forms of sociability arose around these new relations of credit. Some customers seeking loans made appeals to race pride while others begged special consideration on account of race. Mamie Carter of Crozet, Virginia, gladly withdrew her money from the local bank and deposited it with St. Luke: "I been Deposit[ing] in the Crozet Va Bank [Bank of Crozet] some time but think it time for a change."[43] Arthur Bell of Roanoke "desire[d] to help out the colored race all that I can." He needed a fifty-dollar loan, though, to help himself because he had "a long doctor bill and short money."[44] W. L. Young, a dealer in general merchandise and dry goods, wanted to borrow $400 to pay off the remaining balance of another loan and did "not want to borrow from a white bank if I can help it."[45] Members of the community felt proud about being able to withdraw their funds from white banks and get loans from the St. Luke Bank.

A black financial institution was sometimes the lone option for some borrowers to turn to. Richmond B. Garrett of Greensboro, North Carolina, wrote to the bank asking it to give him two ninety-day mortgage loans for a total of $730: "The white banks and money lenders refuse me because I am a Negro." A few brave blacks in Greensboro sued the local banks for overcharging them, a practice that the banks justified by pointing to a special statute allowing them to do so. As collateral, Garrett pledged a lot with a four-room house and an orchard. He needed the mortgage in less than a week, or he could lose his property.[46]

Appeals to race and IOSL affiliation quickly soured, however, if the bank denied a loan. When the bank denied Winnie Harrison's application for a fifteen-dollar loan, she made it clear that she had only made an application to the bank "because it was colored," but, she added, "I will not bother you again."[47] R. D. Pittman of Waverly, Virginia, felt that the lending committee "evidently misunderstood" the collateral he pledged. He added, "To refuse me now, you simply refuse one who has been loyal to this Association and who has aided it in more than one way. I do[n't] ask to be given anything. I come to you a member of my race holding a position. . . . We need not complain with the white man for not keeping us if we will not help each other when we can."[48] Pittman insisted that the committee reconsider his loan request.

The bank clearly saw its membership as an important customer base. By 1903, when the bank opened its doors, the IOSL had grown ninefold under Walker's leadership to 10,200 members. In the early decades of the order, members knew each other intimately; they lived near each other and attended the same churches and schools. Newer councils tended to be created by organizing deputies, paid IOSL staff who received commissions for chartering new councils. Given their rates of growth, leaders of the IOSL and the bank could no longer rely on personal knowledge of their members. The councils maintained only nominal checks on members' behavior through membership and grievance committees. The reasons people sought membership also changed. The death and sickness benefits, not necessarily the rituals and fellowship, attracted many newer members. IOSL members were often members of more than one society, in part to maximize their benefits but also to meet various social obligations. Thus, policing and surveilling members' habits became a challenge for fraternal leaders. Nor could one depend on or expect deep bonds of affection to the IOSL and its values. The bank, then, had to rely on other measures of character to gauge creditworthiness; IOSL membership alone was not enough to illustrate integrity.

Without a standard set of practices in the evolving consumer lending market of the early twentieth century, the bank turned to its own institutions and practices as models. Though it tapped into traditional methods of calculating risk—promoting the common good and relying on social standing to assess creditworthiness—the committee remained suspicious of "traditional" assumptions about black fitness linked to intelligence, morality, and capacity for citizenship. The committee rejected standards in the larger society that systematically judged blacks to be unfit, incorrigible, and ignorant and women to be perpetually dependent, emotional, and irrational. It saw very little that was democratic, virtuous, or liberal about the marketplace for black borrowers, nor could it trust invisible hands to work in blacks' favor. By turning to its own associational configurations, idealized forms, and coded practices, the IOSL mapped its values onto the particular financial exigencies of the new market of consumer credit.[49]

Like other secret societies, the IOSL created rituals, special regalia, secret words, and symbols. A society's rituals helped build and reinforce a collective identity, and it reaffirmed the bonds of mutuality among members. Elsa Barkley Brown notes that the IOSL's "rituals, religious symbolism, and rhetoric" helped build not only the order's collective identity but also its "sense of responsibility to struggle in this world against social, political, and economic oppression."[50] The ritual, or works, of a fraternal organization defined its identity and enacted the core values of the order. "Ritual" connotes religious rites, and all fraternal rituals, to some degree, according to sociologists Bayliss J. Camp and Orit Kent, expressed and enacted "important ideas about individual and collective identity, gender, equality, and collective action."[51] Therefore rituals operated at both the symbolic and the material levels.[52]

Considering African Americans in particular, Alessandra Lorini observes that rituals of race drew on collective experiences, signifying ways that black people sought connection with and affirmation of their connection to the social body. These rituals also analyzed the distribution of power and privilege in larger society. The places in which these rituals took place were autonomous spaces, separate from white surveillance and power. Black people made their own rules, inflected by their religious devotion, progressive democratic ideals, and gendered subjectivities. These rituals were translocal, repeated in different locales, but their content and form remained the same, bound by a strict and elaborate set of rules for their form and content. The fraternal ritual, then, represented a rich resource on which the finance committee could draw to mitigate its lending risks.[53]

As members advanced to higher degrees in the IOSL, the ceremonies became progressively more complex, involved the participation of more

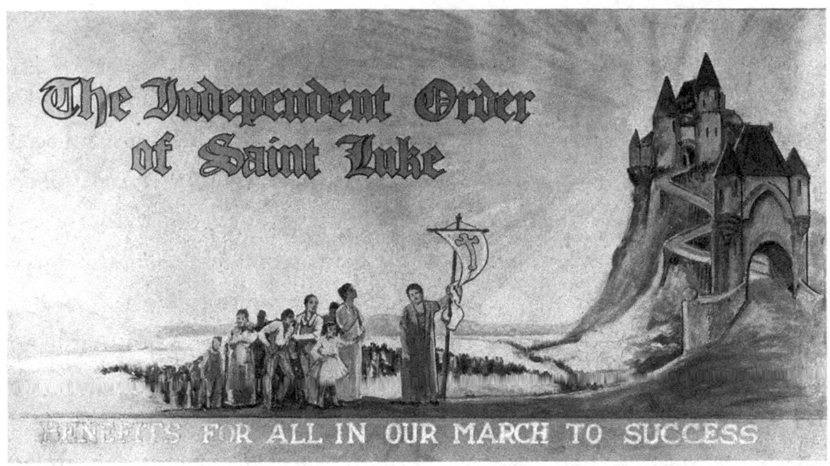

FIGURE 4.3 The image "Benefits for All in Our March to Success" appears to reimagine St. Helena's journey with a figure reminiscent of Maggie Lena Walker leading masses of people to greater heights. At some point subsequent to this photograph, the word "Security" was painted on the top of the buildings. The painting is on display in the National Park Service's Walker House Museum.
Source: V.88.20.29, Valentine Museum.

members, and took longer to perform. In every degree, a senior conductor led the initiate into a room that was set up in a specific configuration and permeated with symbols. The symbols and journeys possessed meaning in multiple valences. The complexity of symbols, challenges along the path, and number of people involved increased with each degree. For example, the simple flowers, water, and coins that represented the IOSL's tenets of love, purity, and charity respectively in the first degree were replaced by the more intricate seraph, fountain, and extended arms in the sixth degree.

A degree candidate's initiation represented a symbolic journey as well. The initiate moved from the position of stranger and outsider to one of union with and acceptance in a community. The fourth and higher degrees also represented searches for knowledge of self and of the higher mysteries. The lower degrees mirrored Abraham's pursuit of the kings who pillaged Sodom and Christ's journey to Jerusalem. The higher degrees emulated Saint Helena's search for the true cross (see fig. 4.3). The symbols on the participants' regalia and in the ritual implements included the all-seeing eye (symbolizing

God's providence), crossed hands (the unity of faith, good works, and prayer), and a partially covered mantel or pillar. The mantel represented St. Luke, but other symbols, such as an embodiment of Memory, stood near the mantel. The IOSL cosmology, though grounded in religious principles, also reflected the realities of black women's experiences. Mary Ann Prout, founder of the order, grounded the ritual search not in Exodus but in the search for the true cross, a search led and sustained by women. The ritual reinforced the important role of women in both the church and the community.[54]

The committee considered the degrees' symbolic meanings and not merely their ranks; ritual degrees were integrative, not hierarchal. Similarly, when the IOSL introduced different classes of insurance plans in the mid-1880s as a sound actuarial practice, it did not necessarily introduce underlying assumptions about the qualitative value of certain classes of lives over others. It did, however, borrow the idea that it could exercise some control over—or at least temper—the worldly forces of greed and selfishness through the fraternal values of charity and equality in the world of commerce. The rituals were about making community, but they were also about taking and mastering risks.

The finance committee considered degrees as a way to balance fraternal values and the imperatives of secular, commercial exchange. The committee emphasized its moral authority, bending the ritual from the esoteric, emotional realm of experience to the practical, experiential utility of weighing risk. The transfiguration undergirded claims that the committee judged individuals not on arbitrary distinctions but on objective measures of achievement. Degreed members completed tests of their character, trustworthiness, and dependability that stood as personal records beyond the confines of the ceremonial chamber. For example, degreed members may have signified their status in coded messages in their loan application letters. The published ritual is replete with secret words and exchanges by which members from different councils and cities might identify themselves to one another. Some member applicants used the closing "L. P. C." (for Love, Purity, and Charity) in formal correspondence to the bank, which may have signified a certain degreed status to the finance committee members. The fraternal degree provided a measure of character, inured with collective values and shaped by race and gender, that held particular underwriting value.[55]

By lending money at fair interest rates and under circumstances that some larger banks may have rejected as too risky, the bank reinforced its commitment to communal values and reaffirmed its role as caretaker of the community. The bank also benefitted from the dedication of IOSL leaders like Walker, Payne, and other women who served on the board and on the finance committee; they did not receive salaries though they worked long hours in the bank's service. The bank positioned itself as a less expensive and less risky option for customers with pressing financial needs compared to many of the options that were then available in black communities, and it did not exploit the vulnerable but helped capable borrowers.

RISK AND RESPECTABILITY DURING THE GREAT MIGRATION

By 1915, the IOSL's membership numbered more than forty thousand, and the bank handled $1.3 million (or about $32 million in today's dollars) in transactions annually. Walker, speaking at the annual IOSL meeting that year, told the members, "This is a commercial age."[56] For all its metaphorical and practical utility, the IOSL myth was still mythical; it could not be counted on for non-IOSL members, nor could it, on its own merit, force delinquent debtors to pay or satisfy regulators' demands. It provided a template and resource for evaluating borrowers based on fraternal and Christian values. The meaning and nature of trust, like risk, are enmeshed in historically specific contexts. Bureaucratic procedures and technical innovations mediated the interrelations of risk taking and trust. The bank capitalized on a decade's worth of borrowers' payment histories, property appraisals, tax records, and insider news about residential and farm developments to help establish another institutional-based resource with which they could evaluate credit references and make underwriting decisions. Technological innovations also greased the wheels of change. Punch cards, addressing machines, and proprietary filing systems helped the bank wend the flow of credit in increasingly dependable ways.

The chief examiner's requirements to reduce past-due paper and a pre–World War I recession forced the bank to adhere to stricter collateral requirements. For example, Burke informed one borrower that his real estate proved inadequate as security for a $300 loan, saying, "The money is tight and the collateral furnished must be first class during these stringent times."[57] By the mid-1910s, then, the bank responded to changes in its customer base, the market, and the industry through a combination of culturally resonant and institutionally tested practices. It combined the personal and the intuitive with the bureaucratic and the statistical.[58]

Like most lenders, the bank's underwriters considered a borrower's personal character and connections. Holding a professional title or public position seemed to be enough to qualify some for a loan. Social standing and title, however, did not always correlate with creditworthiness. The internationally renowned elocutionist and dramatist Henrietta Vinton Davis performed for audiences around the world but struggled to pay back her loans to the bank. When she asked for another extension in early 1913, Burke wrote, "The amount has been so long past due and we have received nothing but promises that we do not feel inclined to grant further time." Burke, however, was inclined to recover the bank's money rather than let Davis off the hook. He gave Davis until early March to pay the debt. His persistence worked. By the end of the month, she paid off the balance of the loan with interest for a total of $27.41.[59] Dr. James Carter tried to pay the interest on the day his note was due, but Burke had already contacted his endorser for payment. Dr. Carter told Burke, "While I know it was your duty to do what you did, still I think you could have favored me."[60] Samuel P. B. Steward, the manager, secretary-treasurer, and owner of Canvassers Tea Company, entreated the board to recognize his "herculean efforts to meet [his] obligations" and extend his note.[61] The difficulties that even the most well-regarded members of the community had in paying back their debts hint at the difficulties that blacks at every income level experienced in meeting their obligations. Their communications with the bank also reveal the hands-on approach the small bank staff took to protect their assets.

In some cases, neither the bank's persistence nor the borrower's professional standing resulted in timely payments. The harried note of Dr. A. Moncrieffee Mitchell of Spring Grove, Virginia, reflected either his desperation or his businesslike efficiency. In a few neat lines, he requested a sixty-day loan to "make a deal on some stock," as he found himself "short" about $200. He pledged not only his own $6,000 worth of property but also his mother-in-law's property in Albermarle. He added as an aside that his wife was "well known to the order."[62] Dr. Mitchell's collateral, his association with the order through his wife, and his respectable position led the finance committee to see him as an acceptable risk. In reality, however, the doctor's precarious financial situation exposed the bank to significant risk over the next eighteen months.

In early 1907, Dr. Mitchell regretted that he had not received money that he expected and therefore needed an extension on his note. He paid six dollars as a good-faith gesture toward the entire balance. He bounced a check soon after and requested a short five-day extension in March. More than two weeks passed before he sent $5.50 along with his fervent hope that some other money that was owed to him would come in soon so that he could pay his note in full.[63] More troubling, Dr. Mitchell's colleague Rev. John Smallwood confidentially questioned Burke about the circumstances surrounding a draft that had been paid to Mitchell. Smallwood, president of the Temperance, Industrial, and Collegiate Institute in Claremont, Virginia, believed that Mitchell had forged his signature on a check in early February 1907, a period that coincided with the time when Mitchell had begged financial distress as a reason he needed extensions on his notes.[64] Thus, personal characteristics and social standing still counted in credit decisions, but they sometimes proved to be unreliable predictors of when or if borrowers would repay their loans.

From the beginning, the finance committee adhered to the industry standard that required at least one endorsement for a loan: a person who vouchsafed the loan in the event that the borrower could not or did not pay. Typically, an endorsement from a well-respected community member was often enough to guarantee a note. Given new pressures from the state and the bank's experience with even well-regarded borrowers who were either slow to pay or failed to pay altogether, one endorsement was not always enough to satisfy the committee. In 1910, Petersburg resident John G. Harris had J. M. B. Holmes endorse his sixty-day thirty-eight-dollar note. Though Holmes held property and was a thirty-year veteran postal carrier, the finance committee did not seem to think this one endorsement enough and asked Harris to secure at least one more. They suggested his wife's countersignature. Harris returned the note with not only the signature of his wife, Susie, but two others for a total of four endorsers.[65]

The committee often requested that married men get their wives' endorsements for their notes. In January 1913, the committee contacted several men to secure their wives' endorsements before they would be approved for loans. The bank also encouraged the wives to "bring us their business."[66] The bank acknowledged women's economic roles in the family, but that acknowledgment also meant that the women were liable if their husbands failed to pay.

The bank acknowledged women's economic roles in different ways. In addition to providing a source for secure borrowing at low rates, it endeavored to treat black women with respect as it encouraged them to save and borrow. The bank did not rely on lending money to only respectable people; rather, it promoted banking and borrowing as respectable activities. Evelyn Brooks Higginbotham's seminal thesis about the politics of respectability also stresses the technologies of power that do physical and psychic violence to black women. These technologies include negative stereotypes deployed in popular movies like *Birth of a Nation* and in stereotypical images of black women's bodies and sexual proclivities that circulated in popular culture, consumer advertising, and national newspapers in the late nineteenth and early twentieth centuries. They extend as well to not only scientific and medical discourses that grounded the poor fitness and vitality of black bodies, families, and communities in the failures of women but also actuarial thinking that viewed women as existentially risky.[67]

The St. Luke Bank's lending practices, rooted in its own fraternal value system and administrative structure, promoted its own technology of power in mobilizing women's economic influence. Gender, character, and credit worked together to enmesh women and their lending institutions in webs of mutuality and obligation. It also reinforced hierarchies and dependencies. The bank rejected models of black women as selfish, spendthrift consumers and refused to allow them to remain or become desperate borrowers, dependent on unsavory or exploitative lenders.[68]

With its location in a remodeled office on Richmond's main business thoroughfare, the bank welcomed women from all economic backgrounds to enjoy equal access to the bank's clean, well-appointed, professional offices. Unlike ladies' departments or rooms in other banks, women were not physically separated from the main banking spaces. At least half a dozen banks in New York and banks in Washington, D.C., and Chicago as well as a few smaller cities operated segregated spaces for their women customers. Some went as far as offering distinctive, "daintily designed" checks especially for women. The St. Luke Bank strove to naturalize women's presence in banking spaces. Though no women worked in the teller cage when the bank opened in 1903, six women worked as clerks, and it was probably not unusual for customers to see women from time to time doing their work in the bank.[69]

One of the bank's primary goals was to increase financial literacy, which served as a marker of respectability for women regardless of socioeconomic class. The St. Luke Bank's borrowers, not all of whom were IOSL members, displayed various levels of financial literacy. Most understood that they needed some type of collateral. Borrowers offered traditional security, such as paid up insurance policies, land, and homes, but some offered assets that were personally valuable to them. Bettie Ransome offered her piano as collateral for a fifty-dollar loan. Charles Jefferson offered to put up his "eleven horses an[d] colts and huge sheep" for a $1,000 loan.[70] While it is not clear in the extant record whether the bank granted Ransome's or Jefferson's requests for funds, the ability to put up personal valuables as collateral would have expanded credit options for lower-income borrowers and for borrowers with assets that did not easily convert to cash. Some women became savvy borrowers and were skilled in securing loans to meet their requirements. Josephine D. C. Cannaday knew that she had strong endorsers and an excellent payment history, so she pressed for a $228 loan within three to four days of her initial request. Belle Fitzgerald wanted to borrow thirty dollars on the same day, as she was behind in some business matters.[71]

The bank also encouraged women, especially IOSL employees, to buy homes. When an IOSL employee earned at least fifty dollars per month, the bank encouraged her to put a minimum amount equal to one month's mortgage payment in the bank. It is not known how much of a down payment the bank required. In the period, a typical homeowner put 50 percent down, made interest payments, and paid a balloon payment of the remaining 50 percent of the sales price after three to five years. Because of the challenge of making a large balloon payment, people often needed to refinance their loans regularly. Some St. Luke Bank customers even pooled their resources to make a down payment and purchased a home collectively. The bank may have offered employees low down payments. It offered women customers very low loan-to-value mortgages. For example, the bank approved Maggie Austin's $2,500 loan for a home that cost $2,800 to build. The bank experienced great success in fulfilling its commitment to increase black homeownership. By the early 1920s, bank customers had paid in full nearly 650 mortgage loans from the St. Luke Bank, and Virginia ranked near the top of states nationally in rates of black homeownership.[72]

The bank committed itself to advancing entrepreneurship, especially among women. A number of businesses held accounts with the bank and borrowed money, but individual borrowers also sought money to open small businesses. Sarah Paige Brown of Jetersville, Virginia, worked as a public school teacher for many years, but her health forced her to give up her profession. She was unable to find other work, so she decided to open a business, "a little grocery." She felt that local blacks in and around the small town of Jetersville would support her new business: "I do not fear a failure," she confidently wrote in her letter to the finance committee. "Success may be slow but it will eventually come to the persevering." In Brown's second appeal for a loan, she did not rely on mere sentiment. She reminded the committee that she was a "sister of the Order," which she felt sure would come to her aid: "I cannot [be] refused the $50 or $75 on reasonable and legal terms."[73] Brown's character references testified to her reputation—and her net worth. "To whom it may concern," wrote one reference, Brown was a "pure honorable Christian woman" who owned "a nice little estate" worth at least $200.[74]

Brown asked for capital, not money. Her strongly worded appeal spoke directly to the aspirations that Walker preached to IOSL members and the black community: starting businesses for the race. Brown also cleverly turned the IOSL's values of love and charity on their heads. Refusal might force her to either give up on her dream or seek funding from less savory sources. If borrowing and lending reinforced hierarchies and dependencies, women and those who depended on them were reduced by their dependence on usurious lenders just as they were undermined by reliance on charity. So that she would not become dependent on charity or subjected to disreputable and exploitative alternate sources of capital, she needed a loan from the bank to fulfill the IOSL's vision and to protect her respectability.

Brown exemplified some of the black women borrowers who turned to the St. Luke Bank for loans. The bank did not map black women onto traditional notions of bourgeois white womanhood. The typical black women who borrowed from the St. Luke Bank worked outside the home. Many were unattached, which gave them greater responsibility and leverage over their household finances. Black women's negotiations with white employers and their efforts to secure widows' pensions and Freedman's Bank refunds helped them better navigate their financial affairs. The work of enlisting witnesses and affidavits for federal pension board investigators; gathering legal documents like marriage licenses, wills, and powers of attorney to affirm their rights to inherit benefits; and negotiating contracts with white employers helped develop their legal and financial identities. Black women's administrative and fundraising work in myriad fraternal, social reform, and church societies and organizations further developed their skills at managing financial affairs. Indeed, the money that went through their hands built halls, schools, and hospitals, and it paid tuition, benefits, and salaries. Finally, most black women, regardless of class, worked outside the home, and many more headed their own households.[75]

The IOSL imagined itself not just as a society that conferred titles and degrees but also as a vehicle for social mobility through building personal wealth, increasing homeownership, and promoting black businesses. It promoted these endeavors as signs of individual and collective achievement. The St. Luke Bank affirmed black women's important economic roles in their families and communities. Its lending decisions respected women's work outside the home. The ability to borrow small sums expanded women's possibilities. A small loan supplemented income from various sources, including work, widows' pensions, and other informal economic activities. Black women did not necessarily experience dramatic shifts in their social and economic status but did gain opportunities to make modest shifts through the ability to own their own homes, educate their children, and participate in leisure. It was better for a woman to borrow twenty dollars and pay it back on time than to allow her family to suffer or seek charity.

For Maggie Lena Walker, respectability had a place in women's uplift, but black women's experiences under racial capitalism posed a threat that comportment alone could not displace. In 1909, after a speech before the Women's Auxiliary of the National Baptist Convention, she clarified the important role of money in black women's lives: "Some women should do housework and be contented, and some women should not engage in business for themselves. Any woman who has executive ability, who is honest, and who has a keen perception and tact in dealing with people can succeed."[76] She did not necessarily believe that all women should enter business or even work outside the home, but all women should be financially literate and empowered. Careful management and planning of every cent earned led to security and helped women create a legacy for their families. In an address to the Virginia Federation of Women's Clubs entitled "Women in Business," Walker stressed that women "helped themselves and husbands and children if [they] earned their own money and [did] not expect to be supported."[77] In a speech entitled "Traps for Women," Walker did not focus on immorality but poverty as the most important threat to women's status. Manners and comportment counted for something, but low wages, economic dependence, and lack of homeownership represented the greatest impediments to women's advancement.[78]

Members of the finance committee shared many elements of Walker's economic vision for women. Their notions of respectability esteemed women's critical economic role and shed some light on why appeals to helplessness from women borrowers' might have been discouraged. In many ways, then, the bank affirmed a kind of middle-class respectability among its women borrowers that privileged the materiality of rustling paper bills and clinking silver coins above the sartorial and genteel. Many of the loans that the finance committee approved acted as missives in the battle against financial indebtedness, illiteracy, and dependence. The bruised honor of Annie J. Evans, whose story opened this chapter, strikes a radically different tone than Sarah Paige Brown's application letter. Brown did not make sentimental appeals to honor, dependence, or vulnerability. Though Brown may have been as self-confident and ambitious as she appeared in print, she certainly understood that she had to appear to the bank as possessing those characteristics. Women had to make appeals that affirmed their independent roles as breadwinners, astute managers of household budgets, and enterprising proprietors if they hoped to gain an approval from the finance committee. Women seeking loans cultivated an economic respectability that included providing acceptable collateral and endorsers.

The reality, however, was that black women remained economically vulnerable. The extant record lists thousands of women's names among the bank's borrowers, but the surviving correspondence includes far fewer women than men appealing to the bank for special consideration when debts became unmanageable. One way to read their absence is that women maintained the appearance of respectability by not communicating financial hardship. Women felt pressure to not highlight their poverty or economic vulnerability in requesting loans, and they felt similar pressures to not reveal their poverty and economic vulnerability as reasons they could not meet their credit obligations. Instead, they repeatedly paid the small fees to extend their notes. After numerous extensions, the bank sometimes asked the women to curtail their notes—to pay off a small portion of the principal balance and refinance the remaining balance.

The fees and extra interest that the bank accrued from extending and curtailing its own notes increased the bank's profits, creating a small but reliable stream of additional money for the bank's lending portfolio. The mutuality aspect of obligation, it seems, bound women in unanticipated ways: they considered it unrespectable to seek help or discuss difficulties in paying back their loans. On one hand, the bank succeeded in expanding the market for working women's credit as a legitimate path for upward mobility. On the other hand, the emphasis on economic respectability forced many women deeper into debt and actually helped the bank's bottom line.[79]

Indeed, the formal and the bureaucratic linked with the cultural and the symbolic to inform notions of risk and responsibility within a collective ethos. The bank's lending policies and practices were highly practical, tailored to the economic needs and social realities of its customers. The extant folders stuffed with letters requesting to extend or curtail notes reveal the practical difficulties that borrowers experienced in meeting their part of the mutual obligation. Those letters also reveal the limits of the bank's sympathetic duty to oblige customers who owed it money.

TESTING THE BONDS OF MUTUALITY: DEBT AND RESPECTABILITY

Debtors employed various tactics to deal with late payments or shortfalls in letters to St. Luke Bank cashier Emmett Burke, whose job included managing collections. Some stressed their personal association to the bank—either as friends of Walker's or Burke's or as members of the IOSL—for some special consideration, particularly if they were unable to pay back their notes or bring overdrafted accounts current. Lillian Payne, arguably Walker's other right hand next to Burke, requested a six-month extension to pay back a $500 note.[80] After a constant stream of letters about late payments and overdrafts, undertaker and fellow St. Luke Bank board member William I. Johnson pleaded with Burke to be "lenient."[81] Walker's close associate Julia Hayes asked her dear friend "Mag" to call and explain the bank's issue with honoring her check; why she encountered such difficulty as an officer of the IOSL "is a mystery," she wrote to Walker.[82] Hayes's private consultation must have gained her some respite because a month later, she made a small payment on her "long past due" note and endorsed another for someone else.[83]

Other delinquent borrowers blamed the bank for undermining their ability to meet their obligations. Customers asked the bank to send periodic reminders in the mail. The bank did not typically send reminders of payments due, expecting that people should remember they were obliged to pay their notes before they were due or, perhaps, to save the bank the expense of postage. At least one customer laid the blame for her delinquency squarely on the bank. Allisen Brown of East Orange, New Jersey, opened her letter with a frank question: "Mr. Burke, will you please tell me what is wrong with you and Mrs. Walker?" The bank had failed to respond to her previous requests for information about her note, stock, and account—or so she claimed. She stressed that she was "a Lady that is trying to work and build alone" and so decided to hold on to her payment until she received some response to her previous requests.[84]

The bank contacted endorsers to collect past-due amounts when customers failed to pay their loans. Delinquent debtors pleaded with the bank not to contact their endorsers. Anderson Branch begged Burke to wait until Saturday when he would come by the bank to pay off his note, adding, "Don't oppress my endorser."[85] Endorsers did not want to be oppressed either. Even Walker and Burke were served notices when borrowers they endorsed failed to pay back their notes on time. When Willa Lee of Clarksburg, West Virginia, failed to pay back $11.20, the bank wrote to Burke and Walker for payment because they had both endorsed Lee's note.[86]

Some endorsers tried to dodge the responsibility before and sometimes even after the borrowers' debts became a personal liability. B. F. Turner endorsed builder Daniel Farrar's note but soon after had second thoughts. Turner wrote to Burke confidentially to "hold it until I see you." Turner may have come across some piece of news that gave him pause about Farrar's ability to pay—or about his own ability or willingness to be held financially liable in the event that Farrar failed to pay off the loan.[87] R. D. Lewis of Scottsville, Virginia, did not dispute that he had endorsed Miss Clark's debt, and he understood that she had not paid. He could not, however, "understand why you [the bank] can't make *her* pay?"[88] Some endorsers argued that they had never actually agreed to be held accountable. W. W. Moore of Pittsburgh, for example, claimed he had never seen George Sallee's note and begged Burke to meet with him privately to discuss the matter when Moore arrived in Richmond.[89]

Endorsers also wrote asking for extensions on debtors' notes. Endorsers cited job troubles, illnesses, and other calamities that kept debtors from paying on time. The endorsers even offered details of their own troubles in hopes of turning the bank's attention back toward the debtors. Edward Wellington Brown, editor of the *Reformer*, the weekly newspaper for the Grand Fountain of the United Order of True Reformers, begged Burke not to hold him to the defaulted twenty-one-dollar note of an ex-*Reformer* employee, C. M. Bowler. However, as a Baptist minister, Brown felt he could not ethically shirk his responsibility: "This is a lesson for me. God being my helper, I shall give satisfaction as to the note."[90] In addition to divine counsel, he asked Burke to transfer Bowler's defaulted note to a new twenty-one-dollar note in Brown's own name and give him thirty days to pay it.[91]

The bank used means of public humiliation, particularly the warrant or protest, to underscore the legal rather than moral aspect of a debtor's obligation. The bank publicly recorded protests with the local chancery or records office, which reinforced the bank's legal claims. A civil servant, often the postal carrier but sometimes a municipal employee or collector, personally delivered protest notices to debtors. The debtors acknowledged receipt by their signatures. The bank had to be careful, however, in mobilizing the state apparatus to collect debts. Most blacks' experiences with police, courts, or municipal authorities were hostile, exploitative, and sometimes even lethal. Suing in a court and using the police to collect the loan principal or appropriate collateral represented extreme action, not just because they were in tension with the bank's values but also because of the potential threat to the debtor. The bank would rather exhaust public pressures or even lose the principal than subject customers to extreme state intervention. But for substantial loan amounts or prime properties in black areas of town, the bank would initiate foreclosure procedures. For example, after several letters in as many months, the bank foreclosed on Maria Chatham's property when she failed to bring her account current.[92]

The protest, or warrant, was usually enough to solicit a response and secure payment from a recalcitrant debtor. One St. Luke Bank protest elicited a bitter complaint from a past-due borrower when the bank's protest arrived in the midst of his protracted battle with his town's officials about back taxes. "I have never before been warranted by any one," he fumed. "I am dealing with white banks but no such dirty acts have ever been served on me like this. . . . I know the law. Warrants are for thieves and rogues. I am not either of those."[93] As much as the bank promoted itself as an alternative to unscrupulous lenders and white banks, borrowers pressed to their limits were quick to associate the bank with the same kind of depredation.

In addition to the impersonal protest, the bank relied on collection agents to recover delinquent debts. It typically used local lawyers but sometimes used collection agents. For example, L. T. Branch of Richmond collected bad notes, bought and sold judgments, and investigated individuals' credit and financial standings. To serve a warrant on a debtor, Branch charged the lender between eighty cents and a dollar per visit. He followed up with debtors periodically and sometimes succeeded in personally collecting the amounts due and forwarding them, minus his fee, to the bank. Effective collectors made an impression and were in demand by lenders. Another business owner asked the bank for help finding a "first-class collector who will take hold of [delinquent accounts] for us."[94] For some borrowers, the sight of Branch or some other collector knocking on the door was enough to compel them to pay.[95]

Sometimes neither attorneys nor collection agents could recover the bank's principal. The bank had asked Dr. J. Meade Benson to get an endorsement from his wife, and it was not long before she began borrowing money from the bank herself. She consistently failed, however, to meet her obligations. When Nellie Benson defaulted on a twenty-five-dollar note, the bank forwarded her account to a local agent in St. Louis for collection. The exasperated agent informed Burke, "All the satisfaction that we have been able to get is smiles and promises."[96]

Middle-class borrowers with steady salaries enabled a particularly effective method of collection: wage garnishment. Rev. J. E. Harper left Richmond owing the bank twenty-six dollars, which had already been a few months past due before his departure. The bank tracked him to his new church in Abbeville, South Carolina, and Burke inquired when he would make good on his past-due note. Harper wrote back that he would pay something soon, but he did not. The bank then contacted the Freedmen's Board of the Presbyterian Church in Pennsylvania, which paid the reverend's salary, and asked the board to deduct the twenty-six dollars from Harper's salary.[97]

Civil servants also made effective collection targets. When two postal carriers, James R. Barrett and James L. Burrell, did not respond to demands to pay their debts, the bank enlisted its attorney James T. Hewin to contact the postmaster general. The postmaster general complied with requests to garnish employees' wages when provided with adequate proof of the claims against them. In 1914, Burke made a pointed threat to Squire Lacy: if Lacy did not pay sixty-five dollars for a check that had been returned for insufficient funds, Burke would personally come to Westpoint, Virginia, to "appear against you." If this happened, Burke warned, "Postmaster General Wilkes writes us that you will have to surrender your contract which you have with the government for delivering mail between Westpoint and Urbanna, V[irgini]a."[98] It appears the bank was not above extorting civil servants to force delinquent debtors to pay their debts.[99]

A shrewd debtor could cast enough doubt to save himself from garnishment. The bank pursued a claim against postal carrier E. H. Weston, who told his superiors that the bank had treated him unfairly and had been slipshod in its recordkeeping. The first assistant postmaster general wrote to the bank, saying that his hands were tied and that the post office could do nothing because Weston "disputes the justness of the account." Weston then engaged attorney George B. White to negotiate with the bank, hoping to pay back less than the principal amount of the loan. The bank refused.[100] Staying ahead of wage garnishment, N. T. Lewis of Richmond assigned half his salary to an attorney, who then distributed the funds to help Lewis pay off his many debtors.[101]

The bank did more than spread risk as a way to mitigate it; it created social knowledge to assess and manage it. In its early years, the bank relied on the IOSL's fraternal ritual and values to manage risk. The discursive elements of the fraternal ritual allowed the bank some latitude in resignifying working people's relationship to capital and credit. Typically on opposite—and unequal—sides, the IOSL allowed its members the power to create businesses and provide services that met their needs. The bank put social knowledge and practices—fraternal values and traditions—in dialogue with local and translocal credit markets.

After the formation of the State Banking Department of Virginia in 1910, the bank had to comply with examinations and demands from the chief examiner. It compiled and maintained records for the examiners. Thus, the bank's lending decisions became more institutionalized. Although the habit of weighing potential risk against the likelihood that borrowers would repay their loans became more systemized and formalized, the bank never rejected whole cloth its sense of obligation to the values of the order. Despite these lofty goals, the class of borrowers that the St. Luke Bank embraced remained high risks, in part due to the vagaries of racism and sexism. Though the bank's decisions about credit and lending crossed multiple dimensions—political, economic, social, and actuarial—they ultimately reaffirmed the tenacity of racial and sexual discrimination.

The vast majority of black women saw little improvement in their labor options as they moved to other cities in the South and North, and the IOSL could take great pride in meeting many of their financial and social goals. By the end of World War I, the IOSL emerged as the largest employer of black women in the city. This professional class of young women enjoyed the economic support and affirmation they received as clients of the bank. They also realized that they had growing options for saving, investing, and spending their money. Contests for the pocketbooks and political consciences of these New Negro women of color ensued, not only in Richmond, but in cities swelling with black migrants, such as Harlem and Chicago. The realities of black women's economic lives in urban spaces made apparent the gaps between the positive rhetoric of the St. Luke Bank and the challenges of living in northern cities. The interwar period challenged the world of transactions in the IOSL moral economy from within and without.

5

"A Good, Strong, Hustling Woman"

FINANCING THE NEW NEGRO IN THE NEW ERA, 1920–1929

When the IOSL renewed its license to conduct business in North Carolina, Maggie Lena Walker used the occasion to reach out to Charlotte Hawkins Brown, the president of Palmer Memorial Institute, a college preparatory school in rural North Carolina. Walker's letter was direct and to the point: "Secure me a good, strong, hustling woman who isn't afraid to travel, talk, and work."[1] Walker likely knew that Brown had raised considerable sums for the institute by stressing an industrial education curriculum to white philanthropists but, in practice, teaching a liberal-arts-based curriculum. For black women, industrial and vocational education at black secondary schools in the early twentieth century consisted mainly of domestic science courses such as sewing and cooking and moral lessons on modesty and cleanliness. If the women did not plan to pursue college studies, most vocational education fitted them for lives as domestic workers in whites' homes or as resourceful housewives. They did not offer business-related courses such as stenography or accounting.[2]

Walker understood that many young women at Palmer Institute and other schools were ambitious but did not want (or were unable) to complete the lengthy education required for traditional avenues of middle-class status, namely nursing and teaching. Nor did they want to practice beauty culture, another career path to middle-class status. Walker imagined the IOSL as a practical school for training and equipping driven, ambitious young women for business careers. From her earliest involvement with the IOSL to experiments such as the Woman's Union to her service with other organizations and institutions throughout her lifetime, Walker helped thousands of "good, strong, hustling" women achieve success in the financial world.

At the beginning of the New Era, the IOSL and the St. Luke Bank were at the peak of their wealth and influence. IOSL membership tipped over eighty-five thousand, and the IOSL and bank combined controlled assets in the millions of dollars. By the end of the decade, however, the Great Depression came early. It hit black workers and businesses hard, crippling most black financial institutions. In the intervening years, financial institutions led by and dependent on black women became highly contested spaces—and conduits of resistance. The young women working at the IOSL and women in its leadership found themselves in the crosscurrents of black economic empowerment and wealth-building strategies that critiqued democratic capitalism and top-down, entrepreneur-led models as legitimate strategies of black economic development.[3]

This chapter considers how workers, entrepreneurs, and activists challenged black-controlled financial institutions' capacity to serve an increasingly urban and northern black population in the 1920s. Entrepreneurs' and activists' strategies reflected anxieties about black women's bodies in urban spaces. Their various investment schemes reflected conflicting attitudes that saw black women as both the victims and the sources of social disorder, as in need of both financial protection and new economic opportunities. Some of the anxieties were legitimate. Unscrupulous labor agents and criminally minded individuals sometimes preyed on women migrants, luring them to cities with promises of respectable, well-paying work but forcing them into low-skilled, poorly paid jobs and even prostitution. Opportunities to secure affordable, quality housing proved difficult as urban populations swelled. Legitimate concerns about the real problems that working women faced, however, sometimes converged with stereotypes and assumptions. Black rural women's alleged lack of intelligence, manners, and virtue shaped moral panic about their capacity to save and spend their money and to make sound investment decisions.

Working women, however, pushed back. They pressed their desires for better career options and housing choices. They rejected efforts to police their behavior and leisure choices. They grew weary of pitches that promoted investment as a marker of citizenship but implied that men were the proper producers and consumers of these investment products. Financial institutions that women led and controlled experimented with innovative ways to raise capital but struggled with inexperience and the intractable problems of racial and sexual discrimination. The IOSL introduced new investment products for its customers that promised greater security but proved unaffordable to most women.

This chapter argues that the various opportunities that opened for women in U.S. finance by the 1920s ultimately failed to sustain the economic security envisioned by entrepreneurs and activists. The opportunities inadequately reckoned with the structural barriers that made it difficult for black women and communities to maximize new investment opportunities and products. The opportunities claimed to offer greater protection and security but often failed to consider working women's own definitions of economic opportunity, stability, and autonomy. The first part of the chapter explores the historical, cultural, and economic factors that gave rise to the New Negro, and it considers the specifically gendered dimensions of the modern identity of the New Negro.

The chapter then considers black women working in the financial industry. Black women dominated as clerks, bookkeepers, cashiers, and office managers. The IOSL was the largest employer of black women in the financial services industry. Its state-of-the-art headquarters, however, revealed a widening generational and ideological divide between the IOSL old guard and New Negro women of color, often younger, college- and vocational-school-educated women who chafed under the expectations and regulations placed on them both inside and outside the workplace.

Next, contests for the hearts, minds, and pocketbooks of black women had always been waged, but they ensued at a frenetic pace after World War I. Consumption and leisure offered more than abstract reassurances of saving and deferred gratification; they offered material expressions of freedom for the New Negro woman. Assertive marketing campaigns promoted investment products aimed at black consumers, including stock investments and whole life insurance. Ambitious upstarts, such as the National Negro Finance Corporation, promised new avenues of credit, wealth, and opportunity outside traditional black banks. With the promise of a "commercial emancipation" for the Negro, promoters relied on gendered discourses to encourage men to take financial risks as a marker of manhood and as an exercise of democratic rights.

Finally, members of the IOSL explored finance and investment options beyond the St. Luke Bank. The IOSL of New York followed in the footsteps of the Right Worthy Grand Council, headquartered in Richmond, by creating a separate, for-profit investment and real estate development arm: the St. Luke Finance Corporation. The corporation responded to the exigencies of life in Harlem, which shared some similarities with conditions in Richmond but differed in significant ways. The independent spirit of the enterprise put it at odds with the IOSL headquarters in Richmond.

THE EMERGENCE OF THE NEW NEGRO

What made the first Great Migration great had a lot to do with the numbers. Estimates vary, but about 1.6 million African Americans left the South and relocated to northeastern and midwestern cities from the mid-1910s through 1930. Scholars cite a number of push and pull factors that both forced blacks to make the move from the South and drew migrants to other regions. The economic factors that figured into migrants' calculus included the search for better economic opportunities and the attractive options that many believed awaited them beyond the confines of the rural and urban South. Natural disasters, pest infestations, and plummeting cotton prices had brought many black tenant farmers and sharecroppers to their knees. Other economic sectors that were heavily dependent on agriculture and on the workers who drew their livelihood from the land had faltered as well. Better-paying jobs awaited workers in cities—in the North and the South. The migration, however, was not limited to rural migrants. Blacks already living in southern cities had equally compelling reasons to look north as well. Low-paying jobs, the lack of job mobility, poor housing conditions, and other economic factors weighed on urban black southerners' decisions to move north.[4]

The allure of personal freedom beckoned to black women. To be sure, black women were not alone in seeking personal freedom. Blacks in general sought escape from the oppression of Jim Crow, which included demeaning racial etiquette, violence, disenfranchisement, and segregation. Black women's desire to escape sexual victimization, particularly at the hands of their employers or partners, provided the key noneconomic motivation for black women to leave the South. Unlike black men, however, for whom northern factory and industrial jobs represented a major economic advantage for migrating, black women's employment options remained similar to the kinds of work they did in the South: domestic and unskilled or low-skill labor. Opportunities for self-making and self-expression, then, were the aspects that made the first Great Migration great, especially for black women.[5]

In these new places, intellectuals and artists proclaimed the arrival of the New Negro. One thing that made the New Negro new was a greater political assertiveness and racial self-awareness. The New Negro traversed diverse political terrain and debated multiple strategies to achieve political, creative, personal, and economic liberation. The political and the economic engaged with claims for personal freedom and self-expression that ran the gamut from the conservative to the radical. Black men and women, however, brought a New Negro sensibility with them and cultivated it in these new spaces. They worked out the contours of modern black identity in urban locales in the North and South.[6]

The movement of more than a million people, however, did not in itself make the New Negro era possible. The Great War played a critical role as well. Mobilization for World War I, from soldiers enlisting to activities on the home front, helped to create, according to Gerald Early, a "truly modern national community with a more informed international consciousness and this, in turn, helped to make the New Negro Movement possible."[7] Women, too, gained a renewed sense of their economic power through home front activities and war loan campaigns. They raised millions of dollars for the war effort despite overt discrimination from war-related organizations, such as the Red Cross and the YWCA. For example, blacks in Evansville, Indiana, raised $600,000 in Red Cross, Patriot Fund, and Liberty Loan Drives, which was $200,000 over their quota. Black housewives set up food clubs in cooperation with the U.S. Food Administration. Their activities, a participant observed, provided clear evidence of the "thrift and economy" of blacks in Evansville. These activities represented "what we are trying to do in anticipation of the future."[8] Aside from displaying black women's formidable fundraising power, Julia Ott notes, these war loan and bond campaigns celebrated cultural pluralism and racial pride and even pushed for "civic inclusion, political rights, and the destruction of Jim Crow."[9] Thus, World War I ignited within New Negro women an assertive political sensibility as well as a reassurance of their economic importance not only to black communities and families but also to the nation.

A grisly undercurrent of violence also helped shaped the New Negros' political sensibility. The postwar economic recession brought difficult times. Swelling populations of black migrants meant fierce competition for jobs and housing. Blacks made assertive claims for economic rights, protested residential segregation, and demanded equitable municipal services. Workers demanded better pay and working conditions, organizing agricultural and industrial labor unions to assert their demands. Outward signs of blacks' economic success combined with their political assertiveness turned some whites feral. They sated their anxieties in a bloodlust of lynching and mob violence. From 1919 to 1921, during a period known as the Red Summer, racial violence erupted in twenty-five cities around the country. Hundreds of blacks lost their lives, and tens of thousands more lost their homes, businesses, and sense of security.[10]

Whites often justified the violence with the "threadbare lie" of black men preying on white women, but the level of destruction in black communities bore out the truer underlying economic dimensions of white domestic terror.[11] The Tulsa race riot of 1921 stands as a poignant conflation of white sexual and economic anxieties. Based on flimsy claims that Dick Rowland battered a white woman elevator operator, the local paper amplified the story into a full-fledged rape. When armed black men resisted whites' attempts to remove Rowland from the jail, mobs of white men, including police and soldiers, directed their anger toward the all-black Greenwood community and its well-respected and nationally known Black Wall Street. For months preceding the specious rape allegations, however, whites had been on edge about blacks' assertions of political and economic autonomy. For example, the African Blood Brotherhood, a black nationalist group that embraced armed self-defense and encouraged patronage of local black businesses as part of its vision of an autonomous, self-determined black nation, had established a chapter in Tulsa.[12]

Black Wall Streets in Durham and Richmond escaped the widespread destruction that engulfed Greenwood, but they did not completely escape extralegal violence and racial tension. During the Red Summer, lynchings occurred near Durham in Franklin, Onslow, Warren, and other counties of North Carolina. Riots also occurred near Richmond in Washington, D.C., and Norfolk. Incendiary headlines in Virginia papers like "Negroes, Armed to Teeth, Fire upon All White Persons" undercut the veneer of civility and led to uncomfortable moments for blacks throughout Virginia and along the East Coast. The New Negro thus emerged from a complicated crucible of opportunity and risk.[13]

FINANCING THE NEW NEGRO WOMAN

Cultural production, particularly in music, literature, and film, as well as commercial amusements represented important new markets in which the enterprising could attract black dollars and constitute the modern sensibility of the New Negro. Black women took advantage of a wide range of educational, civic, and leisure opportunities. They also found jobs in formal and informal black enterprises. Their enthusiastic participation in the marketplace led to moral anxieties, much of it centered on black women's bodies in urban spaces. As historian Anne Stavney notes, "Assertions of black female immorality, impurity, and licentiousness constituted a repeated refrain in white discussions of black America."[14] Middle-class black women reformers often echoed these refrains in both their old and new locales.

In cities of the North and South, black and white reformers worried about black women's appearance, what kinds of music they listened to, the kinds of work they did, and how they spent their spare time. Black women navigated continued sexual and economic exploitation from employers, unscrupulous labor agents, landlords, and con artists in their new destinations. To be sure, the perils and personal freedoms that women migrants sought and that many found were centered on how they earned money and what they did with it.[15]

One important place where reformers and intellectuals encouraged black women to spend money was in black business districts, or Black Wall Streets. For example, the magic of Chicago's Stroll lay not only in the expressive culture on full display in the exaggerated gaits, personal style, and fashion sense of the black men and women who sauntered up and down South State Street. Geography was critical. The Stroll lay in Bronzeville, Chicago's Black Wall Street: a concentration of commercial spaces catering to and owned by black people. Indeed, if Harlem represented the intellectual and artistic epicenter of the New Negro movement in the North, then Chicago was in many ways the movement's economic and political nexus. Stores, restaurants, theaters, professional offices, and service businesses joined financial institutions like insurance offices, banks, and building and loan associations to build up Black Wall Streets in large cities of the North and South, including Jackson Ward in Richmond, Hayti in Durham, and Sweet Auburn in Atlanta. Through appeals to race pride and promises of creating wealth and jobs, Black Wall Streets were *the* places to make, spend, and save money.[16]

Black Wall Streets revealed risks as well. They depended heavily on race-first rhetoric and black customers. Yet the structural problems that black businesses faced—particularly limited and expensive access to credit; undercapitalization; competition from white and immigrant businesses, especially within the black business district; and racial hostility, including extralegal and bureaucratic harassment—adulterated many of the communal benefits that black entrepreneurship claimed to offer. Critics acknowledged the structural barriers but lobbed personal missives as well. Black entrepreneurship represented at best naïve optimism by the aspiring and working classes and at worst pernicious self-interest by the black petit bourgeoisie.

Entrepreneurs, merchants, and professionals created a "racial tariff"—what business scholar and Socialist Abram Harris describes as "higher prices for inferior goods and services."[17] Negro captains of industry were less interested in uplifting the race, providing occupational mobility, or developing the black community than in advancing their own self-interests, critics argued. Though black banks and insurance companies represented millions of dollars of black capital, the apparent failure of black entrepreneurs to match the corporate and industrial empires of titans like Andrew Carnegie and Henry Ford made it impossible for them to create the foundation upon which the prosperity and vitality of every other kind of black business could be sustained.[18]

However, appeals to race pride represented much more than efforts to divert attention away from or to ignore the inherent ethical dilemmas in the exploitative nature of those relations of capital. Black businesses were certainly dependent on black labor and the black market as sources of capital. The black entrepreneurial class placed among the earliest, most sustained, and loudest voices condemning racial capitalism and all its depredations: higher costs for goods and services, low wages, inequitable access to mortgage and consumer credit, and unsafe working conditions.[19]

It is also critical to consider the intentions and goals of blacks who frequented—and even those who criticized—Black Wall Streets. Claudrena Harold's observations about working-class United Negro Improvement Association (UNIA) supporters apply equally to black consumers and investors responding to appeals that they "buy black." Black consumers bought and invested, she says, "with an expansive sense of civic responsibility, extensive organizational experience, an astute awareness of class distinctions within the black community, and an understanding of the ways in which their position in the political economy negatively impacted their life chances and experiences."[20] Black consumers and investors were not simple dupes. They pursued their own self-interests.

Black workers also called into question the democratic potential of capitalism. Those involved in leftist movements criticized the negatives of capitalism. Their experiences with racism and sexism shaped the reforms they promoted. A. Philip Randolph and Chandler Owens, for example, organized the Friends of Negro Freedom in 1920. The Friends embraced black entrepreneurship as a strategy to provide employment and training to black workers. Black Left women such as Claudia Jones called attention to the "superexploitation of black women."[21] She highlighted how black women stood justifiably as vanguards in the movement because of their triple oppression due to their race, class, and gender. Jones's observations called attention to women's important economic roles not only in their families and communities but also to U.S. and global economies. In 1925, Elise Johnson McDougald stressed that black women had always "been the weather-vane, the indicator, showing in which direction the wind of destiny blows."[22] The ways black women made, spent, saved, and invested their money, then, revealed the interconnections and ambiguities of various movements for racial uplift, self-help, and manhood rights. Replete with tensions, black economic nationalism was hardly a unified, ideologically coherent ideology or movement.[23]

THE NEW NEGRO WOMEN OF THE INDEPENDENT ORDER OF ST. LUKE

Reformers and intellectuals tried to keep supposedly vulnerable young women away from commercialized vice through wholesome entertainments centered in lyceums, settlement houses, and other forms of work with women's clubs. Scholars often fail to consider the social activities and clubs that were sponsored by black-owned corporations, particularly black financial institutions. Independent Order of St. Luke employees helped produce pageants, especially for the biennial conventions, and hosted music recitals and other public entertainments in the IOSL's spacious auditorium. The IOSL organized a glee club, a drill team, and the St. Luke Boosters (see fig. 5.1) for its predominately female staff.[24]

Walker mobilized the St. Luke Boosters to represent the IOSL in activities both within the IOSL and in the outside community. The boosters arranged fundraisers for local social service projects. They could also be counted on to make a strong show of force at IOSL rallies outside Richmond. For example, in 1926, the boosters arranged for two busloads of members, staff, and management to travel to Washington, D.C., for a regional rally. While in D.C., the young women clerks stayed at the local YWCA. They enjoyed a night of activities at the local Metropolitan AME Church until two a.m., woke up for a breakfast that was served promptly at 8:30, and had free time for sightseeing until noon.[25]

Boosters also participated in political activism. After passage of the Nineteenth Amendment, black women around the country mobilized to register women voters. Walker had long supported women's suffrage. In an

FIGURE 5.1 The St. Luke boosters, c. 1922. Maggie Lena Walker stands at the end on the far right. The young man in the picture may have been recruited to hide Walker's leg brace. *Source*: MAWA 3127, courtesy of National Park Service, Maggie L. Walker National Historic Site.

address at the 1912 National Association of Colored Women convention in Hampton, Virginia, Walker linked women's political and earning power. She told the audience, "Capital is deaf—and will never hear [black women's] cries, until women force Capital to hear them at the ballot box, and to be just and honest to them as to the men."[26] In 1920, Walker chaired a committee to help register as many black women voters as possible before the registration deadline. Walker relied on the boosters to support and promote the committee's activities. They helped ensure that IOSL employees and members from around the state attended mass meetings. They helped register 4,800 blacks, including 2,401 women, which probably included all of the IOSL's more than one hundred women employees. The women could have registered far more. Segregated lines at the registrar moved slowly for black applicants, and clerks in the registrar's office frequently challenged black women's qualifications. Thousands of Afro-Richmonders signed a petition to press the registrar to appoint black women clerks, but it did not bear fruit.[27]

Clerks in the office made up only a part of the IOSL's workforce. Organizing deputies (ODs) were the most visible, independent, and highly paid positions in the IOSL. ODs earned commissions recruiting new members and planting new councils. They supported the home office in practical and expressive ways, helping to collect dues for new members as well as late or short payments, no matter how small, and delivering benefit checks and policies. ODs often oversaw rituals and helped reinstate lapsed members. Lillian Payne leaned on the ODs to help improve morale among members, offer counsel in disputes, and pray for their district members' individual and group success.

The ODs were working women who were juggling intense professional pressures with personal obligations, which sometimes affected their ability to meet their quotas. They earned bonuses for exceeding quotas, but the job pressures were intense. For example, the 1924 quota called for recruiting two hundred new members, and ODs were expected to double that number for 1925. Lilia Garfield confided, perhaps with a bit of sarcasm, that she had trouble reaching her quota because her "dear Old Daddy" kept her very busy.[28] ODs were the face of IOSL outside Richmond. Unfortunately, the record does not provide a comprehensive list of ODs, but in the 1920s, more than half—at least eighty—were women.[29]

For New Negro women, being an OD was ideal despite the myriad responsibilities. They traveled, entertained, marketed, administered, and organized. They enjoyed a great deal of professional autonomy, and their influence extended beyond their local communities. Some ODs likely supplemented their income with their IOSL work, but especially for those ODs who served full time, the position allowed an escape from domestic, agricultural, and industrial labor.[30]

About sixty other women IOSL employees—more than 90 percent of the office workers—worked in the headquarters in Richmond, and six women clerks worked for the St. Luke Bank. The women appreciated the benefits of working at the IOSL headquarters and the bank. The office and bank buildings provided finely appointed work environments. The St. Luke Bank's interiors boasted "decorative stone arches, . . . brass grills, birch fittings, [and] marble wainscoting."[31] In 1918, black architect Charles T. Russell oversaw renovations to the IOSL building. Walker added a fourth floor, expanded the entire building, and installed an elevator, complete with an operator to run it. The renovated auditorium now seated eight hundred. A café operated out of the IOSL building, and employees could enjoy a private fountain in the building's courtyard.[32]

The modern and the old-fashioned intermingled for the New Negro woman in the financial industry. Black women working clerical jobs tended to be better educated than their white counterparts. Black women also found paths to management positions and opportunities to expand their skills, especially into bookkeeping and accounting positions. Typically at the beginning of women's careers, the conditions and pay for white-collar jobs like the IOSL were far better than for factory jobs and other kinds of low-skilled labor. At some point in her career, however, a woman's pay would not keep up with her experience, which meant that IOSL office jobs were middle class in terms of social stature but working class in terms of pay.[33]

In addition, the women clerks, bookkeepers, and other office workers sometimes chafed under the strict regimen, mountain of work, and pressure to conform to the respectable ideals that had been envisioned by Walker and older women managers. Walker insisted that the women employees wear white shirts and conservative dark skirts (see fig. 5.2). Clerks had to be at their desks by 8:50 A.M. sharp, or they lost a whole day's pay. The workdays at the bank and the IOSL headquarters began with prayer and a devotional. Walker spoke almost every week to the workforce on various topics, including working as a team and promoting the work of the order. She would also offer them advice, from furthering their education to personal relationships. Some of that advice was surely unsolicited and unwelcome. In addition, working at the IOSL entailed some pressure to make financial commitments. Walker insisted that the clerks save at least 5 percent of their earnings, and she sometimes required them to give donations for local causes, such as the fireman's fund in Spring 1921.[34]

The workload was significant. By the mid-1920s, the IOSL had more than eighty-five thousand members in twenty-two states. The bank had total assets of nearly half a million dollars (or about $7 million in 2017 dollars), and the IOSL had $8.6 million (about $121 million in 2017 dollars) of insurance in force. The women clerks handled all claims and queries from customers, verified the circumstances surrounding deaths and sicknesses, and sent reminders and other correspondence to members and councils. They

FIGURE 5.2 IOSL office workers, c. 1924.
Source: Detail from 1925 calendar, *From Their Own Workshop: The Independent Order of St. Luke*. MAWA 0042, courtesy of National Park Service, Maggie L. Walker National Historic Site.

handled the paperwork and managed the needs of nearly 150 organizing deputies and helped prepare materials for audits and state inspections. They often worked long hours without extra pay. The four clerks who worked exclusively with the juvenile division, in addition to their positions in the office, had to be active matrons, or leaders, of juvenile circles.[35]

Not surprisingly, the women grumbled among themselves. Most were too intimidated to confront the formidable Walker personally, but a few gathered the courage to speak out. Estella Anderson complained about work conditions, and she persisted in making her unhappiness known. In 1918, Anderson wrote to Walker, listing a number of grievances, including charges that Walker showed favoritism to certain clerks. The letter upset Walker, and tensions between the two women increased over the next few years. In 1920, Anderson asked for a raise. The record is unclear about whether she received her raise, but Anderson continued to express her displeasure with working conditions. Walker described Anderson as "sullen, insubordinate," and a year after she had requested the raise, Walker said she was still "not doing her best."[36] Walker charged Anderson with insubordination and had a "strong talk" with her. Anderson, not backing down, threatened to talk publicly about negative aspects of the IOSL office work. Walker gave her an ultimatum: "cooperate or leave."[37] Anderson chose to cooperate but did so grudgingly. The "still disgruntled" Anderson was the only clerk to not contribute to the 1921 drive for the fireman's fund.[38]

Lelia Williams Bankett was perhaps Walker's greatest miscalculation, and their fraught relationship reveals the generational divide between the old guard, including Maggie Lena Walker, Patsie Keiley Anderson, and Lillian Payne, and a generation of New Negro women workers in the IOSL (see fig. 5.3). Bankett began working for the IOSL as a stenographer in 1903. Walker encouraged IOSL employees to improve themselves through education, and Bankett attended Hartshorn in Richmond for a short period. She also completed courses at Smith's Business College in Lynchburg, Virginia, a pioneering business vocational school for African Americans.

FIGURE 5.3 Lelia Williams Bankett, c. 1920s.
Source: V.88.20.89, Valentine Museum.

Confident in her skills and talents, in 1920, a then-unmarried Bankett asked for more pay. She probably received a raise because the IOSL did not want to lose an experienced, highly trained employee to the competition. By 1921, Walker reluctantly bowed to the pressure to groom a successor, and Bankett began working as Walker's assistant. Many saw her as the aging Walker's heir apparent. She was clearly talented and capable, which, under normal circumstances, would have won Walker's respect. In 1924, Bankett organized a banquet honoring Walker's silver anniversary as secretary-treasurer, and despite the threat of snow, guests packed the St. Luke Hall—a testament to Bankett's organizing strengths as much as the guests' level of respect for Walker.[39]

Bankett added field secretary to her résumé by the mid-1920s. She recruited extensively in New Negro strongholds like Harlem and Chicago, and she recruited an astounding 4,723 new members to the IOSL in only eighteen months. The message of economic empowerment resonated in old and new ways to recent migrants in their new locales. Bankett undoubtedly stressed the security offered by a financial institution like the IOSL. In Great Migration cities in the Northeast and Midwest, that security served as a hedge against the larger forces of capitalism, particularly growing mechanization and technology that often made workers' jobs more dangerous and made workers themselves more expendable. The national character of the IOSL also gave workers reassurances that they could provide for family members in different parts of the country and in different stages of migration to and from their original locales. Extant records are not available, but it is very likely that St. Luke Bank customers around the country wrote checks on their accounts and sent money to relatives around the country through the bank's correspondent banking relationships with banks in New York and other cities.[40]

By the late 1920s, tensions with Bankett reached a breaking point. Lillian Payne found Bankett hard to work with, but Payne's own desire to succeed Walker may have colored her attitude. Walker and Payne had met as young women in the IOSL in the 1880s, and Payne was effectively Walker's second in command. Walker depended on Payne to oversee rituals and to visit councils outside Virginia, especially as Walker's knee injury made it more difficult for her to walk and travel. Payne served as editor of the

St. Luke Herald for several years, and she served on the St. Luke Bank's board, working on two of its most important committees: finance and auditing. She managed the minute details of thousands of councils, took to the road several times a year to recruit new members and encourage existing ones, and helped supervise workers at headquarters and organizing deputies in the field. Walker and Payne were very close professionally and personally; anyone who crossed Walker crossed Payne as well.[41]

Walker found Bankett impossible. Facing the twilight of her career, Walker came to resent the gifted younger woman. The specific details of what constituted "insubordination," in Walker's estimation, are not apparent.[42] Bankett may have taken workers' concerns seriously, championing their right to wear the latest fashions instead of the "St. Luke uniform" of a white top and conservative skirt. She may have tried to end the near-daily lectures about commitment and proper conduct. Given her ability to attract thousands to the order, Bankett may have had her own plans for national-scale changes to the IOSL. The strong-willed, talented Bankett refused, it seems, to be molded into a carbon copy of Maggie Lena Walker.

To be sure, Bankett's work with the National Ideal Benefit Society by 1927 represented an irreparable breach. It was not unusual for women who were connected to the IOSL to remain active in other societies. Payne, for example, was an officer in a local society and served on the state-level board of the Court of Calanthe, and Walker herself maintained her connections with the United Order of Tents J. R. Giddings and Jolliffe Union. However, Bankett's very public affiliation as the national recruiter for National Ideal Benefit represented to Walker not just divided loyalties but a possible coup. Aware of Bankett's formidable organizing prowess, Walker had reason to feel uneasy. Bankett, too, must have been weary of the constant battles with Walker. Bankett thus seized the chance to build up another organization—and perhaps contemplated growing it so that it would become a serious rival to the IOSL.[43]

In her diary, Walker made an uncharacteristic emotional outburst: "I tried with [Bankett], to make her the best Negro Organizer this country has. I wanted her to be the one woman who would make the St. Luke Order known from coast to coast.—I failed!!"[44] Walker cast Bankett out of her beloved IOSL. In 1928, Walker fired Bankett for "disloyalty": "[Bankett] couldn't subordinate herself.—She wanted more than she could take care of.—She wanted all."[45] Walker's alleged sense of personal failure belied her contentious struggle for power with Bankett. Walker easily adopted new technology and business methods that kept the IOSL and the St. Luke Bank nimble and competitive, but she blinded herself to any shortcomings in her own leadership style and moral vision for the order. However, Bankett's unparalleled success in expanding new markets and the pending economic downturn forced Walker to rehire Bankett in late 1928 or early 1929. In a nod to the younger woman's appeal, Bankett's image preceded Walker's in a *New York Age* story promoting a six week membership drive in New York and throughout the Northeast in early 1929.[46]

The IOSL introduced new insurance policies in the 1920s to provide members with greater options and security. The majority of IOSL members owned Class A policies, which paid $100 each and cost twenty cents per month. In 1922, the IOSL began offering Class B and C policies, which paid $300 and $500 respectively. The policyholder's age at the time of purchase determined the premium paid for these new classes of policies. The IOSL introduced a whole life insurance product in 1928. Whole life, or legal reserve, insurance provided some advantages over the industrial- and endowment-style policies that the IOSL had previously offered. All the premiums paid into the industrial-style policies went toward paying benefits upon death. For people who held their policies for decades, the amount they paid in premiums could exceed the amount of the benefit. The new whole life products offered greater choice through multiple benefit amounts: $100 increments from $100 to $500. They lasted the life of the policyholder, and a portion of the premium paid accumulated cash value against which the policyholder could borrow. Thus, whole life policies were both an investment and a savings product.[47]

Whole life insurance was, however, more expensive. Walker dispatched Payne to canvass Virginia as part of a drive to sign up at least six thousand new policyholders. Payne exploited the usual connections—IOSL councils and circles. Walker also employed a strategy to promote the legal reserve feature similar to one she had used at Corner-Stone and the Woman's Union: she targeted non–St. Luke members. This time, however, she focused on the black middle and professional classes. Walker sent Payne to meet with pastors, teachers, and social workers. Many of the rank-and-file members simply did not understand the new legal reserve benefit. Janie Armistead of the Little David Council No. 835 wrote that "we have some members who can't understand the two hundred dollar policy" despite Payne's recent visit to promote and explain the new benefit.[48] For others, the higher payments, despite the added benefits, proved too expensive for working-class members, many of whom were longtime customers. Fannie Nicholas of Earlysville, Virginia, requested a refund of money she had already paid for her new whole life policy, noting that she and her mother "couldn't keep it up" considering their other expenses.[49] A circle reported that parents and children "are not able to keep up the dues" and wanted their money refunded so that they could purchase lower-priced policies with the IOSL.[50] Payne responded, touting the benefits of the legal reserve, but parents and youths still wanted their money back. One matron warned that if Payne continued to press the legal reserve, the IOSL would "loose [*sic*] eight good members" from among her council.[51] The IOSL experimented with new classes of investment products for members. Its target market of middle- and professional-class non-IOSL members reflected efforts to expand the IOSL's customer base but threatened to leave behind a sizeable portion of its key, longtime constituency: working-class women.

Thus, reformers, civic leaders, and others who expressed concern about how black women earned and spent their money likely saw the IOSL as a beacon for black women. And it was in many ways. One of the few white-collar, professional jobs open to black women, working in the IOSL headquarters allowed those women to escape many of the dangers and difficulties facing many other black women. Managers and other employees arranged social activities for the largely female workforce. Working conditions at the IOSL headquarters, however, brought other challenges. While the IOSL encouraged women employees to save money in St. Luke Bank and the bank helped women to buy their own homes, some women felt that the order did not pay them what they deserved. Walker grew uncomfortable with women who spoke up about unfair treatment or whose ambitions fell outside of her acceptable limits. Black women working in the financial industry navigated difficult terrain. They struggled to meet expectations about their behavior, comportment, and hustle and sometimes had to push back against efforts to limit their ambitions.

"A COMMERCIAL EMANCIPATION" FOR THE NEGRO: FINANCING NEW NEGRO BUSINESS

Maggie Lena Walker probably was no longer surprised that she was the lone woman among the fifty or so business, banking, and insurance leaders attending a banquet in late 1924 in New York City that had been called "to stabilize, strengthen, and protect Negro business."[52] The St. Luke Bank and the IOSL were veritable successes by the mid-1920s. Walker stood as the most powerful black woman in the financial industry. She had worked most of her life to prove that women could excel in the financial world, and her presence lent legitimacy to, if not acknowledgment of, women's critical roles in the financial industry. She surely wondered whether her lifelong efforts counted for much, because here she was again, the only woman in a room full of black men who were charting, as they imagined, the economic future of the race.[53]

The select group of business leaders outlined plans for the National Negro Finance Corporation, a million-dollar corporation that would launch black business into a new financial age. Walker took advantage of the novelty of her presence. She offered the St. Luke Bank as a model for the young finance company to emulate. She told the austere group, "We shall not stop, but put our moneys and brains together and achieve a commercial emancipation."[54] Walker echoed her call to IOSL members two decades earlier, when she had first shared her vision for a bank that was largely owned and run by women for women.[55]

The National Negro Finance Corporation (NNFC) shared ambitious goals with the other black-owned finance company launched in the early 1920s, the Allied Industrial Finance Corporation (AIFC), but bitter rivalries for control over the vision for the future of black business soon emerged between the two companies. The finance companies differed in their opinions about the role that capital and expertise from white investors should play. The effort to save two of the largest black-owned insurance companies from loss to a white-owned company resulted in a battle of wills between the two finance companies. Both the NNFC and AIFC deployed highly gendered rhetoric to legitimize their distinct approaches to preserving black wealth and building black business. Gender and class also converged in heated contests with Marcus Garvey's Negro Factories Corporation and Black Cross Navigation and Trading Company for middle- and working-class investors. Black investors responded in complex ways to the heightened appeals of black-owned finance companies to race pride, racial uplift, and risk. Finally, internal difficulties undermined the finance companies and highlighted the difficulties in achieving a true economic emancipation for black communities.

The origins of the AIFC and the NNFC are important to explore, revealing places where their goals and visions converged and diverged. Both companies grew out of the National Negro Business League (NNBL). Formed in 1900 by Booker T. Washington, the NNBL was the largest association of black businesspeople and professionals. The NNBL oversaw a loose federation of local business clubs and chambers of commerce. Auxiliaries of the NNBL included the National Negro Bankers Association, National Negro Funeral Directors Association, and the National Negro Press Association. Washington served as president of the NNBL until his death in 1915. Emmett J. Scott served as Washington's personal secretary for nearly two decades, and Scott served as secretary of the NNBL.[56]

For some years, even before Washington's death, Emmett Scott had longed to see the NNBL evolve beyond its loosely federated local leagues, largely dormant professional auxiliaries, and camp-style annual meetings. Scott imagined an organization that would provide critical services to black-owned businesses. Once out from under the long and formidable shadow of Washington, Scott attempted to shift the NNBL's center of gravity from Tuskegee to more cosmopolitan climes such as Washington, D.C., or even New York City. He also wanted to reconstitute the executive committee and leadership to tap into the dynamism of a younger generation of self-made men.[57]

Stymied in his efforts to remake the NNBL, in late 1920 Scott organized the AIFC to provide capital to black businesses. Initially, Scott planned to raise the majority of the $3.75 million of capital from white industrialists.

It is very likely that Scott reached out to leading white businessmen and financiers such as the Rockefellers, Julius Rosenwald, George Foster Peabody, and others who had been longtime financial supporters of the NNBL. Scott also dug into his deep contact list of black business owners around the country. When the AIFC formally launched in December 1920, the officers included Emmett Scott as president; Edward C. Brown, founder of Brown Savings Bank in Norfolk, Virginia, and Brown and Stevens Bank in Philadelphia, as chairman of the board; Harry Pace, founder of Black Swan Records and a high-ranking insurance executive, as secretary; and John Nail, a Harlem real estate investor, as treasurer. The AIFC made its headquarters in the sparkling new Southern Aid Building in Washington, D.C., which was completed in 1921.[58]

The AIFC's prospectus boasted that it represented "the first time in history [when] an opportunity is opened to [Negroes] to enter the financial terms on equal terms with all others."[59] The claim implicitly conceded the limitations of black banking. Aggressive lending practices, like those of the St. Luke Bank, drew the censure of state regulators. Some banks had "commercial" in their names, but the title was aspirational rather than actual. Low capitalization limited black banks' ability to lend major sums. Black-owned insurance companies controlled far larger amounts of capital and did invest in local large-scale business and real estate development projects. The AIFC hoped to step into the gap. It planned to lend start-up and operating capital for businesses of various sizes around the nation, reaching markets that did not have or were underserved by existing local black banks. The AIFC was especially interested in capital-intensive businesses such as factories and steamship lines.

Fearful that Scott's AIFC might actually succeed and best the NNBL, in early 1924, Charles C. Spaulding arranged a secret meeting in Durham with a select group of businessmen and then an open, organizational meeting in early June. Durham dominated as the de facto location of leadership, relegating the Tuskegee site to a counseling and inspirational role in the resulting finance corporation. The participants elected Robert R. Moton as temporary president and Spaulding as chair of the executive committee of the new National Negro Finance Corporation. Moton had succeeded Washington as principal of Tuskegee and president of the NNBL. Spaulding, as cofounder of the North Carolina Mutual Insurance Company and president of the Mechanics and Farmers Bank in Durham, was arguably the most well-known and respected black businessman in the country. At a banquet in New York City in November, where Walker as the lone woman declared "a commercial emancipation," a group of about fifty business and civic leaders from around the country officially announced the NNFC.[60]

The goals of the NNFC were even more ambitious than the AIFC's. In addition to providing capital for new black businesses, the NNFC wanted to maintain a corps of industry experts to advise business people. It also wanted "to create and develop a market for listing, exchanging, buying, and selling Negro securities."[61] The NNFC planned to create a stock exchange that would sell stock in and securitize assets backed by Negro businesses. The corporation's prospectus and publicity documents dangled the possibility that the NNFC would invest in non-black-owned businesses but made clear that the NNFC, unlike the AIFC, would not court capital investment from white businessmen and philanthropists. The NNFC wanted to put blacks' assets to work in the larger U.S. financial market, blurring and perhaps even erasing the color line in high finance while compounding the assets of black investors. Future plans included creating an extension bureau to vet black businesses; the NNFC would act as a kind of Dun and Bradstreet to assess, rate, and establish a credit information clearinghouse for black businesses.[62]

In late 1923, a proposed multimillion-dollar merger of two of the top three black-owned life insurance companies accelerated efforts to organize the NNFC. It also fueled an intense competition between the AIFC and the inchoate NNFC. In December 1923, Heman Perry of Standard Life of Atlanta purchased Mississippi Life Insurance Company, which was cofounded and led by Minnie Geddings Cox, formerly of Indianola, Mississippi, but then living in Memphis, Tennessee. Cox's controlling stock in Mississippi Life was worth \$1.8 million (in 2017 dollars). Almost immediately, however, the precarious financial condition of Perry, a man *Forbes* magazine described in 1924 as "the richest Negro in the world," became public knowledge, and white creditors threatened to take over not only both insurance companies but also Perry's other holdings, valued at \$2 million (or \$29 million in 2017 dollars).[63]

The NNFC deployed gendered and racial rhetoric about "saving" black business to build its reputation and undercut the AIFC. The finance company that was able to bail out Standard Life would achieve the ultimate coup. The NNFC's earliest promotional articles grounded its future promise on its "first official act," which was "to save the large estate and business of a widow."[64] The unnamed widow was Minnie Geddings Cox. After the sale of Mississippi Life, her estate still included two dozen properties, including a large plantation, and the Delta Penny Savings Bank in Indianola, Mississippi, a bank she cofounded with her husband in 1903. Neither Cox's estate nor her other businesses were under any threat of loss in her transaction with Perry.

The person who needed a financial rescue was Perry, not Cox. Perry had severely overextended himself in various commercial and residential real estate investment deals, but Perry's precarious financial condition was not necessarily the result of poor business dealings. Organized resistance and market manipulation by white real estate brokers and businessmen had limited him to predatory financing schemes that exposed his principal to great risk and undervalued his properties and other assets. He often relied on easy financing and credit from the bank he founded, Citizens Trust in Atlanta. By late 1923, however, the bank was nearly bankrupt. His creditors, two white-owned trust and insurance companies, threatened to foreclose on Perry to recoup their loan. Both the NNFC organizers and the AIFC worked to raise money to pay off Perry's debt.[65]

The NNFC had not yet been formally organized, but Moton and Spaulding still proceeded with intense negotiations with Julius Rosenwald, John D. Rockefeller Jr., and other white business leaders. The rival AIFC's involvement in the negotiations is more oblique. Moton served on the AIFC board as well. Some AIFC board members engaged in separate talks with the white financiers. The negotiations proved thorny in many ways. Reliance on white financiers for a loan to Perry belied the NNFC's very public rhetoric of its commitment to use blacks' capital for black enterprise. The white financiers controlled the financial cards and made some difficult demands, including requiring Perry to step down. Standard Life, Mississippi Life, and the Service Company (Perry's holding company) would avoid the proverbial frying pan only to fall into the fire: the coterie of white financiers would then own the black businesses.

Rosenwald, Rockefeller, and others pledged to remain private, hidden partners; full credit for the rescue would go to black men and the NNFC. The white financiers offered to lend a little over half a million dollars (or $7.3 million in 2017 dollars) to repay Perry's debt and to preserve "faith in black business."[66] Perry, however, refused to step down. Neither the NNFC nor the AIFC could raise the funds on its own. Both Standard Life and Mississippi Life fell into the hands of Southern Life Insurance Company and Southeastern Trust in 1925, two closely aligned white companies in Tennessee.[67]

The NNFC still managed to get grist for its mill from the failure. A newspaper article that was critical of the NNBL in general nevertheless expressed enthusiasm about the potential benefit of the NNFC. It emphasized that the loss of Standard Life and Mississippi Life could have been avoided if the NNFC had been in operation. The NNFC sidestepped questions about its racial politics in negotiating with white financiers by embracing gendered language focused on saving and protecting a widow. These gendered appeals hearkened to the aggressive marketing tactics of early twentieth-century insurance companies and organizations. In making sympathetic appeals to protecting an unnamed widow, the NNFC traded on the currency of masculine protection and provision. Just as the rhetoric of male protection in the insurance industry constructed men as the proper producers and consumers of financial security products such as insurance policies, in the story of saving a widow's estate, the NNFC promoted men as the legitimate architects of the black community's economic future.[68]

Constructing a desperate, defenseless widow also helped the NNFC repudiate the Universal Negro Improvement Association (UNIA) led by the charismatic Marcus Garvey. The gendered rhetoric dispelled suspicions of capitalist self-interest and tapped into the masculinist appeal that had helped make Garvey so popular. The organizers also hoped to woo investors away from Garvey, whose assertive calls for black pride had helped him raise millions of dollars to support UNIA programs, ancillary businesses, and development projects.

In January 1920, Garvey organized the short-lived Negro Factories Corporation (NFC) to improve "the economic status of the negro race."[69] Capitalized for $1 million, shares cost five dollars each. The NFC operated a laundry, a millinery store, a chain of grocery stores, a restaurant, and the African Communities League, which was the publishing house that printed the daily *Negro Times*. The UNIA also purchased real estate through the NFC. The NFC planned to open factories to manufacture clothing, toiletries, canned goods, and other items. Specifically, these factories would employ thousands of black workers who would produce goods for black consumers in the United States and ship goods overseas on the Black Star Line, Garvey's shipping company. Garvey openly refused white investment capital in the NFC, saying, "The world is looking to see what the New Negro will achieve in the field of commerce."[70] He believed large-scale investment and finance by and among blacks to be essential to the broader purpose of racial uplift and self-help.[71]

In the early 1920s, Garvey made an aggressive push around the country promoting the UNIA and the promise of black investment in cooperative enterprise rather than individual entrepreneurship. With religious zeal, he encouraged working class people to buy stocks in UNIA enterprises, sprinkling his dynamic speeches with allusions to the Bible and U.S. history. Garvey, the NFC, and the UNIA certainly embraced the promise that black business supporters had always believed about the economic potential of a black nation within a nation, but Garvey was not the Moses that many of the black entrepreneurial elites would have chosen. Mismanagement and failure marked a number of UNIA businesses. A school in Monrovia failed. Employees at the Universal Steam Laundry, the first business financed by the NFC, tore clothes, mishandled deliveries, and embezzled funds. Grocery store and restaurant employees stole money and provided poor service. Garvey remained secretive about the businesses' finances, but millions flowed in. Unfortunately, none of the UNIA business ventures or investment schemes ever paid dividends to their largely working-class investors.[72]

Garvey contended with both federal government surveillance and a determined group of critics organized against him. Civil rights and labor activist A. Philip Randolph took issue with what he saw as Garvey's encouragement that blacks satisfy themselves with low wages as a subterfuge to draw white employers' attention away from his efforts to develop a UNIA state in Liberia. Garvey's meetings with white supremacists to support state-funded emigration legislation took much of the remaining luster off his star for Randolph and others.[73]

Garvey's critics had legitimate criticisms about financial mismanagement in the UNIA organization, but jealousies and rivalries did underlie some of their denunciations. The NNFC, AIFC, and NFC drew from the same pool of supporters: working-class blacks. Middle-class business and professional men, like those who organized the AIFC and NNFC, felt threatened by Garvey's prominence—and perhaps even a little humiliated by his fundraising ability. They lobbed criticisms at not only Garvey but also the men and women who invested in the ventures he promoted.

Negative characterizations of UNIA investors underestimated the financial acuity and political astuteness of working-class investors to vet investment appeals and respond in ways that reflected their interests. As investors and workers in the kinds of businesses that the AIFC, NNFC, and NFC tried to create, working-class blacks could claim rights and press demands of the entrepreneurial class from both the boardroom and the factory floor. Their investments provided a foundation from which to fight and challenge the racial power structure, too, particularly the economic dimensions of white supremacy. Investment in black-owned finance corporations gave regular people a sense that they had a modicum of control over the wheels of capitalism.

Garvey's message, despite some restrictive views about the place of women in the movement, did find support among some women members of the black entrepreneurial elite. Both Maggie Lena Walker and cosmetics mogul Madam C. J. Walker—reputed to be the first black woman millionaire—admired Garvey. Garvey's photograph and a copy of his famous editorial "African Fundamentalism" hung prominently in Walker's parlor. Walker may have kept herself apprised of Garvey's activities in Harlem from close associates in the New York City–area IOSL councils, but she was certainly aware of his activities in stronghold Virginia cities and towns like Newport News, Norfolk, and Hampton Roads. Indeed, migrants living in Harlem wrote back home to Richmond about their excitement at seeing Garvey in person, and Amy Jacques Garvey (Marcus's wife) and other UNIA women spoke at mass meetings in St. Luke territories.[74]

The IOSL supported Garvey in other ways. The St. Luke Hall hosted one of the largest UNIA meetings in Virginia. In addition, the *St. Luke Herald* included stories about the UNIA's activities. When W. E. B. Du Bois publicly attacked Garvey in 1924, a *St. Luke Herald* editorial came to Garvey's defense: "Why should we curse and raise hell because Doctor Du Bois returns from Europe and Africa in a quizzical frame of mind?"[75] Scholars consistently cite Booker T. Washington as a critical influence on Garvey, but he also drew inspiration from female contemporaries such as Maggie Lena Walker. To underline Mary G. Rolinson's sage observation that "very little of Garvey's ideology was original," Garvey's ideology and praxis rested on the foundation created by the IOSL's social activities and its business model; Walker's strong support of independent, black economic self-help; and her focus on the needs of working-class people.[76]

Like the Negro Factories Corporation of the UNIA, the AIFC and the NNFC promoted compelling calls for race pride but without the perceived radical political overtones of Garveyism. Both companies hoped to siphon some of the largess from Garvey's coffers into their own and relied on similar appeals to manhood to buttress their efforts. Despite clandestine efforts to secure assistance from white investors, the NNFC and the AIFC advocated—at least publicly—self-help efforts that were independent of white assistance as a cornerstone of manly enterprise.[77]

The AIFC'S and NNFC's appeals targeted both working- and middle-class blacks. Both companies worked hard to win small, individual investors to raise their multimillion-dollar capital requirements, and their ambitions were not unrealistic in the context of the New Era. Business was the heartbeat of the age. President Calvin Coolidge declared that the business of America was business. Many Americans felt compelled by advertising executive Bruce Barton's book in which Jesus is depicted as a businessman and the founder of U.S. business. In a popular 1927 book, William Z. Ripley wrote of the growing interconnections between Main Street and Wall Street. Indeed, the enthusiasm for and commitment to investing in business was even stronger in the black community. Black business had long solicited and depended on, often exclusively, the investments of other blacks.[78]

Blacks had grown accustomed to rhetoric surrounding stock investment that stressed purchase not merely for personal gain but for racial uplift and collective prosperity. The interwar years magnified the altruistic rhetoric. During World War I, for example, blacks responded enthusiastically to campaigns encouraging investment in Liberty Loans and, after the war, in Victory Bonds. In the 1920s, links between race pride and manhood made full-throated endorsements of stock investment as a civic duty and a demonstration of citizenship. For example, the AIFC promoted investing as a "privilege and a right" and as an experiment in "Financial Democracy."[79] The NNFC's prospectus also connected a desire for wealth with the desires of any true citizen, as stressed in a string of descriptors that deserves extended quotation: "Every progressive, thrifty, red blooded, clear headed, liberty loving, property seeking American with grit in his craw and iron in his bones cherishes lofty and laudable ideas; among which are: to live a Christian life; to serve his fellowmen; to acquire sufficient wealth to gratify all normal desires; [and] to create eventually an estate for later years which shall inure to the benefit of those most immediately dear to him."[80] The prospectuses of both finance companies made explicit links between financial and civil responsibilities and rights.

Blacks paid close attention to the multimillion-dollar AIFC and NNFC ventures. The Baltimore *Afro-American* enthused that the community's interest in the NNFC was "phenomenal."[81] The National Negro Insurance Association (NNIA) took time in its 1924 annual meeting to discuss the NNFC. NNIA leaders answered questions from members and policyholders who had heard of the new finance company through enthusiastic coverage in the black press and from personal connections.[82]

Coverage by the press and records of stolen moments at professional meetings reveal a glaring barrier for black investors and the companies seeking their dollars. Neither the AIFC nor the NNFC traded its stock on an exchange. The various stock markets barred the participation of black business as a matter of custom rather than formal restriction. The black investment firms relied on direct marketing to consumers and the personal and professional networks of board members. To put the privilege and right in reach of their potential investors, they allowed investors to buy on the margins like many other financial institutions in the period. Borrowers purchased stocks with borrowed money and on borrowed time. The widespread practice of buying on the margins sowed the seeds of destruction, pushing the economy toward collapse by the end of the decade. The AIFC and NNFC offered very lenient loan terms for investors who did not have the cash to purchase stock. Direct sales and networking effectively limited the pool of potential investors. For the AIFC in particular, blackballing orchestrated in the black press by Robert R. Moton and Albon S. Holsey, Emmett J. Scott's replacement as secretary at Tuskegee Institute and in the NNBL, made it harder to raise adequate capital. For large and small investors in the NNFC, enthusiasm often outsized their capacity to pay. Wanti Gomez, secretary of the NNFC, sent several letters to small subscribers reminding them to fulfill their past-due subscriptions of less than fifty dollars.[83]

Even if subscribers fulfilled their stock subscriptions, there was no guarantee that they would ever see the promised windfalls. Any investment represented a risk for loss. The NNFC, however, recklessly dismissed the financial risks: "There has never been a better opportunity or a better reason offered to members of the race for investment. Every safeguard has been thrown around the organization to protect and conserve the funds and insure the safety of the investment."[84] The NNFC was hardly alone in promising great riches for a small investment and limited risk. It joined other "blue-sky promoters" who endorsed all kinds of money-making schemes.[85] The promise of a commercial emancipation increased the appeal of stock investment but downplayed the associated risks of any speculation. Gambling on the race was no gamble at all but rather an informed, rational, and selfless decision. Charged racial and gender appeals combined with the practice of buying on the margins reflected the reckless overconfidence that made the New Era roar.

The failure of the AIFC in 1925 reinforced critics' claims that black finance firms were not the panacea they promised. Critics characterized all would-be black financiers as rascals who were " 'skinning' the poorest of our people."[86] Others expressed suspicions that the NNFC was not an all-black enterprise. An associate of Moton's asked for assurances for himself and other self-described "Political Militants here in Central Harlem" that the NNFC was not backed by Jews looking to exploit southern Negroes and Negro business men to "get hold of easy money!!!"[87] Such anti-Semitism was not unusual in black business circles and became more bigoted alongside appeals to race pride during the 1920s.[88]

Mismanagement and the inability to raise adequate capital spelled the demise of the NNFC. Stock subscriptions dried up, and stockholders demanded not just dividends but a return of their capital investment. In 1927, a financial statement showed assets of a little more than $4,100 cash on hand and three mortgage bonds totaling nearly $10,000. The NNFC had invested in a bond for the Virginia Theological Seminary and College in Richmond (present-day Virginia Union University) and owned a few stocks in other black businesses. By 1928, the company ceased any pretense of operation.[89]

The Allied Industrial Finance Corporation and the National Negro Finance Corporation failed to effect a commercial emancipation for the race. Rhetoric about manhood and citizenship resonated with black investors, who invested for complex reasons. They were not dupes who fell for questionable schemes but rather calculating and strategic economic actors who were trying to bend capitalism to their needs. Both ventures failed to raise sufficient capital to fund their ambitious schemes, but they were hardly complete failures. They reveal the efforts of the black financial industry to boldly tackle the limitations of racial segregation and a continued commitment to communal-focused approaches to economic development and wealth building.

THE ST. LUKE FINANCE CORPORATION AND THE BUSINESS OF LIVING AND LEISURE IN HARLEM

The world of leisure in Harlem during the New Negro era ranged from the cerebral to the hedonistic. A young woman could listen to renowned intellectuals and literary artists like Hubert Harrison and Langston Hughes speak at the Harlem YMCA or discuss the merits and shortcomings of these writers’ works in the local barber, beauty, and shoe-shine shops that dotted Harlem. She could attend a play, opera, or symphony in one of Harlem’s many stately theaters and halls or catch a western movie, basketball game, or prizefight at the black-owned Renaissance Theater, also known as “the Rennie.” She could attend any number of banquets, galas, reunions, and other events showcasing very public displays of black conspicuous consumption or hold sway in a world of private parlors, house parties, and intellectual salons among Harlem's elite, who were infamously memorialized in works like Carl Van Vechten's *Nigger Heaven*. She might fill her nights attending a rent party, playing cards at a social club party, or gambling at the casino in the Rennie. She could dance into the wee hours of the morning to live or recorded jazz and blues while drinking bootleg liquor at any one of the hundreds of speakeasies and nightclubs in Harlem, or she could find the spirit at a storefront revival. Harlem offered a wide array of commercial amusements; some fulfilled reformers' ideas of wholesome entertainment for young women, and others were characterized by Howard sociologist William Jones as no less than "pathological forms of entertainment."[90]

In Richmond, Maggie Lena Walker ensured that the St. Luke Hall would be the site of enriching entertainment, both financially and morally. In the 1920s, the hall hosted a "New Negro Lectures" series, charging fifty cents to hear speakers such as Chandler Owen and A. Philip Randolph speak on "The New Emancipation" and the "Economic Aspects of the Negro Problem." Local organizations held fundraising exhibitions and concerts at the St. Luke Hall. In other cities, the St. Lukes used occasions such as large meetings to provide entertainments. In Washington, D.C., for example, the St. Lukes ended a convention with a night of activities that included folk singing and a tango dance contest. Children and adults could purchase tickets and were welcome at these events. The IOSL of New York hoped to provide a venue for the kinds of public meetings and activities that grew the order, but it also wanted to capitalize on the vibrant world of leisure in 1920s Harlem. The IOSL in New York used strategies similar to those used in the headquarters in Richmond to address the unique financial and credit needs of its members. Tensions between members of the IOSL in New York and Richmond, however, flared over issues of financial autonomy.[91]

The roots of the New York IOSL sprouted from Virginia soil. By 1900, an estimated 264,000 blacks had left Virginia, many of them settling in Maryland, Pennsylvania, and New York—places that mirror the earliest IOSL strongholds outside of Virginia. Contrary to conventional assumptions about migration, more women than men left Virginia during this early phase of black migration. The men and women who migrated from the South to northern cities before the turn of the twentieth century did so for reasons similar to those who would make the trek a generation later during the first Great Migration: they wanted to escape the humiliations of Jim Crow and find better economic opportunities. These early migrants moved when the age was gilded. The black communities they joined in northern cities were far smaller and would remain small until the years surrounding World War I. They built institutions such as churches, YMCAs, and all manner of societies—secret, lyceum, and reform.[92]

Women who migrated from Virginia to New York near the turn of the twentieth century planted the earliest New York IOSL councils. When Walker took over the IOSL in 1899, she embraced a national vision for the order. To extend the boundaries of the IOSL, she depended on women like Charity Brewer Jones. Charity Brewer was born near Petersburg, Virginia, in 1850 to John and Lucretia Brewer. She married Robert H. Jones, a merchant, in 1873. Death haunted Jones. Her son, Robert Jr., was the only child to survive nine pregnancies. Her personal losses and the solace she found with women in the IOSL may have been one reason Jones was so active in the IOSL. She served as worthy chief (president) of a local IOSL council for a number of years. In the late 1880s, the Jones family moved to New York. For a time, she took in laundry. In late 1903, Walker asked her to reconstitute the Mt. Olivet Council No. 100 and help expand the IOSL in the New York area. Jones, one of the New York stockholders in the St. Luke Bank, persuaded her church, the Mt. Olivet Baptist Church, to buy stock in the bank. Both Jones's husband and son had died by 1909, and she threw herself further into IOSL activities. In two decades, Jones, affectionately known as the "mother" of the St. Luke's in New York, helped grow the IOSL of New York district to nine thousand members and ninety-six councils.[93]

Though Jones was part of an early migrant generation, she owed much of the IOSL's success in New York to the Great Migration. She recruited members to Mt. Olivet Council and helped organize other IOSL councils from among the tens of thousands of migrants who poured into New York City during the early decades of the twentieth century. By the late nineteenth century, blacks were congested in San Juan Hill, the Tenderloin, and Little Africa, but they increasingly found themselves concentrated in Harlem. The black population included longtime residents, southern migrants, and Caribbean immigrants. The areas were run down, overcrowded, and riven by interethnic strife because of competition over limited housing.

An economic downturn in 1902 due to overspeculation helped open up housing for blacks in Harlem, which was at the time a virtually all-white neighborhood. Real estate broker Philip Payton opened the area for blacks by capitalizing on a dispute between two white realtors. One of the realtors, partially to spite the other realtor and partially for the profit potential, allowed Payton to lease an apartment building at 67 West 134th Street. He aggressively marketed the new property, and blacks rushed in to occupy the spacious and finely appointed apartment homes. Later, other white realtors leased and sold other apartments and brownstones in Harlem to Payton. He downplayed the profit motive in his meteoric rise as "the Father of Colored Harlem" and stressed property accumulation as an important way to resist Jim Crow housing conditions in New York City.[94]

The number of black residents in Harlem increased dramatically, but their housing options began to decline by the late 1910s—in numbers and quality—as renters struggled to pay the above-market rents. Studies found that blacks paid more than half their incomes on housing compared to whites, who paid only one-quarter of their incomes. Harlemites subleased their properties to make ends meet, and owners looking to increase their profits subdivided larger units into smaller ones. New housing restrictions and homeowner association activism in other parts of New York City trapped blacks in Harlem. Some landlords took advantage of blacks' limited options and neglected maintenance and upkeep on their properties. By 1920, black Harlemites faced the serious problems of high rents, deteriorating housing stock, and scarcity.[95]

The New York IOSL responded to the unique circumstances of black Harlemites. Under Walker, the St. Luke Association, which was the Right Worthy Grand Council's stock corporation, provided a successful model of cooperative economics. The St. Luke Association had purchased the IOSL headquarters and also invested in and leased commercial and residential property. In Harlem, black churches like St. Philip's Episcopal Church provided a similar model. In 1911, St. Philip's purchased ten apartment buildings on West 135th Street, between Lenox and 7th Avenues, when it built its new church. At the time, the St. Philip's purchase was the largest real estate transaction ever effected by blacks. In an ironic turn, the church evicted white residents in the apartment buildings to make room for black residents, prompting reactionary charges of a "Negro invasion" in the white press.[96]

The New York district's charter limited its ability to engage in moneymaking ventures, but it had not been particularly entrepreneurial. When Dennis Grice assumed leadership of the district in 1916, it had $3.45 in its coffers and was more than $400 in debt. Grice and other members of the district board mulled over their options. Twenty-one members incorporated the St. Luke Finance Corporation in 1918. In addition to boilerplate language about a membership association, the articles of incorporation included specific powers "to own, purchase, buy, lease, or hire real estate for the establishment and maintenance of a meeting place or places for the members."[97] In this way, the new corporation stretched its legal boundaries to enrich members while addressing the needs of an exploding black Harlem community.[98]

The corporation set a limit on the dividends it would pay, marking the venture as being less concerned about profit and more concerned about a socially conscious economic movement. The district board owned the lion's share of stock in the new corporation and did little to sell the remaining stock, which would prove to be part of its undoing. The majority-woman advisory board helped set the finance corporation's priorities. In addition to Dennis Grice, Madaline C. Thomas, Rhoda T. Willis, and Wilhelmina J. Lowe served on the board. Officers included Georgette Young as secretary, Charlotte A. Ford as vice chair, and Lulu Robinson-Jones, Charity Jones's daughter-in-law and a nationally renowned opera singer, as chair of the advisory board (see fig. 5.4). The advisory board had no experience running a finance corporation, but it did have a vision for the business of living and leisure.[99]

Various councils in and around New York City raised $1,000 in working funds for the new venture. Grice and Robinson-Jones organized a reception at Manhattan Casino, which featured music by James Reese Europe, to raise funds. The New York IOSL also borrowed $3,000 from the St. Luke Bank. In 1918, the New York district's first purchase was not a

FIGURE 5.4 Advisory board, New York IOSL, c. 1927. *From left to right,* Madaline Thomas, Dennis Grice, Charlotte Ford (vice chair), Rhoda Willis, Wilhelmina Lowe, John Savage, and Lulu Robinson-Jones (chair).

clubhouse but an apartment building: it purchased the former convent of the Little Sisters of the Assumption at 125 and 127 West 130th Street. The New York IOSL claimed that protecting black Harlemites from rent gouging was a priority over provincial concerns like a meeting space for its membership. To reinforce its claim, the New York IOSL capped apartment rents in the buildings at forty five dollars per month.[100]

By 1920, in the midst of the first Great Migration and the early years of the New Negro era, Harlem was still a mecca in the broadest sense of the term. Blacks could still secure well-paying jobs, and they enjoyed a relatively tolerant racial climate and a cultural renaissance. The mecca failed, however, in terms of housing. Many areas of Harlem had already slid toward decline by the 1920s. Blacks owned about thirty apartment buildings in Harlem between 130th and 150th Streets, a fraction of the housing stock in the community. As Harlem expanded, the St. Luke Finance Corporation tried addressing these shortcomings by expanding its real estate investments. In 1921, it bought the Cassinover, a twenty-four-room apartment building at 257 and 259 West 129th Street (see fig. 5.5). Residents enjoyed an elevator, private hallways, and four- to six-room apartments. The New York IOSL charged eighty-one dollars per month for the larger apartments and reduced

ST. LUKE FRATERNAL BUILDING
NEW YORK DISTRICT

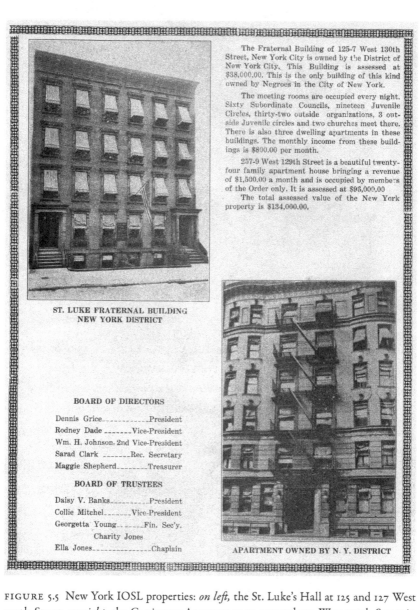

The Fraternal Building of 125-7 West 130th Street, New York City is owned by the District of New York City. This Building is assessed at $38,000.00. This is the only building of this kind owned by Negroes in the City of New York.

The meeting rooms are occupied every night. Sixty Subordinate Councils, nineteen Juvenile Circles, thirty-two outside organizations, 3 outside Juvenile circles and two churches meet there. There is also three dwelling apartments in these buildings. The monthly income from these buildings is $800.00 per month.

257-9 West 129th Street is a beautiful twenty-four family apartment house bringing a revenue of $1,500.00 a month and is occupied by members of the Order only. It is assessed at $96,000.00

The total assessed value of the New York property is $134,000.00.

BOARD OF DIRECTORS

Dennis Grice............President
Rodney Dade ....Vice-President
Wm. H. Johnson, 2nd Vice-President
Sarad Clark ....Rec. Secretary
Maggie Shepherd........Treasurer

BOARD OF TRUSTEES

Daisy V. Banks..........President
Collie Mitchel.......Vice-President
Georgetta Young.......Fin. Sec'y.
Charity Jones
Ella Jones..............Chaplain

APARTMENT OWNED BY N. Y. DISTRICT

FIGURE 5.5 New York IOSL properties: *on left,* the St. Luke's Hall at 125 and 127 West 130th Street, *on right,* the Cassinover Apartments on 257 and 259 West 129th Street in Harlem, c. 1923.
Source: *56th Annual IOSL Souvenir Programme* (1923), Independent Order of St. Luke 1877–1970 (MS1988-121), Virginia Polytechnic Institute and State University.

rents from seventy-five to sixty dollars for the smaller apartments. It also evicted all the Cassinover's white tenants to make room for black tenants. In 1924, the order purchased a combination thirteen-room apartment building, restaurant, and retail store at 301 West 139th Street just west of Striver's Row. By 1929, the New York IOSL's total real estate holdings were worth $300,000 (or $4.4 million in 2017 dollars).[101]

In 1922, the order remodeled its first acquisition, the apartments on West 130th, into a headquarters for the New York district. It became known as St. Luke's Hall, and the IOSL of New York maintained two apartments there. Located in the heart of Harlem's black community, St. Luke's Hall became an important center for enterprise, community activities, and entertainment. In addition to holding IOSL meetings, banquets, and other activities, the hall rented meeting rooms to other groups and churches, and it hosted business and social events in its meeting spaces and auditorium. The hall accommodated everything from pageants to union meetings. For instance, the Trinidad Benevolent Association hosted a reception for Dr. F. E. Bass, past mayor of the Port of Spain, and the Brotherhood of Sleeping Car Porters and Maids held its regular meetings and hosted mass rallies and other public events there. During a dispute between black garment workers and members of the Communist Party U.S.A., the International Ladies Garment Workers Union acted as mediator between the two at a meeting in St. Luke's Hall.[102]

Maggie Lena Walker's strict moral code forbade what she considered unwholesome amusements in Richmond's St. Luke Hall, but the New York IOSL hoped to capitalize on Harlem's vibrant nightlife. In 1924, the New York IOSL spent another $70,000 to remodel the building, adding a one-thousand-seat auditorium, a two-hundred-seat dining room, and a floor of offices and remodeling nine club rooms. Grice also applied for a dance hall license, which he or some other New York IOSL members likely paid bribes to get the license.[103]

The New York IOSL's efforts did not escape notice or censure. In a session of the Interdenominational Ministers Conference, a number of ministers roundly condemned the New York IOSL's plans to open a dance hall and some of its other recreational activities. Rev. Richard M. Bolden of First Emmanuel Church called out St. Luke's Hall as a place where "bootlegging, bold prostitution, [and] cabarets" belied its "saintly" name. Frederick Asbury Cullen, the reverend of Salem Methodist Episcopal Church and adoptive father of Harlem Renaissance poet Countee Cullen, called St. Luke's Hall nothing less than one of the "Hell holes of God."[104]

In addition to bootlegged liquor, it is also very likely that tenants in the restaurant, stores, and office spaces in St. Luke's Hall and the order's apartment buildings ran numbers. Numbers, also known as playing the numbers or policy, was an extralegal lottery gambling game. Players waged a small sum of money and selected a combination of numbers, usually three. If their numbers hit in various combinations, they could win as much as six hundred times their initial wager. As historian LaShawn Harris notes, numbers allowed working- and middle-class players alike the chance "to pursue personal pleasures and amusements and still preserve outward images of respectability."[105] At its peak in the 1920s, numbers represented an estimated $100 million annual business (or $1.4 billion in 2017 dollars), employing tens of thousands of employees nationally.[106]

As the country slid toward economic decline, the structural weaknesses of the St. Luke Finance Corporation hastened the company's economic disintegration. The board's failure to sell all of the corporation's stock left it undercapitalized and with inadequate funds despite the fact that it claimed more than $10,000 in annual profits from renting space in the hall and apartments in its buildings. The order dipped into those revenues not only to pay its mortgage but also to fund other commitments, such as providing charitable assistance to nearly five hundred families and paying the salaries of a top-heavy workforce of twenty-three employees. In the summer of 1924, the St. Luke Finance Corporation board took out two second mortgages to help fund remodels. It did so without the proper authority, vetting, and sanction of the New York IOSL membership.[107]

Most troubling, however, in order to help the finance corporation, the advisory board instituted a rudimentary bond offering. The bond resembled a combination thrift club and raffle. The board solicited other IOSL councils to buy memberships to the district's board of directors for a $100 loan to be paid back at the end of five years. Each new board member was then required to produce at least one other new board member for another $100 loan. The advisory board was able to raise only about $2,500 through this scheme, and the board of directors bloated from twenty to forty-five members, which violated the order's constitution.[108]

The St. Luke Finance Corporation then offered several thousand so-called refunding notes to the public. The refunding notes could be purchased in five-dollar denominations at 5 percent interest for five-year terms. The board may have modeled this plan on Marcus Garvey and the UNIA's Black Star Line, Negro Factories Corporation, and Black Cross Navigation and Trading Corporation. The refunding notes doubled as membership certificates: holders became members of the New York IOSL and loaned money to the order at the same time. The district raised an estimated $80,000 from the refunding notes scheme. The incredible amounts raised highlight the democratization of investing in black communities and the commitment of the working and middle classes to self-help.[109]

The large amounts might also reveal some duplicitous, extralegal financialization. The board kept the proceeds of the refunding notes in the Harlem branch of the Chelsea Exchange Bank, the same bank used by Casper Holstein, the infamous Harlem policy king. Holstein's occupation was no secret, and the willingness of the Chelsea Bank to help launder funds appears obvious. While the Harlem branch of the Chelsea Bank had little trouble accepting blacks' money, it had a poor reputation for extending even small amounts of credit to its thousands of black depositors. The expenditures to the IOSL of New York were not standard practice for the Chelsea, and the amount—$1.2 million in 2017 dollars—was significant as well. The New York district's membership numbers did grow during the mid-1920s, but it seems unlikely that a sizeable number of members purchased such a significant number of notes—$80,000 worth of five-dollar notes—in such a short time. The notes may have been a subterfuge for money borrowed from a policy banker such as Holstein, to whom millions of dollars of cash flowed each month. The fact that the New York district did not keep its funds in the St. Luke Bank also raises some suspicion that it tried to keep its financial dealings veiled from IOSL superiors in Richmond.[110]

Problems for the St. Luke Finance Corporation escalated when some members holding the refunding notes demanded repayment of the money they had loaned the order. At least one tenant in St. Luke's Hall complained about his office lease and, dissatisfied with the advisory board's response, complained to city officials about the New York district's finances. It is also likely that the country's economic downturn, coupled with investigations into the UNIA's finances, left the creative finance schemes of black fraternal groups vulnerable to scrutiny. It does not appear that the order failed to pay any claims, but its complex indebtedness did place all IOSL councils in the New York district in jeopardy with the chance that death claims might go unpaid, which was more than enough justification for New York officials to take action. The state attorney general served Grice with papers requesting that he appear in court to answer questions about the order's finances in late June 1928. After two hearings, Judge Walsh determined the order insolvent and appointed a receiver, who ordered the district to sell its two apartment buildings.[111]

When the St. Luke Finance Corporation went under, the RWG Council in Richmond quickly distanced itself from the New York IOSL's financial problems. Only a few years before, the RWG Council had praised the New York district's economic success and paid it the highest compliment in 1925 by holding its biennial meeting in the newly remodeled St. Luke's Hall in Harlem. The meeting was the first convention ever held outside of Virginia. The IOSL's 1927 souvenir program included pictures of the New York district's hall and the Cassinover as well as images and names of the district's board of directors and advisory board. In the midst of the New York IOSL's legal troubles, however, St. Luke Bank board member Dr. Leon Reid criticized the New York members for "using the Order to their personal advantage."[112] Maggie Lena Walker sent a telegram to prominent black newspapers in which she chastised the New York district for repeating the mistakes of fraternal orders who had lost sight of their first responsibility: members. She wrote, "They [the orders] began to reach out and to speculate and invest their moneys in things as an auxiliary to their fraternal work"—seemingly forgetting that the New York IOSL had been modeled on her initiatives or that some saw her as guilty of the very same overreach.[113]

In the 1920s, blacks' reliance on banks increased. Their deposits rose significantly, in part because many found well-paying jobs by migrating north. Most northern and midwestern cities did not have black-owned banks. Blacks deposited their money in local institutions but also maintained accounts in black banks in the South. In places like Illinois, Indiana, Michigan, and New York, where the IOSL boasted a significant number of members, blacks maintained and relied on their bank accounts and insurance policies back home in the South, resulting in a boom for black women who worked for not only the IOSL and the St. Luke Bank but also other black financial institutions.[114]

By 1930, according to the U.S. Census, nearly 2,600 black women worked in the financial industry. They represented a tiny fraction of all men and women in the industry (0.35 percent) and trailed significantly behind white women (39.3 percent). All women, white and black, dominated in support service jobs in the industry, such as bookkeepers and stenographers. Yet jobs in the financial sector allowed some to escape from many of the harsh and dangerous working conditions that most black women faced. The various opportunities that were opened for women to save and invest included products marketed by insurance companies, finance corporations, and other businesses. They failed, ultimately, to sustain the economic security envisioned by entrepreneurs and activists because they inadequately reckoned with the structural barriers—mainly low wages, racial segregation, and sexual discrimination—that made it difficult for black women in particular, no matter how hard they hustled, to maximize these new opportunities and products.[115]

Epilogue

By the late 1920s, only three black banks still stood in Richmond, only one of which had been open before 1920: the St. Luke Bank, Second Street Savings, and Commercial Bank and Trust.[1] Maggie Lena Walker had lived through the very public failure of the True Reformers Bank in 1910, and the failure of the Mechanics Savings Bank in 1922 proved another hard loss to bear. After Mechanics Savings failed, Walker approached the presidents of the two other black banks about the prospect of merging their three banks.

It certainly made financial sense. St. Luke, Second Street, and Commercial controlled the assets of three highly successful insurance organizations: the Independent Order of St. Luke, Richmond Beneficial, and Southern Aid respectively. They all held deposit accounts in varying amounts in each other's institutions and worked cooperatively on large financing ventures. Between 1926 and 1928, Second Street and Commercial suffered significant losses in their loan portfolios. A merger with the stronger St. Luke Bank was a proposition that made sense for the two struggling banks. The bank presidents had other reasons to consider a merger: St. Luke board members expressed concern about white bankers' machinations to open a segregated bank branch in the empty Mechanics Savings Bank property. So, in late 1929, the St. Luke Bank and Second Street Savings Bank merged to form

Consolidated Bank and Trust Company. As the economic downturn worsened in the early 1930s, Commercial Bank continued to flail, finally merging with Consolidated in 1931. The Consolidated merger helped secure the financial futures of tens of thousands of depositors in Richmond and around the country.[2]

Consolidated stood as a testimony to three decades of Walker's tenacity. Her vision of a bank created by and for black working women, however, was fast becoming a faded memory. Second Street and Commercial did not have any women board members, and Walker's death in 1934 left only five women on Consolidated's thirty-eight member board. Black women did make up most of the shareholders in the St. Luke Bank, but most held only a few shares, and women represented only a fraction of shareholders in Second Street and Commercial Banks. Black women were becoming peripheral in the financial institution that had historically made their needs central.[3]

To be sure, Consolidated remained committed to extending credit and making loans. During the 1930s, like other lenders, it had difficulties getting Federal Housing Administration (FHA) insurance for loans to blacks except in segregated areas. The bank approached other federal credit modernization programs with caution. For example, it did not join President Herbert Hoover's National Credit Corporation, and the IOSL did not immediately join the Federal Home Loan Bank Board (FHLB) even though the chair of the FHLB board singled out African American homeowners as a group that would particularly benefit from its assistance. Consolidated also resisted the Virginia state bank examiner's demands that it participate in the preferred stock program of President Franklin Roosevelt's Reconstruction Finance Corporation, which the board saw as a threat to its autonomy. Unlike other strong black-owned lenders, such as North Carolina Mutual in Durham and Universal Life in Memphis, Consolidated chose not to make aggressive moves to secure federal funding for large-scale multiple- and single-family housing projects.[4]

The St. Luke Bank's legacy as a source of credit and loans did not disappear, however. The bank's gendered economic practices became institutionalized in Consolidated's underwriting standards and practices. Consolidated continued to vet every loan by committee and then brought each up for a vote by the board. During the 1930s, the bank averaged more than fifty new loans per month. It handled scores of requests for renewals and extensions of previous loans each month as well. The laborious process, made more so by the large board of directors, was intended to take into account local conditions and accurately assess borrowers' creditworthiness. It likely saved the bank from failing during the Great Depression. It assured a steady flow of credit and money to needy borrowers and proved profitable to the bank as well: Consolidated's assets more than quadrupled between 1931 and 1950, and its income doubled.[5]

It would be seventy years before Consolidated elected another woman president. In 2004, Kim D. Saunders became the president and chief executive officer of Consolidated. The directors brought Saunders on board to revive the bank, which was struggling with a portfolio of poorly performing loans and regulators' demands. Saunders could not orchestrate a quick turnaround to longstanding problems, and the bank changed hands in 2005 and then again in 2011, when Premier Financial Bancorp merged Consolidated with four other banks to form Premier Bank.[6]

So what is the importance of one savings bank that was organized and led by black women for the first thirty-one of its 108 years? *Banking on Freedom* has demonstrated the ways in which gender and race shaped and were shaped by finance capitalism. Race and gender drove distinctions between savings and wealth, money and capital. Finance capitalism indexed black women as special categories of risk. In every register of the word, womanness and blackness together signified the need to take precaution. They were a gamble. Danger. But black women wrested other meanings from the word. Opportunity. Profit. Power.

Few could effectively argue that gender and race no longer matter in building wealth, but what is less clear is how to decouple them. The subprime mortgage crisis revealed the frustrating mix of risk and opportunity. Subprime mortgages had helped achieve something that the federal government and private banks had not: they put a large number of black people into homes in a very short time. In late 2003, black homeownership rates reached their highest in U.S. history; nearly half of all black families (49.4 percent) owned their own homes, and families headed by black women made up a sizeable portion of that number (about 20 percent). Some estimates have concluded that half the loans on these homes qualified as subprime.[7]

The battle for equitable solutions continues. Some of the keys to unlocking the problems of the present lie in the past. It is no accident that history of capitalism studies have made such a strong pull on our historical imagination at this moment. Labor, political, and social histories animate history of capitalism studies. Their semiotics give scholars powerful tools to put the economy and politics in conversation by mining the materially and ideologically fungible natures of money and power over time. Like the ledger, however, history of capitalism studies alternately reveal and obscure. When they ignore gender and race, they can mask the power embodied in relationships around capital.

I have argued against an assumption that is implicit in too many histories: that capitalism equals freedom, innovation, progress. I might seem to contradict myself since I have argued throughout *Banking on Freedom* that black women used finance to carve out possibilities in society and the economy. But what I have tried to do is unpack how and why black women had to act in strategic, deliberate, and innovative ways, as well as how they could be reactive and repressive at the same time. I have tried to stress the ways that wealth, value, and risk are gendered, raced, and classed codes. They continue to be so. It is critical not merely to acknowledge the limitations of race and gender but also to demonstrate alternative ways in which people have defined their value, produced their own knowledge, and worked around restrictions.

Appendix

I offer these tables as a snapshot of the economic conditions of black banks in Richmond. I do not include contextual data about other banks in the city or state because the length and detail of the tables would be prohibitive. Capitalization of black banks matched other small and even some large banks in the city, but black banks' assets, investments, and deposits, with unique exceptions like the True Reformers Savings Bank, were significantly smaller than other banks of comparable size.

TABLE A.1 Assets of Black Banks in Richmond, 1904–1919

Year	True Reformers	Nickel Savings	Mechanics Savings	St. Luke	Total
1904	$518,330	$15,400	$64,110	$37,870	$635,710
1905	$541,558	$16,977	$95,196	$53,348	$707,079
1906	$557,289	$23,909	$108,274	$53,673	$743,145
1907	$561,288	$25,335	$140,735	$78,647	$806,005
1908	$452,179	$29,955	$140,605	$86,778	$709,517
1909	$451,267	$28,323	$147,315	$102,552	$729,457
1910	—	$47,517	$214,085	$120,813	$382,415
1911	—	—	$231,060	$141,589	$372,649
1912	—	—	$226,126	$173,168	$399,294
1913	—	—	$206,637	$195,915	$402,552
1914	—	—	$218,383	$204,113	$422,496
1915	—	—	$229,988	$190,211	$420,199
1916	—	—	$280,082	$216,896	$496,978
1917	—	—	$330,560	$247,470	$578,030
1918	—	—	$467,398	$302,756	$770,154
1919	—	—	$605,337	$440,636	$1,045,973

Source: Reports, Virginia State Corporation Commission, Bureau of Banking, reprinted in Jesse E. Fleming, "A History of Consolidated Bank and Trust Company" (MA thesis, Rutgers University, 1972).

TABLE A.2 Assets of Black Banks in Richmond, 1920–1930

Year	Mechanics Savings	Second Street	Commercial	St. Luke	Total
1920	$720,478	$38,880	$82,286	$529,883	$1,371,527
1921	$648,807	$126,818	$137,015	$515,187	$1,427,827
1922	—	$140,888	$183,579	$455,873	$780,340
1923	—	$179,638	$254,066	$473,600	$907,304
1924	—	$184,657	$302,694	$495,116	$982,467
1925	—	$184,471	$401,416	$475,305	$1,061,192
1926	—	$214,774	$474,982	$484,662	$1,174,418
1927	—	$239,756	$492,714	$498,907	$1,231,377
1928	—	$203,812	$471,802	$479,841	$1,155,455
1929	—	$162,177	$431,251	$454,542	$1,047,970
1930	—	Merged	$357,229	$564,263*	$921,492

* For Consolidated Bank; includes assets of merger of Second Street and St. Luke banks.

Source: Reports, Virginia State Corporation Commission, Bureau of Banking, reprinted in Jesse E. Fleming, "A History of Consolidated Bank and Trust Company" (MA thesis, Rutgers University, 1972).

Notes

INTRODUCTION

1. Name changed.
2. Nick Chiles, "Devastating Examples of Systemic Racism in Generations," *Atlanta Black Star*, January 27, 2015, http://atlantablackstar.com/2015/01/27/black-families-continue-forced-homes-across-america-foreclosure-crisis-one-devastating-examples-systemic-racism-generations/.
3. Sandra Phillips, "The Subprime Mortgage Calamity and the African American Woman," *Review of Black Political Economy* 39, no. 2 (June 2012): 227–37.
4. An estimated 9.3 million people lost their homes. David Dayen, "Obama Failed to Mitigate America's Foreclosure Crisis," *The Atlantic*, December 14, 2016, https://www.theatlantic.com/politics/archive/2016/12/obamas-failure-to-mitigate-americas-foreclosure-crisis/510485/; Amaad Rivera, Brenda Cotto-Escalera, Anisha Desai, Jeannette Huezo, and Dedrick Muhamma, *Foreclosed: State of the Dream 2008* (Boston: United for a Fair Economy, 2008), http://files.faireconomy.org/files/pdf/StateOfDream_01_16_08_Web.pdf; John Leland, "Baltimore Finds Subprime Crisis Snags Women," *New York Times*, January 15, 2008, http://www.nytimes.com/2008/01/15/us/15mortgage.html; Avis Jones-DeWeever, "Losing Ground: Women and the Foreclosure Crisis," National Council of Jewish Women, n.d., http://www.ncjw.org/content_1441.cfm, accessed January 25, 2017.
5. Some ethnic entrepreneurship strategies that blacks were not able to exploit as effectively include acting as middlemen, maintaining finance and business networks with home countries, harnessing kinship networks, and monopolizing certain businesses within an enclave or segregated neighborhood. In asserting the unique racial experiences of blacks, I am not suggesting that ethnic-immigrant entrepreneurs were not subjected to racialization or negatively affected by segregation in custom and law. John

Sibley Butler, *Entrepreneurship and Self-Help Among Black Americans: A Reconsideration of Race and Economics*, rev. ed. (Albany: State University of New York Press, 2005), 29, 74–75, 77–82, 151; Ivan H. Light, *Ethnic Enterprise in America: Business and Welfare Among Chinese, Japanese and Blacks* (Berkeley: University of California Press, 1972); Illsoo Kim, *New Urban Immigrants: The Korean Community in New York* (Princeton, N.J.: Princeton University Press, 1981), 112–13, 131, 140, 145; Robert W. Fairlie, *Ethnic and Racial Entrepreneurship: A Study of Historical and Contemporary Differences* (New York: Garland, 1996); Steven J. Gold. "A Critical Race Theory Approach to Black American Entrepreneurship," *Ethnic and Racial Studies* 39, no. 9 (2016): 1697–718.

Ethnic immigrants discriminated against blacks—a key practice in defining and affirming the ethnics' whiteness. The literature is extensive, but some works are particularly instructive. Eric Lott, *Love and Theft: Blackface Minstrelsy and the American Working Class* (New York: Oxford University Press, 1993); Matthew Frye Jacobson, *Whiteness of a Different Color: European Immigrants and the Alchemy of Race* (Cambridge, Mass.: Harvard University Press, 1998); David R. Roediger, *The Wages of Whiteness: Race and the Making of the American Working Class*, rev. ed. (London: Verso, 2007).

6. Edward Ayers, *The Promise of the New South: Life After Reconstruction* (New York: Oxford University Press, 1992); Glenda Gilmore, *Gender and Jim Crow: Women and the Politics of White Supremacy in North Carolina, 1896–1920* (Chapel Hill: University of North Carolina Press, 1996); Leon F. Litwack, *Trouble in Mind: Black Southerners in the Age of Jim Crow* (New York: Vintage, 1998); Mia Bay, "'If Iola Were a Man': Gender, Jim Crow and Public Protest in the Work of Ida B. Wells," in *Becoming Visible: Women's Presence in Late Nineteenth-Century America*, ed. Janet Floyd, R. J. Ellis, and Lindsey Traub (New York: Rodopi, 2001), 105–28; C. Vann Woodward, *The Strange Career of Jim Crow: A Commemorative Edition* (New York: Oxford University Press, 2002).
7. Joseph A. Pierce, *Negro Business and Business Education: Their Prospect and Prospective Development* (New York: Harper, 1947); Abram Harris, *The Negro as Capitalist: A Study of Banking and Business Among American Negroes* (1936; College Park, Md.: McGrath, 1968); E. F. Frazier, *Black Bourgeoisie* (1957; New York: Collier, 1962); Earl Ofari, *The Myth of Black Capitalism* (New York: Monthly Review, 1970); Manning Marable, *How Capitalism Underdeveloped Black America: Problems in Race, Political Economy, and Society*, rev. ed. (Cambridge, Mass.: South End, 2000); Mehrsa Baradaran, *The Color of Money: Black Banks and the Racial Wealth Gap* (Cambridge, Mass.: Harvard University Press, 2017).
8. Caley Horan, "Actuarial Age: Insurance and the Emergence of Neoliberalism in the Postwar United States" (PhD diss., University of Minnesota, 2011), 111–14, 170–76, 185–88; Devin Fergus, "The Ghetto Tax: Auto Insurance, Postal Code Profiling, and the Hidden History of Wealth Transfer in America," in *Beyond Discrimination: Racial Inequality in a Post-Racist Era*, ed. Fredrick C. Harris and Robert C. Lieberman (New York: Russell Sage, 2013), 277–316.
9. In 1903, the bank opened as the St. Luke Penny Savings Bank. In 1910, the bank changed its name to the St. Luke Bank and Trust Company. In the early 1930s, the St. Luke Bank absorbed two other black banks and changed its name to Consolidated Bank and Trust. Consolidated Bank enjoyed the distinction of being the oldest continually operating, black-controlled bank in the United States until 2005, when Abigail Adams National

Bank, the largest women-owned bank in the country, purchased it. Consolidated Bank continued to operate under its own name until 2011, when Premier Bank purchased both banks.

Sarah Howe's Ladies Deposit Company (organized in 1878) and Women's Bank of Boston (organized in 1884) were not banks but Ponzi schemes that defrauded thousands of women depositors of more than $300,000. At least one white woman preceded Walker's accomplishment: Anna Mebus Martin and her two sons established the Commercial Bank of Mason in Mason County, Texas, in 1901; Martin served as president until her death in 1925. George Robb, *Ladies of the Ticker: Women and Wall Street from the Gilded Age to the Great Depression* (Champaign: University of Illinois Press, 2017), 87–92; "Mason Matters," *American-Statesman* (Austin, Tex.), June 18, 1901, 4; Deborah S. Large, "Martin, Anna Henriette Mebus," *Handbook of Texas* Online, Texas State Historical Association, June 15, 2010, modified April 27, 2016, http://www.tshaonline.org/handbook/online/articles/fmaax.

10. Gertrude Woodruff Marlowe, *A Right Worthy Grand Mission: Maggie Lena Walker and the Quest for Black Economic Empowerment* (Washington, D.C.: Howard University Press, 2003); Elsa Barkley Brown, "Womanist Consciousness: Maggie Lena Walker and the Independent Order of Saint Luke," *Signs* 14 (Spring 1989): 610–33; Brown, "Constructing a Life and a Community: A Partial Story of Maggie Lena Walker," *OAH Magazine of History* 7, no. 4 (Summer 1993): 28–31; Angel Kwolek-Folland, "The African American Financial Industries: Issues of Class, Race, and Gender in the Early Twentieth Century," *Business and Economic History* 23, no. 2 (Winter 1994): 85–106, here 93–97, 100–101, 103–4.
11. Gilmore, *Gender and Jim Crow.*
12. Erin Chapman, *Prove It on Me: New Negroes, Sex, and Popular Culture in the 1920s* (New York: Oxford University Press, 2012), 9.
13. W. E. B. Du Bois, *Black Reconstruction*, (Millwood, N.Y.: Kraus-Thomson, 1976); Du Bois, "Negroes and the Crisis of Capitalism in the U.S.," *Monthly Review* 4, no. 12 (April 1953), reprint, 54, no. 11 (April 2003), https://monthlyreview.org/2003/04/01/negroes-and-the-crisis-of-capitalism-in-the-united-states/; C. L. R. James, *The Black Jacobins: Toussaint L'Ouverture and the San Domingo Revolution* (New York: Dial, 1938); Eric Eustace Williams, *Capitalism and Slavery* (Chapel Hill: University of North Carolina Press, 1944). The recent scholarship on slavery and capitalism, which owes much to Du Bois, James, and Williams, continues to grow; a good sampling and overview can be found in Sven Beckert and Seth Rockman, eds., *Slavery's Capitalism: A New History of American Economic Development* (Philadelphia: University of Pennsylvania Press, 2016).
14. On real estate finance, see Richard Rothstein, *The Color of Law: A Forgotten History of How Our Government Segregated America* (New York: Liveright, 2017); Paige Glotzer, "Exclusion in Arcadia: How Suburban Developers Circulated Ideas About Discrimination, 1890–1950," *Journal of Urban History* 41, no. 3 (2015): 479–94; N. D. B. Connolly, *A World More Concrete: Real Estate and the Remaking of Jim Crow South Florida* (Chicago: University of Chicago Press, 2014); Adam Gordon, "The Creation of Homeownership: How New Deal Changes in Banking Regulation Simultaneously Made Homeownership Accessible to Whites and Out of Reach for Blacks," *Yale Law Journal* 115, no. 1 (2005): 186–226; Kevin Fox Gotham, *Race, Real Estate, and Uneven Development* (Albany: State University of New York Press, 2002). On credit

access, see Louis Hyman, "Legitimating the Credit Infrastructure: Race, Gender, and Credit Access," in *Debtor Nation: The History of America in Red Ink* (Princeton, N.J.: Princeton University Press, 2011), 173–219. On actuarial criminology, the literature is framed largely in social scientific paradigms. The emphasis on governmentality draws in but does not often make central the roles of capitalism and financialization. See overviews in Jonathan Simon, "Reversal of Fortune: The Resurgence of Individual Risk Assessment in Criminal Justice," *Annual Review of Law and Social Science* 1 (December 2005): 397–421; David Garland, "'Governmentality' and the Problem of Crime: Foucault, Criminology, Sociology," *Theoretical Criminology* 1, no. 2: 173–214. On social impact bonds, see Zenia Kish and Justin Leroy, "Bonded Life: Technologies of Racial Finance from Slave Insurance to Philanthrocapital," *Cultural Studies* 29, no. 5 (March 2015): 630–51.

1. "I AM YET WAITIN": AFRICAN AMERICAN WOMEN AND FREE LABOR BANKING EXPERIMENTS IN THE EMANCIPATION-ERA SOUTH, 1860s–1900

1. All quotes, with original spelling, from Mrs. H. T. Scott to Treasury Department, July 13, 1920, in the Freedman's Savings and Trust Company: Letters Received by the Commissioners, 1870–1914, Part 1: Correspondence, Loans, and Bank Books (Bethesda, Md.: UPA Collection from LexisNexis, 2005–), microfilm, hereafter Freedman's Bank Commissioners Letters. Also see Scott to Treasury Department, May 10, May 24, June 12, 1920; Commissioner [John S. Williams] to Mrs. H. T. Scott, May 10, July 22, 1920, Freedman's Bank Commissioners Letters; Record no. 803 for Adaline Washington opened September 3, 1872, Shreveport Branch, series M816, roll 12, p. 553, in Registers of Signatures of Depositors in Branches of the Freedman's Savings and Trust Company, 1865–1874, microfilm, National Archives and Records Administration, Washington, D. C, hereafter Freedman's Bank Registers. All contemporary dollar amounts calculated using Westegg Inflation Calculator, http://www.westegg.com/inflation/.
2. Some might argue that blacks did achieve economic self-sufficiency. Early on, for example, they were able to dictate terms that were important to them, such as choosing with whom to enter a contract, allowing wives to not do fieldwork, or sending children to school. Others, particularly a small group of black men, were able to purchase land. It is important to acknowledge that the terms of many contracts and the exceptional opportunities to purchase large tracts of land discriminated against women. In addition, the failure to redistribute land, exploitative labor contracts, crop liens, and other depredations highlight the incredible odds that most blacks faced in their efforts to achieve economic self-sufficiency. Willie Lee Rose, *Rehearsal for Reconstruction: The Port Royal Experiment* (Indianapolis: Bobbs-Merrill, 1964), 65.
3. Free-labor ideologues like General Otis O. Howard and others drew comparisons between black workers on southern plantations and white northern industrial workers. Pragmatism motivated northern industrialists; they wanted to test the theory that paid labor was less expensive than enslaved labor. On the racial dimensions of free-labor ideology, see Julie Saville, *The Work of Reconstruction: From Slave to Wage-Laborer in South Carolina, 1860–1870* (Cambridge: Cambridge University Press, 1994); Eric Foner, *Reconstruction: America's Unfinished Revolution, 1863–1877* (New York: Harper

Collins, 2002), esp. chap. 4, "Ambiguities of Free Labor," 124–75. On gender, race, and free labor, see Amy Dru Stanley, "The Labor Question and the Sale of Self," in *From Bondage to Contract: Wage Labor, Marriage, and the Market in the Era of Slave Emancipation* (Cambridge: Cambridge University Press, 1998), 60–97; Susan Eva O'Donovan, "Black Women and the Domestication of Free Labor," in *Becoming Free in the Cotton South* (Cambridge, Mass.: Harvard University Press, 2007), 162–207; Mary Farmer-Kaiser, "'The Women Are the Controlling Spirits': Freedwomen, Free Labor, and the Freedmen's Bureau," in *Freedwomen and the Freedmen's Bureau: Race, Gender, and Public Policy in the Age of Emancipation* (New York: Fordham University Press, 2010), 64–94. For examples of free-labor experiments rooted in land redistribution, see Rose, *Rehearsal for Reconstruction*; Janet Sharp Hermann, *The Pursuit of a Dream* (Oxford: Oxford University Press, 1981).

4. See Special Orders no. 15, reprinted in John Eaton and Ethel Osgood Mason, *Grant, Lincoln, and the Freedman: Reminiscences of the Civil War with Special Reference to the Work for the Contrabands and Freedman of the Mississippi Valley* (New York: Longmans, Green, 1907), 5.
5. Louis Gerteis, *From Contraband to Freedman: Federal Policy Toward Southern Blacks, 1861–1865* (Westport, Conn.: Greenwood, 1973).
6. Contraband were not legally U.S. citizens. While the First Confiscation Act of 1861 freed slaves of Confederates who used their enslaved property in the war effort, Abraham Lincoln and Congress hesitated to enact more aggressive emancipation efforts. The Second Confiscation Act of 1862 did not address the issue of emancipation directly, but it did allow black men to enlist. It also allowed Union soldiers to protect self-emancipated blacks in their lines from rebel slaveholders. Slaveholders who professed allegiance to the Union, however, were able to search for and have their enslaved property returned.
7. General John E. Wool created the first fund for freedpeople at Fortress Monroe. Wool, who took over the fort after General Benjamin Butler's reassignment, continued Butler's policy of accepting black refugees as contraband of war. In October 1861, Wool issued Special Order no. 72, which instituted a mandatory work policy for self emancipated people. A portion of their wages would be set aside in a fund to care for the infirm and those not able to work. In practice, however, the quartermaster held all the workers' wages and deducted the costs of rations and board. Quartermasters shorted blacks' wages, shorted their rations, and embezzled from the fund. Blacks complained to visiting church missionaries. "Special Order no. 72," in *War of the Rebellion: Compilation of the Official Records of the Union and Confederate Armies*, series 2, vol. 1 (Washington, D.C.: General Printing Office, 1894), 774, hereafter *Official Records*; "Africans in Fort Monroe Military District: A Letter from the Secretary of War," H.R. Doc. 85, 37th Cong., 2nd Sess. (Washington, D.C.: General Printing Office, 1863); Robert Francis Engs, *Freedom's First Generation: Black Hampton, Virginia, 1861–1890* (New York: Fordham University Press, 2004), 30–32; Cassandra L. Newby-Alexander, *An African American History of the Civil War in Hampton Roads* (Charleston, S.C.: History, 2010), 33.
8. Eaton and Mason, *Grant, Lincoln, and the Freedmen*, 13–15, 23–24, 126–32, 128n1, 194; "Abstract of the Preliminary Report," *The Liberator*, August 14, 1863; American Freedmen's Inquiry Commission, *Preliminary Report Touching the Condition and Management of Emancipated Refugees* [. . .] (New York: J. F. Trow, 1863), 20; "Appeal on Behalf of the Freedman," *The Liberator*, November 3, 1865.

9. John Eaton to John A. Rawlins, April 29, 1863, American Freedmen's Inquiry Commission, Testimony, file 4, quoted in John Cimprich, *Slavery's End in Tennessee, 1861–1865* (University: University of Alabama Press, 1985), 61, 63.
10. Eaton and Mason, *Grant, Lincoln, and the Freedmen*, 14.
11. Eaton and Mason, 139–40, 154, 156–60; Barbara Jeanne Fields, *Slavery and Freedom on the Middle Ground: Maryland During the Nineteenth Century* (New Haven, Conn.: Yale University Press, 1985), 139–56; Richard Paul Fuke, "Planters, Apprenticeship, and Forced Labor: The Black Family Under Pressure in Post-Emancipation Maryland," *Agricultural History* 62, no. 4 (Fall 1988): 57–74; Noralee Frankel, *Freedom's Women: Black Women and Families in Civil War Era Mississippi* (Bloomington: University of Indiana Press, 1999); Thavolia Glymph, *Out of the House of Bondage: The Transformation of the Plantation Household* (New York: Cambridge University Press, 2008).
12. Eaton and Mason, 128.
13. Because of Howard's position as head of the bureau, many fail to acknowledge or parse his use of freedpeople's own funds to help build black educational institutions like Howard and Fisk Universities. The 1870 investigation into his spending makes clearer the different expenditures. Eaton and Mason, 69; House of Representatives, "Charges Against Gen. Howard, July 13, 1870 [. . .]," H.R. Rep. 121, 41st Cong., 2nd Sess., in *Index of Reports of the House of Representatives*, vol. 3 (Washington, D.C.: General Printing Office, 1870).
14. Nathaniel P. Banks, "General Orders no. 23," Headquarters, Department of the Gulf, 19th Army Corps, New-Orleans, [La.], February 3, 1864, reprinted in *Emancipated Labor in Louisiana* ([Boston?], 1864), 37–41, here 39, in John Shaw Pierson Civil War Collection, Rare Books and Special Collections, Firestone Library, Princeton University.
15. Jonathan Levy, *Freaks of Fortune: The Emerging World of Capitalism and Risk in America* (Cambridge, Mass.: Harvard University Press, 2012), 113.
16. Blacks complained about subpar provisions and unfair treatment. Quote in Banks, *Emancipated Labor in Louisiana*, 12. See also Banks, 11–13, 15–16, 19; "Gen. Banks Labor System Philanthropy Run Mad," *New York Times*, July 23, 1864; "Later from New-Orleans," *New York Times*, February 11, 1864; Abram Harris, *The Negro as Capitalist: A Study of Banking and Business Among American Negroes* (1936; College Park, Md.: McGrath, 1968), 26–27.
17. John Davis, "Bankless in Beaufort: A Reexamination of the 1873 Failure of the Freedman's Savings Branch at Beaufort, South Carolina," *South Carolina Historical Magazine* 104, no. 1 (2003): 25–55, here 29–31.
18. The idea of creating separate institutions by race also reflects the popularity and growth of immigrant, ethnic, and religious savings institutions from the 1880s to World War I. See Levy, *Freaks of Fortune*, 106, 115–17; Sheldon M. Garon, *Beyond Our Means: Why America Spends While the World Saves* (Princeton, N.J.: Princeton University Press, 2012), 89–90; William Velvel Moskoff and Carol Gayle, "An Immigrant Bank in Philadelphia Serving Russian Jews: The Blitzstein Bank (1891–1930)," *Pennsylvania History* 81, no. 2 (2014): 226–47, here 228–30.
19. Brig. Gen. R. Saxton to Hon. Edwin M. Stanton, December 30, 1864, in *Official Records*, series 3, vol. 4, 1022–31, here 1022.
20. Quoted in Marland E. Buckner Jr., "Liberty and Economy in Lowcountry South Carolina: The Case of the Freedmen's Bank," in *Keep Your Head to the Sky: Interpreting*

African American Home Ground, ed. Grey Gundaker and Tynes Cowan (Charlottesville: University of Virginia Press, 1998), 211–26, here 222.

21. The quartermaster often did not have enough currency to meet payroll. Butler noted that troops were "almost in a state of insurrection." Benjamin Franklin Butler, *Autobiography and Personal Reminiscences of Major-General Benj. F. Butler: Butler's Book* (Boston: A. M. Thayer, 1892), 508, 514–15, insurrection quote on 514.

22. Butler also discovered that when soldiers did receive their pay, they sent it back home or to banks in New York and Boston using Adams Express; see Benjamin Butler to John M. Forbes, December 8, 1863, reprinted in Benjamin Franklin Butler, ed., *Private and Official Correspondence of Gen. Benjamin F. Butler, During the Period of the Civil War*, vol. 3, February 1863–March 1864 (Norwood, Mass.: Plimpton, 1917), 222–23.

Figures for the bank in New Orleans are not known. The Military and Free Labor Bank in Norfolk had more modest success compared to Beaufort. In less than a year of operation, black soldiers and freedpeople deposited more than $8,000 in the bank. "Address of the American Freedmen's Aid Commission," *The Liberator*, December 1, 1865; Harris, *The Negro as Capitalist*, 27; Davis, "Bankless in Beaufort, 31; Levy, *Freaks of Fortune*, 113; Richard Bailey, *Neither Carpetbaggers Nor Scalawags: Black Officeholders During the Reconstruction of Alabama 1867–1878*, 5th ed. (Montgomery, Ala.: New South, 2010), 165; Carl R. Osthaus, *Freedmen, Philanthropy, and Fraud: A History of the Freedman's Savings Bank* (Urbana: University of Illinois Press, 1976), 1–3. Also see Buckner, "Liberty and Economy in Lowcountry South Carolina," 211–26.

On currency in the southern economy during the Civil War, see Karin Lurvink, "Strapped for Cash: Non-Cash Payments on Louisiana Cotton Plantations, 1865–1908," *Tijdschrift voor sociale en economische geschiedenis* 11, no. 3 (2014): 123–51, here 127–30; Gary M. Pecquet, "Money in the Trans-Mississippi Confederacy and the Confederate Currency Reform Act of 1864," *Explorations in Economic History* 24, no. 2 (April 1987): 218–43.

23. Roderick A. McDonald, "Independent Economic Production by Slaves on Antebellum Louisiana Sugar Plantations," in *The Slaves' Economy: Independent Production by Slaves in the Americas*, ed. Ira Berlin and Philip D. Morgan (London: Frank Cass, 1991), 182–208, here 201. For examples of antebellum to late eighteenth-century black banking, see Berlin and Morgan, *The Slaves' Economy*; Harris, *The Negro as Capitalist*, 17, 20–23; Juliet E. K. Walker, *The History of Black Business in America: Capitalism, Race, and Entrepreneurship, vol. 1, To 1865* (Chapel Hill: University of North Carolina, 2010), 112–18, 170–71; Barbara P. Josiah, "Providing for the Future: The World of the African American Depositors of Washington, D.C.'s Freedmen's Savings Bank, 1865–1874," *Journal of African American History* 89, no. 1 (Winter 2004): 1–16, here 1, 3–4. For specific examples of individual free black and enslaved people's banking activities, see William Johnson, *The Barber of Natchez*, ed. Edwin Adams Davis and William Ransom Hogan (Baton Rouge: Louisiana State University Press, 1973), esp. 38, 42, 95, 157, 231, 254–56; Charles B. Dew, "Part 2: The Slaves," in *Bond of Iron: Master and Slave at Buffalo Forge* (New York: W. W. Norton, 1994), 171–240; Marcus Anthony Allen, "Cautiously Capitalistic: Black Economic Agency at the Savings Bank of Baltimore, 1850–1900" (PhD diss., Morgan State University, 2013).

24. Free blacks also circulated shinplasters, which were extralegal promissory notes. Josiah, "Providing for the Future," 1; Walker, *The History of Black Business*, xv–xvi, 111–17; Martin R. Delany, *The Condition, Elevation, Emigration, and Destiny of the Colored*

People of the United States (1852; New York: Arno, 1968), 94–98; Carla L. Peterson, "Capitalism, Black (Under)Development, and the Production of the African-American Novel in the 1850s," *American Literary History* 4, no. 4 (Winter 1992): 559–83, here 569. On the gendered dimensions of shinplaster exchange, see Robert J. Gamble, "The Promiscuous Economy: Commercial and Cultural Landscapes of Secondhand in the Antebellum City," in *Capitalism by Gaslight: Illuminating the Economy of Nineteenth-Century America*, ed. Brian P. Luskey and Wendy A. Woloson (Philadelphia: University of Pennsylvania Press, 2015), 31–52, here 43.

25. "Art[icle] III. The Freedmen and Free Labor in the South," *Christian Examiner*, May 1864, 344–73, here 349.
26. Overwork describes incentives paid to enslaved people for performing above a quota or baseline of work set by the master or overseer. Enslaved people also hired out their free time to earn extra money. Market activities included selling food, produce, handmade goods, and the like. John Campbell fittingly describes slave market activities in South Carolina as a "terrain of freedom." Slaveholders and politicians recognized enslaved people's market exchanges as a source of empowerment. Municipal laws and codes tried to prevent blacks from purchasing goods that whites felt were too dangerous (e.g., liquor), to restrict with whom blacks should trade (e.g., poor whites), and to deride how blacks spent their money (e.g., gambling). Campbell also acknowledges the class-like divisions and inequalities created between and among enslaved communities by their market activities. See John Campbell, "'As a Kind of Free Man': Slaves' Market-Related Activities in the South Carolina Upcountry, 1800–1860," *Slavery and Abolition* 12, no.1 (June 2008): 131–69, here "terrain" quote 131, discussion of slave exchange 138, inequalities 158n42.
27. Jacquelyn Jones, "A Spirit of Enterprise: The African-American Challenge to the Confederate Project in Civil War–Era Savannah," in *African American Life in the Georgia Lowcountry: The Atlantic World and the Gullah Geechee*, ed. Philip D. Morgan (Athens: University of Georgia Press, 2010), 188–223, here 189–90, 192–93, 203.
28. [Name-redacted] letter to Maj.-Gen. Nathaniel Banks, October 3, 1864, in Banks, *Emancipated Labor in Louisiana*, 44; Susie King Taylor, *Reminiscences of My Life in Camp* [. . .] (Boston, 1902), 16; Garon, *Beyond Our Means*, 53–55, 62–65, 90–92, 149; Frankel, *Freedom's Women*, 28–29, 46–48, 51–53; Stephen B. Sledge, "The Bitter Fruit of Secession: The Union Army's Wartime Occupation of Southeastern Virginia" (PhD diss., George Mason University, 2012), 381–82.
29. I borrow this insight from the notion that citizens in a neoliberal regime resist the "reductive utilitarian calculus" of commodification. See Kevin Thompson, "Resiliency and Freedom: Response to Pat O'Malley's 'From Risk to Resilience,'" *Carceral Notebooks* 7 (2011): 69–75, http://www.thecarceral.org/cn7_Thompson.pdf.
30. "An Act to Incorporate the Freedman's Savings and Trust Company, March 3, 1865," *The Statutes at Large, Treaties, and Proclamations of the United States* [. . .] (Boston: Little, Brown, 1866), 13:510–12.
31. Frederick Douglass, *Life and Times of Frederick Douglass* [. . .] (Hartford, Conn.: Park, 1882), 487.
32. Anson Sperry, an army paymaster, first suggested merging the three free labor and military banks to create a national bank. In early 1865, John Alvord, a minister, succeeded in convincing philanthropists and financiers in New York to support a savings bank for freedpeople. The bill creating the bank passed easily through Congress, and Lincoln

signed it on March 3, 1865. The Freedman's Bank's headquarters moved from New York City to Washington, D.C., in 1868.

33. Harris, *The Negro as Capitalist*, 25–45; Osthaus, *Freedmen, Philanthropy, and Fraud*; Levy, *Freaks of Fortune*, 104–49.
34. F. Colburn Adams, *"White Man Bery Unsartin"; "Nigger Haint Got No Friends, No How": The Blackest Chapter in the History of the Republican Party: The Men Who Robbed and Combined to Rob the Freedmen of Their Hard Earnings* (Washington, D.C.: Judd and Detweiler, 1878).
35. Levy, *Freaks of Fortune*, 107.
36. "Items of Interest from the Branches of the Freedman's Savings and Trust Company," *National Savings Bank*, June 1, 1868, 1–2, here 1; Harris, *The Negro as Capitalist*; Osthaus, *Freedmen, Philanthropy, and Fraud*.
37. Women also faced difficulties when they exercised economic autonomy. They opened individual accounts to protect funds from abusive or exploitative partners, and they sometimes suffered abuse at the hands of husbands and partners for opening individual accounts. Tracey M. Weis, "Negotiating Freedom: Domestic Service and the Landscape of Labor and Household Relations in Richmond, Virginia, 1850–1880" (PhD diss., Rutgers University, 1994), 131.
38. Quote from Account no. 5904-8413 for Milly Chapman opened November 1, 1871, p. 535, Vicksburg Branch, Freedman's Bank Registers; see also Account no. 2564 for Milly Chapman opened May 24, 1869, p. 175, Vicksburg Branch, Freedman's Bank Registers; Passbook of Milly Chapman, Freedman's Bank Commissioners Letters.
39. Record 5669 for Ladies Beneficial Society No. 1 opened April 3, 1873, Nashville Branch, Freedman's Bank Registers, series M816, roll 25, p. 173; Passbook for Ladies Beneficial Society No. 1, Freedman's Bank Commissioners Letters.
40. Alfred N. [unreadable] to Gen. O. O. Howard, August 9, 1866; Richard [unreadable] to [cut off], undated, Freedman's Bank Commissioners Letters.
41. Of the sixty-one thousand deposits that remained when the bank closed, less than 5 percent were of sizeable sums. About thirty thousand depositors averaged around fifty dollars in their accounts, and fifteen thousand held less than five dollars. The average deposit was only forty dollars. Abby L. Gilbert, "The Comptroller of the Currency and the Freedman's Savings Bank," *Journal of Negro History* 57, no. 2 (April 1972): 125–43, here 126; "The Freedman's Savings Bank," *Banker's Magazine* 29 (June 1875): 936–39, here 938.
42. Passbooks of Louisa Wood, no. 5370; Susan Ackes, no. 2747; Sarah Brickhouse, no. 3623; Frances Carey, no. 967, Freedman's Bank Commissioners Letters.
43. Allen also notes that the interest-building strategy was not unique to black savers, and he acknowledges some of the limitations of the practice. Allen, "Cautiously Capitalistic," 2–4, 3–4n3, 8; Levy, *Freaks of Fortune*, 116. Also see Freedman's Bank Registers.
44. Levy emphasizes savings banks' anachronistic place in the capitalist transformations occurring in the U.S. political economy, often serving as tributaries to commercial banks. He also notes that working-class whites tended not to use savings banks for expenses related to "accidents, sickness, or old age" (137). Blacks reacted similarly, though Levy attributes it to their desire to buy land. Secret and workingman societies, which served as inchoate labor unions, proved important as well. Levy, 108, 116, 135.
45. In Mobile, a clerk noted that one of the largest categories of withdrawal, besides personal use, was speculation. In Richmond, nearly three-quarters of depositors withdrew

money to invest in real estate and businesses. By 1870, trustees reported that blacks withdrew $663,000 (about $13 million in 2017 dollars) for land purchases. Robert Somers, *The Southern States Since the War, 1870–1* (London: Macmillan, 1871), 54; "Items of Interest from the Branches"; "Our Report," *National Savings Bank*, June 1, 1868, 2; William Henry Brown, *The Education and Economic Development of the Negro in Virginia*, Phelps-Stokes Fellowship Papers 6 ([Charlottesville, Va.?]: [Suber-Arundale], [1923?]), 119; Levy, *Freaks of Fortune*, 134.

46. "Address of the American Freemen's Aid Commission," *The Liberator*, December 1, 1865; Elsa Barkley Brown, "Negotiating and Transforming the Public Sphere: African American Political Life in the Transition from Slavery to Freedom," *Public Culture* 7 (1994): 107–46, here 190–10; Angela Davis, "Reflections on the Black Woman's Role in the Community of Slaves," *Massachusetts Review* 13, nos. 1/2 (Winter–Spring 1972): 81–100; Deborah Gray White, *Ar'n't I a Woman? Female Slaves in the Plantation South*, rev. ed. (1985; New York: W. W. Norton, 1995); Stanley, *From Bondage to Contract*; Jessica R. Cattelino, "Casino Roots: The Cultural Production of Twentieth-Century Seminole Economic Development," in *Native Pathways: American Indian Culture and Economic Development in the Twentieth Century*, ed. Brian Hosmer and Colleen O Neill (Boulder: University Press of Colorado, 2004), 66–90, here 70. See debates about the relative equity among black men and women in David Barry Gaspar and Darlene Clark Hine, eds. *More than Chattel: Black Women and Slavery in the Americas* (Bloomington: Indiana University Press, 1996).
47. J. C. Embry, "The Freedman's Bank a Success," *Christian Recorder*, February 27, 1873, 1.
48. Jesse Stiller, "The Freedman's Savings Bank: Good Intentions Were Not Enough; A Noble Experiment Goes Awry," Office of the Comptroller of the Currency, https://www.occ.treas.gov/about/what-we-do/history/freedman-savings-bank.html; Levy, *Freaks of Fortune*, 129–44.
49. Levy makes the cogent observation that Henry Cooke's control of blacks' capital revealed a social power reminiscent of slaveholders' power. I disagree, however, with the absolute nature of that power. Freedpeople's resistance clearly indicated its limits. Levy, 143.
50. If the designated heirs or closest living relatives of the deceased account holder were also deceased, close relatives could also make claims.
51. Lucy Ann Seymour to Mr. Knox, June 19, 1882; January 22, 1883, Freedman's Bank Commissioners Letters.
52. J. B. Nowlin to Commissioners, August 2, 1883, Freedman's Bank Commissioners Letters.
53. W. W. Fleming [?] to Charles D. Dawes, December 15, 1899, Freedman's Bank Commissioners Letters.
54. George W. [unreadable] to John Jay Knox, September 10, 1883, Freedman's Bank Commissioners Letters.
55. J. H. Deveaux to Commissioners, August 9, 1901, Freedman's Bank Commissioners Letters.
56. Charles G. Dawes to J. H. Deveaux, August 13, 1901; Eliza Talbot passbook for account no. 8265; Isaac Datts to Commissioners, August 23, 1901; Deveaux to Commissioners; [unreadable name] to J. H. Deveaux, June 19, 1901; Lucy Houston affidavit, Freedman's Bank Commissioners Letters; Record no. 8265, Eliza Talbot, Freedman's Bank Registers.

57. Contemporary estimates place the appropriated value of enslaved labor as $7–$15 trillion in 2017 dollars. The methods of valuation and calculations vary and are controversial. See Ronald P. Salzberger and Mary Turck, eds., *Reparations for Slavery: A Reader* (Lanham, Md.: Rowman and Littlefield, 2004); essays in "African Americans and Movements for Reparations: Past, Present, and Future," special issue, *Journal of African American History* 97, nos. 1–2 (Winter–Spring 2012); Thomas Craemer, "Estimating Slavery Reparations: Present Value Comparisons of Historical Multigenerational Reparations Policies," *Social Science Quarterly* 96, no. 2 (June 2015): 639–55. See also Mary Frances Berry, *My Face Is Black Is True: Callie House and the Struggle for Ex-Slave Reparations* (New York: Knopf, 2005).
58. Record no. 2962, Kate Barber, [Anne Arundel County,] Maryland, Freedman's Bank Registers; Joseph Jackson to Commissioners, August 3, 1884; J. R. Carson to Commissioners, July 28, 1884; Lucy Barber to Commissioners, July 28, 1884; H. W. Cannon to J. R. Carson, July 17, 1884; R. H. Leipold to J. R. Carson, July 31, 1884, Freedman's Bank Commissioners Letters.
59. Charles Spencer to Commissioners, June 30, 1885, Freedman's Bank Commissioners Letters.
60. R. H. T. Leipold to J. R. Chalmers, March 23, 1878; inventory of the sixty books in Lehman and Hartigan to R. H. T. Leipold, March 9, 1878, Freedman's Bank Commissioners Letters.
61. Harriett Mitchell to Commissioner, April 3, 1899, Freedman's Bank Commissioners Letters.
62. W. W. Fleming [?] to Charles D. Dawes, December 15, 1899, Freedman's Bank Commissioners Letters; "New Savings Bank Law of New York," *Banker's Magazine* 29 (June 1875), 939–42, here 942.
63. H. C. Myers to John J. Knox, August 5, 1882, Freedman's Bank Commissioners Letters. Also see complaints by Jerusalem Benevolent Association of New Orleans that claim agent James Allan absconded with its refund, H. N. Frisbie, Attorney, to John Jay Knox, July 3, 1883, Freedman's Bank Commissioners Letters.
64. Moyers was disbarred at least once for stealing a Civil War widow's pension; see W. W. Dudley to H. M. Teller, February 7, 1883, in U.S. House of Representatives, *Irregular Practices of Certain Attorneys* [. . .]*: Letter from the Secretary of the Interior,* H. R. Doc. 172, 48th Cong., 1st Sess., 971. Affidavit of Britton Jones, April 12, 1878; Morris and Whitfield, Attorneys, to R. H. T. Leipold and Robert Purvis, February 28, 1878; Morris and Whitfield to Leipold, [illegible] 1, 1878, January 22, 1878, Freedman's Bank Commissioners Letters; "Griffith, Benjamin W.," *Mississippi: Comprising Sketches of Towns, Events, Institutions, and Persons* [. . .], vol. 3, ed. Dunbar Rowland (Atlanta: Southern Historical Publishing, 1907), 286–88.
65. Elsa Barkley Brown discusses at length black public culture in the years after the Civil War. She writes, "African American women in Virginia, Mississippi, South Carolina, and elsewhere understood themselves to have a vital stake in African American men's franchise. The fact that only men had been granted the vote did not at all mean that only men should exercise the vote." On notion of a shared franchise, see Brown, "Negotiating and Transforming the Public Sphere," quote herein on 123. Record no. 7850 Hart Naylor opened February 28, 1873; record no. 7851 Jefferson Warren opened February 28, 1873, in series M816, roll 15, p. 663, Vicksburg Branch, Freedman's Bank Registers; Julius Jones to Commissioners, February 2, 1878; James Thornton to J. J. Creswell and others,

August 30, 1876; George H. Brown to R. H. Leipold, May 18, 1878, Freedman's Bank Commissioners Letters.

66. W. W. Fleming [?] to Charles D. Dawes, December 15, 1899, Freedman's Bank Commissioners Letters.
67. Quote in Fleming [?] to Dawes; "The Freedman's Bank Victims," *Weekly Clarion* (Jackson, Miss.), January 23, 1878, 2.
68. "Carter in Custody," *New Orleans Times-Democrat*, March 11, 1883; H. C. Myer, Elliott and Tucker Law Firm, to Commissioners, September 5, 1882; Louis Carter to John Jay Knox, September 11, 1882; Meyers to Knox, March 24, 1883; N. Toulouse Velese [?] to John Jay Knox, September 12, 1882, Freedman's Bank Commissioners Letters.
69. All quotes in A. W. Sperry to G. W. Stickney, October 10, 1873; W. F. Bronaugh to R. H. T. Leipold, September 5, 1874; promise to pay from Bronaugh to the Freedman's Bank, December 18, 1872, Freedman's Bank Commissioners Letters.
70. Morgan owed his office to black voters. Their votes helped the Republican win significantly over the incumbent, Frank Hilliard, and then their guns helped oust an obstinate Hilliard after the election. Armed black men fatally shot Hilliard during the armed conflict; see Nicholas Lemann, *Redemption: The Last Battle of the Civil War* (New York: Farrar, Straus and Giroux, 2006), 101–2.
71. Both quotes in Sophia Johnson to R. H. T. Leipold, March 16, 1875, Freedman's Bank Commissioners Letters.

2. "WHO IS SO HELPLESS AS THE NEGRO WOMAN?": THE INDEPENDENT ORDER OF ST. LUKE AND THE QUEST FOR ECONOMIC SECURITY, 1856–1902

1. This introduction is a work of creative nonfiction, also known as evocative history. From very sparse details, I have grounded Elizabeth Draper's experience in the realities of life for many enslaved African American women. I work against sentimental depictions of Draper's relationship with Cuthbert. I disagree with scholars and popular sources who suggest that Draper and Eccles Cuthbert would have married if not for the laws forbidding interracial marriage. Sexual violence represented an ever-present threat in the lives of enslaved black women. Draper's actions toward Cuthbert signal that she was his victim, not partner. Based on subsequent censuses and her death certificate, Draper would have been eleven and a half years old when she gave birth to her daughter. I choose to use other estimates of Draper's age in 1864. See Maggie Lena Walker Diary 1925, Independent Order of St. Luke Records, National Park Service, Maggie L. Walker National Historic Site, Richmond, Virginia, archive hereafter referenced as NPS Walker House; obituary, "Death of Colonel Eccles Cuthbert," *Washington, D.C. Times*, July 14, 1902, 1; Elizabeth Draper Mitchell's death certificate, Ancestry.com, accessed March 29, 2016; Gertrude Woodruff Marlowe, *A Right Worthy Grand Mission: Maggie Lena Walker and the Quest for Black Economic Empowerment* (Washington, D.C.: Howard University Press, 2003), 2; Elizabeth Van Lew, excerpt from "A Yankee Spy in Richmond: The Civil War Diary of 'Crazy Bet' Van Lew," January 24, 1864, 54, Central Rappahannock Regional Library (blog), posted September 13, 2018, https://www.librarypoint.org/blogs/post/a-yankee-spy-in-richmond/?source=fic.

   On the lore around the Forresters saving the U.S. flag, see Theresa M. Guzman-Stokes, "A Flag and a Family: Richard Gill Forrester, 1847–1906," *Virginia Cavalcade*

47, no. 2 (Spring 1998): 52–63; Gregg D. Kimball, *American City, Southern Place: A Cultural History of Antebellum Richmond* (Athens: University of Georgia Press, 2000), 254–55. None of these sources mention the industrial sewing school. However, see reference to the unmarried brother of one of the women in the school who had hidden a flag throughout the war and brought it to school in "Virginia Matters," *Boston Christian Watchman*, January 24, 1867, 6. On the school name, see image, "Glimpses at the Freedmen—The Freedmen's Union Industrial School, Richmond, Va. from a sketch by Ja[me]s E. Taylor," Library of Congress, LC-USZ62-37860.

2. "Extracts from [Right Worthy Grand Secretary's] Report," reprinted in "Record of 1901," *Fiftieth Anniversary, Golden Jubilee Historical Report of the R[ight] W[orthy] G[rand] Council, I[ndependent] O[rder of] St. Luke, 1867–1917* (Richmond: Everett Waddey Co., [1917?]), 23, emphasis added, hereafter *IOSL Fiftieth Anniversary Report*, box 14, folder 5, item A-0228, Independent Order of St. Luke Records, NPS Walker House.
3. On the society's origin in Bethel, see Elsa Barkley Brown, "Uncle Ned's Children: Negotiating Community and Freedom in Postemancipation Richmond, Virginia" (PhD diss., Kent State University, 1994), 500, though Brown places the formation of the society in 1867. On the 1856 date, see Lawrence Mamiya, "A Social History of the Bethel African Methodist Episcopal Church in Baltimore: The House of God and the Struggle for Freedom," in *American Congregations*, vol. 1, *Portraits of Twelve Religious Communities*, ed. James P. Wind and James W. Lewis (Chicago: University of Chicago Press, 1994), 221–92, here 246. On children's membership in the society, see James Handy, *Scraps of African Methodist Episcopal History* (Philadelphia: AME Book Concern, [1902]), 344. On the important role of secular and religious mutual aid societies in Bethel AME in Baltimore, see Mamiya, 245–47.
4. The Bethel AME Church's origins lay in a 1785 prayer group that met at the Strawberry Alley meetinghouse and among other groups of blacks who rejected segregated services at two local Methodist churches in Baltimore. The groups joined to form the Colored Methodist Society in 1787; by 1797, the society renamed itself the Bethel Free African Society. Bethel AME formally incorporated on April 16, 1816. On the church's early history, see Mamiya, 221–92, 223–26; Christopher Phillips, *Freedom's Port: The African American Community of Baltimore, 1790–1860* (Urbana: University of Illinois Press, 1997), 128–30. On Prout's early connection to Bethel, see Benjamin T. Tanner, "Miss Mary Prout," *An Apology for African Methodism* (Baltimore, 1867), 445–46, here 445; Jualynne E. Dodson, *Engendering Church: Women, Power, and African Methodism* (Lanham, Md.: Rowman and Littlefield, 2002), 12–13, 24, 27.
5. Daniel Coker, "Sermon Delivered Extempore in the African Bethel Church in the City of Baltimore [. . .], on the 21st of January, 1816 [. . .]," in *A Documentary History of the Negro People in the United States*, ed. Herbert Aptheker (New York: Citadel, 1951), 1:67–69, here 68.
6. On Prout's life, see Tanner, "Miss Mary Prout," 445–46; Handy, *Scraps of African Methodist Episcopal History*, 344, 346; Jeff Crocombe, "Prout, Mary Ann," in *African American National Biography*, ed. Henry Louis Gates Jr. and Evelyn Brooks Higginbotham (New York: Oxford University Press, 2008), 460–61; Margaret Reid, "Mary Ann Prout (1801–1884)," *Notable Black American Women*, ed. Jessye Carney Smith (Detroit: Gale Research, 1991), 897–98.
7. Of the sources providing biographical details about Prout, two claim she was born a slave, and some give Baltimore as her birthplace. The circumstances of Prout's early life

and family, particularly her older brothers' involvement with the colonization movement and the near-free-labor economy that prevailed in northern Baltimore, support my claim that Prout was born a free woman of color. On claims of an enslaved childhood, see Sylvia Dannett, *Profiles of Negro Womanhood: 1619–1900* (Yonkers, N.Y.: Educational Heritage, 1964), 1:141; Wendell Phillips Dabney, *Maggie L. Walker and the I. O. of Saint Luke: The Woman and Her Work* (Cincinnati, Oh.: Dabney, 1927), 118. See Jacob Prout, James Prout, Robert Prout, Sarah Prout, and William Prout households, 1800 U.S. Census, Anne Arundel County, Maryland, series M32, roll 9, p. 96; Barbara Jeanne Fields, *Slavery and Freedom on the Middle Ground: Maryland During the Nineteenth Century* (New Haven, Conn.: Yale University Press, 1985).

8. For example, members of the Bethel AME congregation organized the Chesapeake and Marine Railway and Drydock Company in 1866. Organizers raised more than $10,000 among Bethel members and other black churches to help capitalize the company. Mamiya, "A Social History," 241–45; Felix James, "The Civil and Political Activities of George A. Myers," *Journal of Negro History* 58, no. 2 (April 1973): 166–78; Bettye C. Thomas, "A Nineteenth Century Black Operated Shipyard, 1866–1884: Reflections upon Its Inception and Ownership," *Journal of Negro History* 19, no.1 (January 1974): 1–12.
9. An 1841 Baltimore County ordinance outlawed blacks' participation in secret societies. In addition to a fine, free people of color could be enslaved and sold outside the state; enslaved offenders would receive thirty-nine lashes and could be sold out of the state. Whites who allowed black societies to meet or who did not report them or break them up could be fined up to $500 and imprisoned. Officials' exception for societies that they felt were strictly beneficial probably reflected their desire to relieve the city of financial responsibility for the indigent. James Martin Wright, *The Free Negro in Maryland, 1634–1860*, Studies in History Economics and Public Law 97, no. 3 (New York: Columbia University, 1921), 250–51; Jeffrey R. Brackett, *The Negro in Maryland: A Study of the Institution of Slavery* (Baltimore, Md.: N. Murray; Johns Hopkins University, 1889), 200–201, 203–4; Mamiya, 229.
10. Maggie L. Walker maintained that Prout originally wanted St. Luke to remain an all-female society. See Walker, "[Comments]," *IOSL Fiftieth Anniversary Report*, 1.
11. Tanner, "Miss Mary Prout," 446; Daniel Alexander Payne, *Recollections of Seventy Years*, ed. C. S. Smith (Nashville, Tenn.: AME Sunday School Union, 1888), 224; Mamiya, "A Social History," 239–41.
12. On women's activities in the nineteenth-century AME church, see Dodson, *Engendering Church*, 12–13, 28–29, 78. Consider also black women in the Baptist church; see Evelyn Brooks Higginbotham, *Righteous Discontent: The Women's Movement in the Black Baptist Church, 1880–1920* (Cambridge, Mass.: Harvard University Press, 1993).
13. The 1880 census lists her as a widowed "doctoress" living with her niece, but references contemporary to Prout state that she never married. Record for Mary E. Brown, 1880 U.S. Census, 14-WD Baltimore (Independent City), Maryland, series T9, roll 502, p. 331. On black women's antebellum organizations, see Shirley Yee, *Black Women Abolitionists: A Study in Activism, 1828–1860* (Nashville: University of Tennessee Press, 1992), 2–3; Martha S. Jones, *All Bound Up Together: The Woman Question in African American Public Culture, 1830–1900* (Chapel Hill: University of North Carolina Press, 2007). On attitudes about gender and nineteenth-century capitalism, see George Robb,

Ladies of the Ticker: Women and Wall Street from the Gilded Age to the Great Depression (Champaign: University of Illinois Press, 2017), 132–42.

14. Prout raised thousands of dollars for the women's home through a three-day community fair in 1867, equivalent to at least $44,500 in 2017 dollars. Tanner, "Miss Mary Prout," 446; Richard Paul Fuke, *Imperfect Equality: African Americans and the Confines of White Racial Attitudes in Postemancipation Maryland* (New York: Fordham University Press, 1999), 125–26; Dodson, *Engendering Church*, 66. On the entrepreneurial aspects of black women's church societies, see W. E. B. Du Bois, *Some Efforts of American Negroes for Their Own Social Betterment*, Atlanta University Publications 3 (Atlanta: Atlanta University Press, 1898), 5–44; Susan Yohn, "'Let Christian Women Set the Example in Their Own Gifts': The 'Business' of Protestant Women's Organizations," in *Women and Twentieth-Century Protestantism*, ed. Virginia Brereton and Margaret Bendroth (Urbana: University of Illinois Press, 2002), 213–35.
15. In Philadelphia, societies like the African Female Union and the Sisters of Dorcas collected one dollar in quarterly fees, payable at 12.5¢ per month. In the early decades of the 1800s, mite or cent societies were also very popular among women's church groups that raised funds for missionary work. In the 1880s and 1890s, black washerwomen and domestics in the South earned on average between four and eight dollars per month, though a few might earn as much as twelve dollars per month. Given black women's meager wages and demanding expenses, their commitment to pay even a fraction of their income every month was significant. Bettye Collier-Thomas, *Jesus, Jobs, and Justice: African American Women and Religion* (New York: Knopf, 2010), 39. On mite societies, see George Winfred Hervey, *The Story of Baptist Missions in Foreign Lands* [. . .] (St. Louis, Mo.: Chancy R. Barns, 1884), 180, 188–89; Stephanie McCurry, *Masters of Small Worlds: Yeoman Households, Gender Relations and the Political Culture of the Antebellum South Carolina Low Country* (New York: Oxford University Press, 1995), 189. On washerwomen's wages, see Tera Hunter, *To 'Joy My Freedom: Southern Black Women's Lives and Labors After the Civil War* (Cambridge, Mass.: Harvard University Press, 1997), 52–53.
16. The black population of Baltimore swelled by nearly twelve thousand between 1860 and 1870, from 27,898 to 39,558. Mamiya, "A Social History," 229–47; Carol V. R. George, "Widening the Circle: The Black Church and the Abolitionist Crusade, 1830–1860," in *Antislavery Reconsidered: New Perspectives on the Abolitionists*, ed. Michael Fellman (Baton Rouge: Louisiana State University Press, 1979), 75–95; Howard Holman Bell, *Survey of the Negro Convention Movement, 1830–1861* (1953; New York: Arno, 1969), 146–47; Fuke, *Imperfect Equality*, 112–16; Fields, *Slavery and Freedom on the Middle Ground*, 108–9, 111.
17. The Freedmen's Bureau in Maryland did help some women challenge apprenticeship contracts, though it was generally unsuccessful. See Fields, 139–56; Richard Paul Fuke, "Planters, Apprenticeship, and Forced Labor: The Black Family Under Pressure in Postemancipation Maryland," *Agricultural History* 62, no. 4 (Fall 1988): 57–74.
18. Noralee Frankel, *Freedom's Women: Black Women and Families in Civil War Era Mississippi* (Bloomington: University of Indiana Press, 1999), 30; Thavolia Glymph, *Out of the House of Bondage: The Transformation of the Plantation Household* (New York: Cambridge University Press, 2008), esp. chaps. 5–6; Hunter, *To 'Joy My Freedom*, esp. chap. 3; Dabney, *Maggie L. Walker*, 118.

19. Seth Rockman, *Scraping By: Wage Labor, Slavery, and Survival in Early Baltimore* (Baltimore, Md.: Johns Hopkins University Press, 2009).
20. Black workingman groups existed before the Civil War. M. Ray Della Jr., "The Problems of Negro Labor in the 1850s," *Maryland Historical Magazine* 66, no. 1 (Spring 1971): 14–32; Fields, *Slavery and Freedom on the Middle Ground*, 38; Fuke, *Imperfect Equality*; Joseph L. Browne, "'The Expenses Are Borne by Parents': Freedmen's Schools in Southern Maryland, 1865–1870," *Maryland Historical Magazine* 86, no. 4 (Winter 1991): 407–22, 180. On the Colored National Labor Union, see James, "The Civil and Political Activities"; Eric Foner, *Organized Labor and the Black Worker, 1619–1973*, 2nd ed. (New York: International, 1982), esp. chap. 5.

    Fraternal and workingmen's cooperative insurance witnessed explosive growth after the Civil War. On the AUOW, see "Ancient United Order of Workmen," Encyclopedia Dubuque, http://www.encyclopediadubuque.org/index.php?title=ANCIENT_ORDER_OF_UNITED_WORKMEN_(A.O.U.W.); "Ancient United Order of Workmen," Phoenix Masonry Masonic Museum, http://www.phoenixmasonry.org/masonicmuseum/fraternalism/aouw.htm; Walter Basye, *History and Operation of Fraternal Insurance* (Rochester, N.Y.: Fraternal Monitor, 1919), 14; David T. Beito, *From Mutual Aid to the Welfare State: Fraternal Societies and Social Services, 1890–1967* (Chapel Hill: University of North Carolina Press, 2000), 12–13. Also see John Witt, *The Accidental Republic: Crippled Workingmen, Destitute Widows, and the Remaking of American Law* (Cambridge, Mass.: Harvard University Press, 2000), esp. chap. 3.
21. Exceptions include work on nineteenth-century washerwomen's strikes and collective organizing. See the chapter "'Washing Amazons' and Organized Protests," in Hunter, *To 'Joy My Freedom*, 74–97.
22. "Testimony of Mrs. George Ward," U.S. Government, *Report of the Committee of the Senate upon the Relations Between Labor and Capital and Testimony Taken by the Committee* (Washington, D.C.: Government Printing Office, 1885), 4: 315, 345–44, cited in Glymph, *Out of the House of Bondage*, 152.
23. On conflicts between white women employers and black women domestics in the antebellum and postbellum South, see Hunter, *To 'Joy My Freedom*; Glymph; Tracey M. Weis, "Negotiating Freedom: Domestic Service and the Landscape of Labor and Household Relations in Richmond, Virginia, 1850–1880" (PhD diss., Rutgers University, 1994).
24. "An Appeal from the Richmond Negroes for Protection," *New York Tribune*, June 12, 1865, 8; John O'Brien, *From Bondage to Citizenship: The Richmond Black Community, 1865–67* (New York: Garland, 1990), 148–52, 154, 160–66, 175–80; Weis, 130–31; Elsa Barkley Brown, "Negotiating and Transforming the Public Sphere: African American Political Life in the Transition from Slavery to Freedom" *Public Culture* 7 (1994): 107–46; Lewis Randolph and Gayle T. Tate, *Rights for a Season: The Politics of Race, Class and Gender in Richmond, Virginia* (Knoxville: University of Tennessee Press, 2003), 82–86, 91–92, 95; Carey H. Latimore, *The Role of Southern Free Blacks During the Civil War Era: The Life of Free African Americans in Richmond, Virginia 1850 to 1876* (Lewiston, N.Y.: Edwin Mellon, 2015), 130–31, 134, 138–42.
25. In 1840, industrial firms held more than half (55 percent) of enslaved men. In 1860, enslaved people comprised 83 percent of workers in tobacco manufacturing in Richmond. Brown, "Uncle Ned's Children," 2, 161–62; Weis, 15–21, 90, 298; Peter J. Rachleff,

Black Labor in the South: Richmond, Virginia, 1865–1890 (Philadelphia: Temple University Press, 1984), 5–6.

26. Richard Gustavus Forrester grew up in Richmond in relative privilege, living among a small, accomplished group of free blacks in a home he inherited from his white aunt. His father was Gustavus Myers, a prominent Jewish attorney and civic and fraternal leader in Richmond, and his mother was the free black house servant of Myers's cousin Gustavus Forrester. Richard married Narcissa, the daughter of Ellen Wilson, a free black woman, and wealthy Jewish merchant and philanthropist Judah Touro, both of New Orleans. Richard and Narcissa had twenty children. William M. T. Forrester was born in Richmond in March 1847. A barber and regalia manufacturer, William married Eliza in 1867, and they had two children. On the Forresters, see Theresa and Keith Stokes, "Fourth Generation—The Forresters of Richmond," http://www.eyesofglory.com/fourth-generation/; Steve Clark, "Richard Gustavus Forrester," *Richmond Times-Dispatch*, February 25, 2002, https://www.richmond.com/special-section/black-history/richard-gustavus-forrester/article_62144000-3217-56ee-81ff-a44ef6cda978.html; Willi[a]m M. T. Forrester Household, 1900 U.S. Census, Henrico County, Monroe-WD, Richmond, Virginia; Account 1045, William M. Forrester Record in 1870; Account 1800, Richard Forrester Record in 1870, Registers of Signatures of Depositors in Branches of the Freedman's Savings and Trust Company, 1865–1874, National Archives and Records Administration, Washington, D.C., microfilm.
27. "Right worthy grand" (or RWG) designated state-level leadership positions in the IOSL. Unfortunately, IOSL reports from 1867 to the mid-1870s and 1910 to 1914 are missing from the National Park Service's archival copy of the *IOSL Fiftieth Anniversary Report*.
28. St. Luke's Lodge No. 9 Record, Account 1800, U.S. Freedmen Bank Records.
29. W. M. T. Forrester, *Degree Ritual of the Independent Order of St. Luke* [. . .], rev. ed. ([Richmond?], 1894), box 1, folder 1, p. 13, Independent Order of St. Luke Collection, 1877–1970, MS 1988–121, Special Collections, University Libraries, Virginia Polytechnic Institute and State University.
30. On Maggie Lena Walker's early life and her father, see Marlowe, *A Right Worthy Grand Mission*; Dabney, *Maggie L. Walker*; Elsa Barkley Brown, "Womanist Consciousness: Maggie Lena Walker and the Independent Order of Saint Luke" *Signs* 14 (1989): 610–33; Brown, "Constructing a Life and a Community: A Partial Story of Maggie Lena Walker," *OAH Magazine of History* 7, no. 4 (Summer 1993): 28–31.
31. Three councils founded by Carter, including the Prout Council, survived at least through World War I. Walker, "History," *IOSL Fiftieth Anniversary Report*, 6, and related annual convention minutes.
32. William P. Burrell and D. E. Johnson, *Twenty-Five Years History of the Grand Fountain, 1881–1905* (Richmond, Va.: Grand Fountain of the True Reformers, 1909), 69, 74, 125, 148.
33. Women were also instrumental to spreading the True Reformers in other ways. For example, leading women such as plantation owner Caroline Williams in Guinea, Virginia, and Emily Monroe in the District of Columbia introduced True Reformers founder William W. Browne to leading businesspeople, pastors, and educators in their communities. Burrell and Johnson, 398; "Officers Elected," *Richmond Planet*, August 22, 1896, 4. On women's assistance to Browne, see Burrell and Johnson, 136–37, 145.

34. On the Ancient Order of United Workmen, see note 20 above. Dryden helped found the Widows' and Orphans' Friendly Society in Newark, New Jersey, in 1873; it changed its name in 1875 to the Prudential Friendly Society. In 1877, Dryden incorporated the Prudential Life Insurance Company of America. It was one of the first major companies in the United States to offer insurance benefits to working-class Americans. Within ten years, Prudential had more than one million policies in force and emerged as one of the largest and most influential insurance companies in the world. See Frederick Ludwig Hoffman, *History of the Prudential Insurance Company of America (Industrial Insurance), 1875–1900* (Newark, N.J.: Prudential, 1900), 37–38. For an interactive time line of Prudential's history, see "Prudential History," http://corporate.prudential.com/view/page/corp/31790.

    On Browne, see David M. Fahey, ed., *The Black Lodge in White America: "True Reformer" Browne and His Economic Strategy* (Dayton, Oh.: Wright State University Press, 1994); W. W. Browne and D. Webster Davis, *The Life and Public Services of Rev. William Washington Browne* (Philadelphia: AME Book Concern, 1910). On Bush, see A. E. Bush and P. L. Dorman, *History of the Mosaic Templars of America: Its Founders and Officials* (Little Rock, Ark.: Central, 1924; reprint, Fayetteville: University of Arkansas Press, 2008), http://www.mosaictemplarspreservation.org/history_mosaic/history.pdf; C. Calvin Smith, "John E. Bush: The Politician and the Man, 1880–1916," *Arkansas Historical Quarterly* 54 (Summer 1995): 115–33. Stringer has been called "the father of black Masonry in the South." On Stringer, see Marilyn T. Peebles, *The Alabama Knights of Pythias of North America, South America, Europe, Asia, Africa, and Australia: A Brief History* (Lanham, Md.: University Press of America, 2012), 7–15, father quote on 9; George Alexander Sewell and Margaret L. Dwight, eds., *Mississippi Black History Makers*, rev. ed. (Jackson: University of Mississippi Press, 1984), 49–51.
35. David T. Beito notes that many white and ethnic fraternalists were also suspicious of the new insurance schemes and initially resisted participation. W. T. Andrews, "Insurance and Real Estate," *Report of the Fifth Annual Convention of the National Negro Business League, Held at Atlanta, Georgia* (Boston: Charles Alexander, 1906), 35; Beito, *From Mutual Aid*, 207–8.
36. *Virginia Star* (Richmond), November 18, 1882, 2, Miscellaneous Negro Newspapers, Committee on Negro Studies of the American Council of Learned Societies, Virginia Historical Society, Richmond, Virginia, hereafter Miscellaneous Negro Papers.
37. Charles H. Brooks, *The Official History and Manual of the Grand United Order of Odd Fellows in America* (Philadelphia, 1902), 156.
38. An endowment and life insurance plan are similar in that they accumulate cash value and pay a lump sum benefit on the death of the insured. However, an endowment plan lasts for a certain coverage period, say ten or twenty years, while a life insurance plan lasts through the life of the individual.
39. Committee on Endowment Report, *IOSL Fiftieth Anniversary Report*, 8.
40. Committee on Endowment Report; lists of reporting councils throughout *IOSL Fiftieth Anniversary Report*; Marlowe, *A Right Worthy Grand Mission*, 12.
41. Marlowe, 12, 37. On trust in early insurance, see Viviana A. Zelizer, "Human Values and the Market: The Case of Life Insurance and Death in 19th-Century," *American Journal of Sociology* 84, no. 3 (November 1978): 591–610; Penelope Gwynn Ismay, "Trust Among Strangers: Securing British Modernity 'by Way of Friendly Society,' 1780s–1870s" (PhD diss., University of California at Berkeley, 2010).

Early life insurance executives did not rely solely on values-laden sentiment; they built confidence and trust in their products through other methods such as scientific narratives. See Sharon Ann Murphy, *Investing in Life: Insurance in Antebellum America* (Baltimore, Md.: Johns Hopkins University Press, 2010).

42. For comparison, black teachers in Virginia earned less than $200 a year in the 1890s. See table 4.1, "Annual Salaries of Public School Teachers: Selected Southern States, 1890–1950 (in 1950 Dollars)," in Robert A. Margo, *Race and Schooling in the South, 1880–1950: An Economic History* (Chicago: University of Chicago Press, 1990), 54.
43. "Record of 1885," *IOSL Fiftieth Anniversary Report*, quote on 9.
44. "Record of 1887," *IOSL Fiftieth Anniversary Report*, 10–11.
45. "Record of 1888," *IOSL Fiftieth Anniversary Report*, 11.
46. Forrester moved into national prominence in the Odd Fellows in 1875 when the order elected him to the Grand Directors Board. He was elected deputy grand master in 1880 and elected grand master for a record seven consecutive terms, 1882–1893. See Brooks, *The Official History and Manual of the Grand United Order of Odd Fellows in America*, 156, 167, 235; "W. M. T. Forrester Elected Again," *Richmond Planet*, October 18, 1890, 1; "Odd Fellows Day," *Richmond Planet*, June 30, 1894.
47. Given transnational and translocal membership, these notions of manhood were linked to regional, national, international, and diasporic notions of masculinity. Martin Summers, *Manliness and Its Discontents: The Black Middle Class and the Transformation of Masculinity, 1900–1930* (Chapel Hill: University of North Carolina Press, 2004), 1.
48. On gender and civic identity in fraternal societies, see Summers; Peter P. Hinks and Stephen Kantrowitz, eds., *All Men Free and Brethren: Essays on the History of African American Freemasonry* (Ithaca, NY. Cornell University Press, 2013); John M. Giggie, *After Redemption: Jim Crow and the Transformation of African American Religion in the Delta, 1875–1915* (New York: Oxford University Press, 2007), 59–60, 69.
49. It is not known whether Elizabeth accepted any financial support from Cuthbert or whether he ever offered any. "[Mr. Eccles Cuthbert]," *Richmond Dispatch*, July 15, 1902, 3; Maggie Lena Walker Diary, August 21, 1925.

Cuthbert was born in Ireland around 1840 and immigrated to the United States when he was a boy. His family settled in South Carolina. He joined a local militia in 1860 and formally enlisted in the First Regiment, South Carolina Infantry, First Provisional Army of the Confederacy in Abbeville, South Carolina, in 1862. He recovered from wounds received in battle at Chimborazo Hospital in Richmond. It was around that time that he boarded with the wealthy Van Lews. Scholarship characterizing Cuthbert as an abolitionist embraces an idealistic view. While some Scots-Irish living in the South were Unionists, many linked southern secession with Irish separation from Britain. Extant newspaper accounts reveal Cuthbert's support for secession, and he joined a local militia before the conflict at Fort Sumter. He also penned a series of sympathetic reports about South Carolina and the 1876 election for the *New York Herald*. To be sure, his enlistment, his strong vocal support of secession, and his rejection of any federal role in southern politics may have represented the exigent, self-interested calculations of an immigrant casting his lots in the postbellum South. On Cuthbert's alleged abolitionist leanings, see Muriel Miller Branch. "Maggie Lena Walker (1864–1934)," Encyclopedia Virginia, Virginia Foundation for the Humanities, http://www.encyclopediavirginia.org/Maggie_Lena_Walker_1864-1934; Irish in the antebellum South in Arthur Mitchell, *South Carolina Irish* (Charleston, S.C.: History Press, 2010);

Cuthbert's 1876-era reports in Bruce Chesterman, "Progress Dooms Another Landmark," *Richmond Times-Dispatch*, January 13, 1935, 45; "A Well-Merited Honor," *Richmond Dispatch*, April 17, 1877, 3. On Cuthbert, see "United States Civil War Soldiers Index, 1861–1865," Eccles Cuthbert, National Archives and Records Administration, M381, roll 8, FHL microfilm 881974; Historical Commission of South Carolina, *South Carolina Troops in Confederate Service* (Columbia, S.C.: R. L. Bryan, 1913), 1: 338–39, 339n1; "Mr. Cuthbert in Carolina," *State* (Columbia, S.C.), July 21, 1902, 4; "The Death of Colonel Eccles Cuthbert" *Richmond Dispatch*, July 15, 1902, 3.

50. "Nothing but Leaves," address, 1909, quoted in Marlowe, *A Right Worthy Grand Mission*, 5.
51. Inklings of Maggie Lena's future assertiveness became evident while she was in high school. She and lifelong friend Wendell Dabney organized one of the first student protests against segregation. When the school scheduled her graduation in a racially segregated venue, she and Dabney led a protest against holding graduation ceremonies in a racially segregated venue. Marlowe, 15–17.
52. "Leah's Council, 161, I. O. St. Luke," *Richmond Planet*, May 8, 1897, 1; "Register Vernon's Speech," *Washington Bee*, January 9, 1909, 4.
53. Marlowe, *A Right Worthy Grand Mission*; Dabney, *Maggie L. Walker*; John N. Ingham and Lynne B. Feldman, eds., "Walker, Maggie Lena (July 15, 1867–December 15, 1934)," in *African-American Business Leaders: A Biographical Dictionary* (Westport, Conn.: Greenwood, 1994), 670–679; Gertrude W. Marlowe, "Walker, Maggie Lena," *Black Women in America*, ed. Darlene Clark Hine, Oxford African American Studies Center, http://www.oxfordaasc.com.ezproxy.lib.utexas.edu/article/opr/t0003/e0454; Brown, "Womanist Consciousness"; Brown, "Constructing a Life and a Community."
54. "The Ladies Organize," *Richmond Planet*, August 17, 1895, 1. Also see Suzanne Lebsock, *A Murder in Virginia: Southern Justice on Trial* (New York: W. W. Norton, 2004).
55. Funeral Program, Maggie Lena Walker [December 1934], file Maggie L. Walker, Vertical Files, Valentine Richmond History Center.
56. Ads for Woman's Corner-Stone Beneficial Association, *Richmond Planet*, April 10, 1897, 4; October 16, 1897, 3; December 25, 1897, 2; March 1, 1902, 6; February 27, 1904, 6; "Resignation," *Richmond Planet*, July 16, 1898, 5; "In Union There is Strength," *Richmond Planet*, July 16, 1898, 8. On Jones, see "A Founding Family Part 3: The Jonses," Virginia Union University Archives and Special Collections, https://vuuarchives.wordpress.com/2017/02/17/a-founding-family-part-3-the-joneses/. On Anderson, see *Twentieth Annual Report of the Superintendent of the Public Schools, Richmond, 1889* ([Richmond?], [1889?]), 27.
57. The sources do not reveal the exact date that the Woman's Union Grocery Store opened, but it is reasonable to assume that it was at least imagined in the 1898 charter and may have started business in the same year or soon after. Listing for rooms in *Hill's Richmond* (Virginia) *City Directory* (Richmond: Hill Directory Company, 1900), HeritageQuest.com; brief mention of Anderson as store manager in August Meier and Elliott Rudwick, "Negro Boycotts of Segregated Streetcars in Virginia, 1904–1907," *Virginia Magazine of History and Biography* 81 (October 1973): 479–87, here 483; ad, Woman's Grocery, *True Reformer* (Richmond, Va.), January 28, 1903, 4, Miscellaneous Negro Newspapers.
58. "Record of 1895," *IOSL Fiftieth Anniversary Report*, 14.
59. "Record of 1885," "Record of 1895," "Record of 1897," *IOSL Fiftieth Anniversary Report*, 9, 14, 15–16; Marlowe, *A Right Worthy Grand Mission*, 35, 38–39.

60. Marlowe, 37, 39–40, 41.
61. "W. M. T. Forrester," *IOSL Fiftieth Anniversary Report*, 6.
62. The St. Luke Association incorporated in 1897 as a stock company, capitalized for $50,000. The association purchased the building for $4,000 ($117,000 in 2016 dollars) for $500 down and $500 with interest every six months. "Record of 1897," "St. Luke Association, of Richmond, Va., Inc.," *IOSL Fiftieth Anniversary Report*, 19, 70–72; Marlowe, *A Right Worthy Grand Mission*, 41–42, 115.
63. "Record of 1897," *IOSL Fiftieth Anniversary Report*, 15.
64. Bowser worked as a schoolteacher and helped found the first professional association for black schoolteachers in Virginia in 1887. In 1895, she founded the Richmond Woman's League, supported mothers' clubs, and helped charter the National Association of Colored Women. Marlowe, *A Right Worthy Grand Mission*, 42.
65. To reassert the GUOSL's authority, Prout's niece Lucy Vincent changed her title to "right worthy grand supreme chief." Marlowe, 42–43; "Record of 1895," *IOSL Fiftieth Anniversary Report*, 13–14; "Grand Council Speaks," *Richmond Planet*, September 16, 1899, 8; "Supreme Council Explains Strange Action of Councils," *Richmond Planet*, September 9, 1899, 8.
66. Both quotes from "Record of 1899," *IOSL Fiftieth Anniversary Report*, 20.
67. Marlowe, *Right Worthy Grand Mission*, 46; "Record of 1899," *IOSL Fiftieth Anniversary Report*, 20; Brown, "Uncle Ned's Children," 499.
68. "Record of 1900," *IOSL Fiftieth Anniversary Report*, 20–22, diligent quote on 20; Brown, "Uncle Ned's Children," 6–7; Record for Ella Onley, 1900 U.S. Census, Henrico County, Marshall-WD Richmond, series T623, roll 1737, p. 68.
69. "Our Mission," undated editorial, *St. Luke Herald*, quoted in *IOSL Fiftieth Anniversary Report*, 26.
70. "Record of 1900," *IOSL Fiftieth Anniversary Report*, 20.
71. See "St. Luke Brevities," *Richmond Planet*, January 6, 1900, 3; "I. O. St. Luke Notes—Death Claims Paid," *Richmond Planet*, April 20, 1901, 8.
72. Brown, "Uncle Ned's Children," 6–7; "Record of 1900," *IOSL Fiftieth Anniversary Report*, 20.
73. "Record of 1907," *IOSL Fiftieth Anniversary Report*, 33.
74. "Record of 1900," *IOSL Fiftieth Anniversary Report*, 21–22.
75. "Record of 1900."
76. I was not able to find additional biographical information about most of these women. "Record of 1902," *IOSL Fiftieth Anniversary Report*, 25.

3. "LET US HAVE A BANK": ST. LUKE PENNY SAVINGS BANK, ECONOMIC ACTIVISM, AND STATE REGULATION, 1903 TO WORLD WAR I

1. This introduction is a work of creative nonfiction. The board of directors approved having school-age girls from the juvenile circles deliver invitations for the bank's opening. Minutes for October 5, 1903, St. Luke's Penny Savings, Board of Directors Meeting Minutes, hereafter St. Luke Bank Board Minutes, [August 19, 1903–January 31, 1913,] 7–8, Consolidated Bank and Trust Records, c. 1903–1993, Special Collections, L. Douglas Wilder Library, Virginia Union University, Richmond, Virginia, hereafter CB&T Records.

2. "Extracts from [RWG Secretary's] Report," reprinted in "Record of 1901," *Fiftieth Anniversary, Golden Jubilee Historical Report of the R[ight] W[orthy] G[rand] Council, I[ndependent] O[rder of] St. Luke, 1867–1917* (Richmond: Everett Waddey, [1917?]), box 14, folder 5, item A-0228, p. 23, Independent Order of St. Luke Records, hereafter *IOSL Fiftieth Anniversary Report,* Maggie Lena Walker Historical Site, National Park Service, Richmond Virginia, hereafter NPS Walker House.
3. Sheldon M. Garon, *Beyond Our Means: Why America Spends While the World Saves* (Princeton, N.J.: Princeton University Press, 2012); Nicholas Osborne, "Little Capitalists: The Social Economy of Saving in the United States, 1816–1914" (PhD diss., Columbia University, 2014); Jonathan Levy, *Freaks of Fortune: The Emerging World of Capitalism and Risk in America* (Cambridge, Mass.: Harvard University Press, 2012), 125–48.
4. John Mercer Langston of Richmond served as a trustee. It is unclear whether Langston actually had any experience with the day-to-day operations of the Freedman Bank. A sizeable number of Freedman Bank branches had blacks working as tellers, clerks, and bookkeepers by 1870. Washington, D.C.; Richmond; and Norfolk had a large number of black men who served on the Freedman's Bank advisory committees and boards. Abram Harris, *The Negro as Capitalist: A Study of Banking and Business Among American Negroes* (1936; College Park, Md.: McGrath, 1968), 45. ["Negro Banks,"] *Report of the Eleventh Annual Convention of the National Negro Business League Held in New York, New York, August 17–19, 1910* (Nashville: AME Sunday School Union, 1911), 176–77; Negro Bankers Symposium in *Report of the Seventh Annual Convention of the National Negro Business League Held in Atlanta, Georgia, August 29–31, 1906* (Boston: Charles Alexander, 1906), 156–92.
5. Cuthbert was an ex-Confederate, first-generation Irish immigrant who earned a reputation as "one of the best-known newspaper men in the country." In the mid-1890s, he moved from Richmond to the District of Columbia. As a well-known, popular, and constant presence in the capital, he added politicians and business leaders to his wide network of professional and personal contacts. Quote in "Death of Colonel Eccles Cuthbert," *Washington, D.C., Times,* July 14, 1902, 1.
6. All quotes from Ann Field Alexander, "Black Protest in the New South: John Mitchell, Jr., 1863–1929, and the *Richmond Planet*" (PhD diss., Duke University, 1972), 335.
7. Quote in Ann Field Alexander, *Race Man: The Rise and Fall of the "Fighting Editor" John Mitchell Jr.* (Charlottesville: University of Virginia Press, 2002), 72; "Obituary [Critty Williams]," *Richmond Dispatch,* February 11, 1900, 14.

   On southern white elite responses to race relations in the period, see Clayton McClure Brooks, "Conversations Across the Color Line: Interracial Cooperation and the Making of Segregation in Virginia, 1900–1930" (PhD diss., University of Virginia, 2006); Stephen Kantrowitz, "One Man's Mob Is Another Man's Militia: Violence, Manhood, and Authority in Reconstruction South Carolina," in *Jumpin' Jim Crow: Southern Politics from Civil War to Civil Rights,* ed. Jane Elizabeth Dailey, Glenda Elizabeth Gilmore, and Bryant Simon Princeton (Princeton, N.J.: Princeton University Press, 2000), 67–87.
8. By the 1920s, women from broader social backgrounds gained access to the banks' ladies rooms and services, and banks hired more women tellers and employees. Richard N. Germain, *Dollars Through the Doors: A Pre-1930 History of Bank Marketing in America* (Westport, Conn.: Greenwood, 1996), 78–83; Nancy Marie Robertson, "'The Principles

of Sound Banking and Financial Noblesse Oblige': Women's Departments in U.S. Banks at the Turn of the Twentieth Century," in *Women and Their Money, 1700–1950: Essays on Women and Finance*, ed. Anne Laurence, Josephine Maltby, and Janette Rutterford (London: Routledge, 2009), 243–53. On women's departments at brokerage firms, see George Robb, *Ladies of the Ticker: Women and Wall Street from the Gilded Age to the Great Depression* (Champaign: University of Illinois Press, 2017), 71, 74–75.

9. Minutes for August 19, 1903, St. Luke Bank Board Minutes, 3–4.
10. Minutes for August 19, 1903, 3–4; Minutes for October 5, 1903, 7–8; Minutes of December 5, 1903, 9–10, St. Luke Bank Board Minutes; Mary Maclin Smith to Emmett C. Burke, [c. 1912–1913], folder [Letters 1912] R, box Letters, 1912–1913, 1 of 2, CB&T Records.
11. Minutes for August 21, 1903, 5; Minutes of December 5, 1903, 9, in St. Luke Bank Board Minutes.
12. Minutes of December 5, 1903, 9; Minutes of January 8, 1904, 9, St. Luke Bank Board Minutes; "Record of 1904," *IOSL Fiftieth Anniversary Report*, 29.
13. Minutes of August 26, 1904, 12, St. Luke Bank Board Minutes.
14. "[Time Was When the Northern Negro]," *Washington, D.C. Colored American*, September 5, 1903, 8.
15. Daily Balance [Ledger], 1903–1909, box 15 Ledgers, CB&T Records; "New Institution of Colored Order of St. Luke Opened Today," *Richmond News Leader*, November 2, 1903, transcribed in Jesse E. Fleming, "A History of Consolidated Bank and Trust Company: A Minority Bank" (MA thesis, Rutgers University, 1972), 25–26; "Record of 1904," *IOSL Fiftieth Anniversary Report*, 29; Gertrude Woodruff Marlowe, *A Right Worthy Grand Mission: Maggie Lena Walker and the Quest for Black Economic Empowerment* (Washington, D.C.: Howard University Press, 2003), 92, 104n92; Minutes for August 19, 1903, 3–4; Minutes for October 5, 1903, 7–8; Minutes of December 5, 1903, 9–10, St. Luke Bank Board Minutes; Mary Maclin Smith to Emmett C. Burke, n.d., folder [Letters 1912] R, box Letters, 1912–1913, 1 of 2, CB&T Records.
16. [St. Luke Penny Savings] Bank Ledger, 1–7, box Consolidated Bank Ledger, 1903–1907, CB&T Records.
17. The board limited the number of shares sold to non-IOSL members to five shares, and nonmembers could own no more than one-quarter of the total capital stock. See "Report of Stockholders, 1904," and various stock certificate receipts, folder Letter Box E 1904, box Letter Box 1908 [*sic*]; St. Luke's [*sic*] Penny Savings Stock Certificate Book [1–500]; Minutes for August 19, 1903, 4, CB&T Records; Marlowe, *Right Worthy Grand Mission*, 99; Elsa Barkley Brown, "Womanist Consciousness: Maggie Lena Walker and the Independent Order of Saint Luke," *Signs* 14 (1989): 620.
18. William P. Burrell and D. E. Johnson, *Twenty-Five Years History of the Grand Fountain of the United Order of True Reformers, 1881–1905* (Richmond, Va.: Grand United Order of True Reformers, 1909), 496–97; Minutes for June 18, 1906, 20; Minutes for November 5, 1906, 27, St. Luke Bank Board Minutes; Marlowe, 91–92.
19. The St. Luke Bank opened an account at the clearinghouse bank, and the clearinghouse bank credited and debited the St. Luke Bank's account depending on the checks, deposits, and other financial transactions that the agent bank handled. M. C. Dowling to St. Luke Penny Savings Bank, October 16, 1910, folder [4], box Letter Box, 1906–1911; A. Robyn to Emmett C. Burke, October 23, 1908, folder Letter Box D 1908 J, box

Letter Box, 1908; F. K. Sands to St. Luke Penny Savings Bank, March 8, March 13, 1905, folder Letter Box 2 1906–1907 A, box Letter Box 1, 1906–1907; John Gardin to St. Luke Penny Savings Bank, August 28, 1912, folder Letters 1912 N, box Letters, 1912–1913, 1 of 2; O. Baylor Hill to St. Luke Savings Bank, December 20, 1906, folder Letter Box 1 A–C, box Letter Box 1, 1906–1907, CB&T Records; "Book [Bank?] Assets and Liabilities, July 31, 1917," *IOSL Fiftieth Anniversary Report*, 68.

20. Minutes for June 5, 1907, St. Luke Bank Board Minutes.
21. The bank had cumulative deposits of $87,892.53 between the bank's opening on November 3, 1903, and November 30, 1904. St. Luke Daily Bank Balance Ledger, 1903–1909, 1–14, CB&T Records.
22. First Annual Meeting of St. Luke Penny Savings Bank Stockholders, January 14, 1905, St. Luke Bank Board Minutes, 14–15.
23. In late 1909, the price of stock increased from $10 to $12.50 per share. Minutes for April 6, 1904, 11; June 18, 1906, 21; December 5, 1906, 28; August 5, 1909, St. Luke Bank Board Minutes; "Colored Woman's Appeal," *New York Times*, August 10, 1903; St. Luke Bank Daily Balance Ledger, 1903–1909; Note, October 11, 1910, folder [17], box Letter Box, 1906–1911, CB&T Records.
24. Mollison's father, attorney Willis E. Mollison, founded the Knights of Honor Bank in 1892. The Knights of Honor of the World Savings Bank was the first black bank founded in Mississippi and the second fraternal bank founded in the United States.
25. Minutes for June 18, 1906, St. Luke Bank Board Minutes, 20, CB&T Records.
26. It is not clear when or if Winfree had ever worked at a bank. All quotations Minutes for June 18, 1906, St. Luke Bank Board Minutes, 20–21; "Manchester Letter," *Richmond Planet*, March 7, 1896, 4.
27. C. A. Winfree to the President and Board of Directors of the St. Luke Penny Savings Bank, September 5, 1906, folder Letter Box 1 M–Z, box Letter Box 1, 1906–1907, CB&T Records.
28. C. A. Winfree to the President and Board of Directors, September 5, 1906; Minutes for November 5, 1906, St. Luke Bank Board Minutes, 27. About Dawson's IOSL organizing, see "IO St. Luke Notes—Death Claims Paid," *Richmond Planet*, April 20, 1901, 8.
29. The RWG Council paid three-quarters of the assistant cashier's salary. "Record of 1904," *IOSL Fiftieth Anniversary Report*, 29.
30. Minutes of February 14, 1906, St. Luke Bank Board Minutes, 19–20.
31. Maggie Lena Walker to Emmett C. Burke, n.d., folder [17], box Letter Box, 1906–1911, CB&T Records.
32. True Reformers took in $1,269.28 on its first day, and Mechanics Savings took in $5,000 in one week. It is not known how much customers deposited in Nickel Savings on its first day. Grand Fountain [United Order of True Reformers], *1619–1907: From Slavery to Bankers* (Richmond: Reformers, [1907?]), 17, https://hdl.handle.net/2027/emu.010000576508; James D. Watkinson, "William Washington Browne and the True Reformers of Richmond, Virginia," *Virginia Magazine of History and Biography* 97, no. 3 (July 1989): 375–98, here 387; Alexander, *Race Man*, 155; Marlowe, *Right Worthy Grand Mission*, 129.
33. Harry H. Pace, "The Business of Banking Among Negroes," *Crisis* (February 1927): 184–88, here 187; Nickel Savings Bank ad, *Richmond Planet*, February 10, 1900, 6; Minutes of August 6, 1906, 22; Minutes of August 12, 1906, 23; Minutes of August 20, 1909, 24; Minutes of August 14, 1909, St. Luke Bank Board Minutes; James Ezekiel

Bowen to Emmett C. Burke, October 9, 1906; Josephine D. Chambers to Burke, February 5, February 7, March 11, 1907, folder Letter Box 1 A–C, box Letter Box 1, 1906–1907, CB&T Records.

Some prominent IOSL members in Washington, D.C., such as Calvin Chase, did not believe it advisable to open a branch. See Marlowe, *Right Worthy Grand Mission*, 81, 113.

34. For decades, fraternal orders escaped much of the regulatory scrutiny states directed toward insurance companies, requiring little more than a charter and licensing fees. By the early 1900s, however, the reform impulse gained intense momentum, influenced in no small measure by the Armstrong Committee investigation of financial companies in New York. See New York [State] Legislature and William W. Armstrong, *Joint Hearing of Special Insurance Investigation and Assembly Insurance Committee on Proposed Legislation Arising out of the Insurance Investigation of 1905–1906*, 2 vols. (Albany, 1906); Mark J. Roe, *Strong Managers, Weak Owners: The Political Roots of American Corporate Finance* (Princeton, N.J.: Princeton University Press, 1994), 63–73; Kenneth J. Meier, *The Political Economy of Regulation: The Case of Insurance* (Albany: State University of New York Press, 1988), 57–59.
35. Young's name has been deduced from North Carolina Insurance Commission records. "Record of 1907," *IOSL Fiftieth Anniversary Report*, 32.
36. Neither the *IOSL Fiftieth Anniversary Report* nor Walter Weare mentions the name of the insurance company that met its demise at the hands of the state insurance commission. The most likely candidate is People's Benevolent and Relief Association of Charlotte. Started in 1897, People's quickly became a success with ten thousand policyholders, six full time staff, and nearly one hundred agents. It met some state requirements and dodged others, but by 1906, it could not to comply with multiple requirements from the North Carolina Insurance Commission. The North Carolina Mutual and Provident Association (later North Carolina Mutual Life Insurance Company) purchased People's Benevolent. Walter B. Weare, *Black Business in the New South: A Social History of the North Carolina Mutual Life Insurance Company* (Urbana: University of Illinois Press, 1993), 74–75, 108; State of North Carolina, "An Act for Relief of Peoples Benevolent and Relief Association," in *Private Laws of the State of North Carolina Passed by the General Assembly* [. . .] (Raleigh: E. M. Uzzle, 1903), 28–29; People's Benevolent ad, New York Public Library Digital Collections, http://digitalcollections.nypl.org/items/510d47e4-745c-a3d9-e040-e00a18064a99.
37. Extralegal violence accompanied Representative McMichael's legislation. In Early County, Georgia, whites bombed seven black fraternal halls, claiming that the societies encouraged blacks to hold out for minimum wages and shielded from arrest blacks who had been accused of crimes against whites. The society that helped organize the boycott may have been the Grand United Order of Odd Fellows. Letter to the editor from J. B. B., *Atlanta Independent*, July 27, 1907, 6; Clarence A. Bacote, "Some Aspects of Negro Life in Georgia, 1880–1908," *Journal of Negro History* 43, no. 3 (1958): 186–213, here 199–202; "E. H. McMichael," *Marion County (Georgia) Patriot*, July 26, 1907, 4.
38. "Record of 1907," *IOSL Fiftieth Anniversary Report*, 32, emphasis added.
39. "Record of 1907."
40. Advocates imagined democratic capitalism as a system that promoted both economic and political liberty and social innovation through free enterprise. Legal challenges to

the race-based discriminatory practices of insurance companies emerged in the 1880s. Insurance companies avoided sanction through extralegal practices, such as forbidding agents from writing policies for blacks, withdrawing their business from states, and adopting other practices to undercut the legal scrutiny. See Mary L. Heen, "Ending Jim Crow Life Insurance Rates," *Northwestern Journal of Law and Social Policy* 4, no. 360 (Fall 2009): 360–99, here 363, http://scholarlycommons.law.northwestern.edu/njlsp/vol4/iss2/3.

41. *Report of the Proceedings and Debates of the Constitutional Convention of the Commonwealth of Virginia, 1901–1902*, vol. 2 (Richmond: Hermitage, 1906), quote on 2141, 2160–61.
42. Glass also hoped to rid the rolls of poor and working-class whites; he added, "And next to this achievement [i.e., removing black voters] in vital consequence will be the inability of unworthy men of our own race . . . to cheat their way into prominence." The Glass Plan, which included an understanding clause, poll taxes, and other voter suppression methods, became part of Virginia's constitution. In 1902, Virginia legislators appointed Glass, publisher and owner of two newspapers in Lynchburg, to the state's Banking and Currency Committee. "[Speech of Delegate Carter Glass on] Elective Franchise," April 4, 1902, in *Report of the Proceedings*, 3075–77, here 3076. On Glass, see Ronald L. Heinemann, "Carter Glass (1858–1946)," Encyclopedia Virginia, Virginia Foundation for the Humanities, August 20, 2015, http://www.encyclopediavirginia.org/Glass_Carter_1858-1946, accessed January 15, 2017.
43. The new provisions also removed 50 percent of the white electorate. Jane Elizabeth Dailey, *Before Jim Crow: The Politics of Race in Postemancipation Virginia* (Chapel Hill: University of North Carolina Press, 2000), 162–66; Lewis Randolph and Gayle T. Tate, *Rights for a Season: The Politics of Race, Class and Gender in Richmond, Virginia* (Knoxville: University of Tennessee Press, 2003), 105–8. Also see Allan G. Gruchy, *Supervision and Control of Virginia State Banks* (New York: Appleton-Century, 1937).
44. "To Make Test Case: Negroes Threaten to Agitate 'Till the Very Foundation of the Republic Trembles,'" *Rockingham Register* (Harrisonburg, Va.), February 3, 1905, 2.
45. "To Make Test Case"; Randolph and Tate, *Rights for a Season*, 106; Dailey, *Before Jim Crow*, 165.
46. August Meier and Elliott Rudwick, "Negro Boycotts of Segregated Streetcars in Virginia, 1904–1907," *Virginia Magazine of History and Biography* 81, no. 4 (October 1973): 479–87, here 479–81; Blair L. M. Kelley, *Right to Ride: Streetcar Boycotts and African American Citizenship in the Era of "Plessy v Ferguson"* (Chapel Hill: University of North Carolina Press, 2010), 122–25, 142–47; Alexander, *Race Man*, 133–42.
47. John Mitchell, "The Separate Cars and the Negro," *Richmond Planet*, October 27, 1900, 4, quoted in Kelley, *A Right to Ride*, 133.
48. Marlowe, *Right Worthy Grand Mission*, 94.
49. Marlowe, 93–94; John H. Burrows, *The Necessity of Myth: A History of the National Negro Business League, 1900–45* (Auburn, Ala.: Hickory Hill, 1988), 78; "Record of 1904," *IOSL Fiftieth Anniversary Report*, 29.
50. "New Negro Enterprise: Richmond Colored Women Secure Charter for a Big Store," *Washington Post*, March 12, 1905, 98; Marlowe, 96–97, 111–15.
51. Minutes of May 8, 1905, St. Luke Bank Board Minutes, 17.
52. By late summer 1905, the bank's previous landlord, John Mitchell Jr., founder and president of the Mechanics Savings Bank, purchased two properties near the emporium

location—not on Broad Street but a block away. United Aid and Insurance Company, a black-owned company, purchased another nearby parcel and established its headquarters there. The Negro Development Corporation also leased space near the *Planet* office. Minutes of August 1, 1905, St. Luke Bank Board Minutes, 18–19; "Old Dominion Capital Comments: Business Organizations Buying Select Properties [. . .]," *New York Age*, July 27, 1905, 8; Negro Development Corporation shown on map of community, "Map 4. Maggie Lena Walker's Neighborhood, 1905–1915," in Elsa Barkley Brown, "Uncle Ned's Children: Negotiating Community and Freedom in Postemancipation Richmond, Virginia," (PhD diss., Kent State University, 1994), 525.

53. Shoe wholesaler Wingo, Ellett, and Crump sued the emporium for $960.47 in late September 1905. See undated clipping "Creditors Are After St. Luke's Emporium," *Richmond News Leader*, n.d., enclosed in George St. Julian Stephens to Maggie Lena Walker, item A-0530, folder 21, box 3, Walker Papers, NPS Walker House; Marlowe, *Right Worthy Grand Mission*, 98–99.

54. On black women and black public culture, see Alessandra Lorini, *Rituals of Race: American Public Culture and the Search for Racial Democracy* (Charlottesville: University Virginia Press, 1999); Martha S. Jones, *All Bound Up Together: The Woman Question in African American Public Culture, 1830–1900* (Chapel Hill: University of North Carolina Press, 2007).

55. Similarly, Davarian Baldwin's the concept of "marketplace intellectual life" represents the interface between cultural practices, cultural production, and the mass consumer marketplace. Indeed, Baldwin stresses that contestations in the marketplace led blacks to see "race-based cooperative and capitalist strategies as possible solutions toward autonomy and self control." Baldwin, *Chicago's New Negroes: Modernity, the Great Migration, and Black Urban Life* (Chapel Hill: University of North Carolina Press, 2007), 5–7, 10–13, 18, here 7. In addition, Erin Chapman's discussion of the "sex-race marketplace" underscores the commodification of black women's bodies, images, and style. Linked with Michele Mitchell's notion of a "social history of thought," these concepts influence my ideas about the intersections of gender, race, and class with knowledge production in market contexts. Erin Chapman, *Prove It on Me: New Negroes, Sex, and Popular Culture in the 1920s* (New York: Oxford University Press, 2012); Michelle Mitchell, *Righteous Propagation: African Americans and the Politics of Racial Destiny After Reconstruction* (Chapel Hill: University of North Carolina Press, 2004), 13–14. Also see James R. Grossman, *Land of Hope: Chicago, Black Southerners, and the Great Migration* (Chicago: University of Chicago Press, 1989), 130–60, 261–62.

On the politics of race and consumption, see Grace Elizabeth Hale, "'For Colored' and 'For White': Segregating Consumption in the South," in Dailey, Gilmore, and Simon, *Jumpin' Jim Crow*, 162–82; Lizabeth Cohen, *A Consumers' Republic: The Politics of Mass Consumption in Postwar America* (New York: Alfred A. Knopf, 2003); Kate Dossett, "Luxuriant Growth: The Walkers and Black Economic Nationalism," in *Bridging Race Divides: Black Nationalism, Feminism, and Integration in the United States, 1896–1935* (Gainesville: University Press of Florida, 2008), 107–49; LaShawn Harris, *Sex Workers, Psychics, and Numbers Runners: Black Women in New York City's Underground Economy* (Urbana: University of Illinois Press, 2016).

56. Though largely critical of the affected intimacy, exclusivity, and flattened hierarchies of secret groups, Jürgen Habermas demonstrates the ways these groups acted as institutional forms and, although private, were nevertheless part of and constitutive of the

public sphere. Habermas, *The Structural Transformation of the Public Sphere: An Inquiry into a Category of Bourgeois Society*, trans. Thomas Burger (Cambridge: Massachusetts Institute of Technology Press, 1989), esp. "Institutions of the Public Sphere," 31–43; Baldwin, *Chicago's New Negroes*, 5–7; Jessica R. Cattelino, "Casino Roots: The Cultural Production of Twentieth-Century Seminole Economic Development," in *Native Pathways: American Indian Culture and Economic Development in the Twentieth Century*, ed. Brian Hosmer and Colleen O Neill, (Boulder: University Press of Colorado, 2004), 81.

57. Calamity quote in Minutes of August 1, 1905, 20; Minutes of February 14, 1906, 19, St. Luke Bank Board Minutes.
58. A *New York Times* article reports that Dixon said, "The colored women and girls in the South had not yet been civilized enough to know the meaning of virtue." Dixon wrote *The Clansmen* and later collaborated on the screenplay for *Birth of a Nation*, the 1915 film based on his novel. Walker does not mention Dixon by name or restate what Dixon said, but he is the most likely source of the comments that upset her and other black women. "Thomas Dixon's 'Way Out,'" *Index of Current Literature*, ed. Edward J. Wheeler, 60 (January–June 1906): 359–60, quote on 360; "Hot Talk in Church After Dixon Spoke," *New York Times*, January 29, 1906.
59. "Benaiah's Honor," folder 24, box 3, 3, Walker Papers, NPS Walker House.
60. "Benaiah's Honor," 4.
61. "Benaiah's Honor," 4–5.
62. "Benaiah's Honor," 6.
63. "Benaiah's Honor," 9, emphasis in original.
64. "Benaiah's Honor," 19–20.
65. See letters from Matron Sadie Moulton, Robert Moulton Circle, to Maggie Lena Walker, undated, item A-0534; M. E. Wright, Shady Grove Circle No. 389, to Walker, April 7, 1908, Item A-0532; W. L. White to Walker, April 19, 1908, item A-0529; M[arietta]. L. Chiles and Kate Thomas, Heliotrope Council No. 160, March 14, 1908, item A-0526, folder 21, box 3, Walker Papers, NPS Walker House.
66. See "Letter and Circular from the Insurance Commissioner of the State of Virginia," November 27, 1909, item A-1049, Walker Papers, NPS Walker House; David T. Beito, *From Mutual Aid to the Welfare State: Fraternal Societies and Social Services, 1890–1967* (Chapel Hill: University of North Carolina Press, 2000), 211.
67. "Maggie Walker Fined in Court," *Richmond News-Leader*, November 18, 1909, clipping in Maggie L. Walker (hereafter MLW File), Vertical Files, Valentine Museum and Richmond History Center, Richmond, Va. (hereafter Valentine).
68. "Maggie Walker Fined in Court"; "Warrants for Maggie Walker: Colored Woman Charged with Violating Insurance Regulations of the State," *Richmond News-Leader*, [November 1909,] clipping in MLW File, Valentine.
69. A series of high-profile and embarrassing bank failures in 1908 forced legislators to consider strengthening state oversight of the state's banks. For example, the failure of the Bank of Mecklenburg in 1908 led to a widely publicized trial that resulted in criminal charges and jail time. "Big Business in Va. Banks," *Richmond Times Dispatch*, July 23, 1911, 12. On links between professionalism, class, and social power, see Terence C. Halliday, "Professions, Class and Capitalism," *European Journal of Sociology / Archives Européennes De Sociologie / Europäisches Archiv Für Soziologie* 24, no. 2 (1983): 321–46. On banking division actions, Chief Examiner to Virginia Safe Deposit and Trust

Corp., July 25, 1910; Chief Examiner to Citizens Bank, July 25, 1910; Chief Examiner to Cheiton Banking, July 25, 1910; Chief Examiner to Commercial Bank, July 29, 1910; Chief Examiner to Farmers and Merchants Bank, August 6, 1910; Chief Examiner to Hanover Bank, September 29, 1910, Virginia State Corporation Commission, Record Group 112, vol. July–Aug.–Sept. 1910, Letters of the Virginia Bureau of Banking, 1910–1918, State Records Center, hereafter SCC Banking Bureau Letters.

70. Barksdale gave the bank thirty days to institute a list of changes, including collecting more than $10,000 in past-due loans, requiring additional payments by stockholders to cover inflated and erroneous ledger items, and collecting another $5,000 to cover a failing stock. Chief Examiner to State Bank of Columbia, July 25, September 29, 1910, vol. July–Aug.–Sept. 1910, SCC Banking Bureau Letters.

71. Chief Examiner to Farmers Bank of Butterworth, July 25, 1910; Chief Examiner to Farmers and Merchants State Bank, July 25, August 6, 1910, Chief Examiner to Bank of Amherst, July 25, 1910; Chief Examiner to Meherrin Valley Bank, July 25, 1910; Chief Examiner to Peoples Savings Bank and Trust, July 25, 1910; Chief Examiner to Peoples Bank, July 25, August 6, 1910; Chief Examiner to Bank of Bristol, July 26, August 10, 1910; Chief Examiner to Bank of Appomattox, August 3, 1910; Chief Examiner to First State Bank, September 16, 1910; Chief Examiner to Hanover Bank, September 29, 1910, vol. July–Aug.–Sept. 1910, SCC Banking Bureau Letters.

72. Chief Examiner to Bank of Capron, August 6, 1910; Chief Examiner to N. M. Horton, August 3, August 10, 1910; Chief Examiner to Chesterfield County Bank, August 22, 1910; Chief Examiner to Messrs. Leedy & Bery, September 28, 1910; Division Clerk to R. T. Wilson, July 26, 1910, vol. July–Aug.–Sept. 1910, SCC Banking Bureau Letters.

73. Chief Examiner to Bank of Elba, December 14, 1910, vol. Oct.–Sept. [*sic*] 1910, SCC Banking Bureau Letters.

74. Chief Examiner to L. E. Mumford Banking, November 23, 1910, vol. Oct.–Sept. [*sic*] 1910, SCC Banking Bureau Letters; M. E. Bristow, "Banking on the Eastern Shore," *Richchap*, December [Year?], reprinted in University of Virginia, "The Countryside Transformed: The Railroad and the Eastern Shore of Virginia 1870–1935," Southern Spaces, http://eshore.iath.virginia.edu/node/1884.

75. Chief Examiner to Bank of Elba; Chief Examiner to Mumford; Chief Examiner to Dickenson County Bank, August 6, 1910; Chief Examiner to Messrs. Henry J. Tynan & Co., August 29, 1910, vol. July–Aug.–Sept. 1910, SCC Banking Bureau Letters.

76. Chief Examiner to Messrs. Henry J. Tynan, August 24, 29, 1910, vol. July–Aug.–Sept. 1910, SCC Banking Bureau Letters.

77. Quote in Joseph Button, "Report [of the Insurance Committee], May 1, 1911," in *Fifth Annual Report of the Commissioner of Insurance of Virginia* . . .[1910–11], by Virginia Bureau of Insurance (Richmond: Davis Bottom, 1911), iii–xiii, here xii; special, early attention requested in Marlowe, *Right Worthy Grand Mission*, 117.

78. Publicly, the United Order of True Reformers appeared indomitable. In addition to its pioneering bank and insurance company, it owned a hotel, a newspaper, a regalia business, a building and loan association, a general store, an old folks' home, and an extensive portfolio of improved and unimproved property. Unfortunately, the society practiced poor accounting and record keeping. It suffered low profits due to high death rates and inadequate medical examinations on the insurance side and overexpansion and mismanagement on the banking side. Officers of the bank increased their salaries

at will, took out mortgages without the proper vetting, inflated the appraised value of Reformers' property holdings, and embezzled money. When the True Reformers failed, their $451,000 in assets represented 62 percent of the combined assets of all the black banks in Richmond. Downfall quote in Wendell P. Dabney, *Maggie L. Walker and the I. O. of Saint Luke: The Woman and Her Work* (Cincinnati: Dabney, 1927), 39; Alexander, *Race Man*, 177; Fleming, "A History of Consolidated Bank and Trust Company," 16, 34; David M. Fahey, ed., *The Black Lodge in White America: "True Reformer" Browne and His Economic Strategy* (Dayton, Oh.: Wright State University Press, 1994), 32–37; Watkinson, "William Washington Browne," 395–96; "The True Reformers," *Washington (D.C.) Bee*, November 5, 1910, 4.

79. A 1910 article lists only twelve banks, and therefore the assets of some of the banks are missing from these figures. "Negro Banks of Virginia," *New York Age*, January 27, 1910, 1. The total resources of the 247 banks in Virginia as of November 1910 was $68.7 million. See Virginia State Corporation Commission, "Summary," *Statements Showing the Condition of the Incorporated State Banks* [. . .], *Year Ending December 31, 1910* (Richmond: Davis Bottom, 1911), 114.

80. The Imperial Grand United Order of Abraham's worthy secretary reported that the bank had $10,548 in paid-in capital, but examiners discovered that only $1,048 was actually accounted for. Of that amount, all of it had been spent on fixtures, leaving the bank with a $300 deficit. The examiner gave the bank ten days to collect in cash the worthy secretary's $9,500 note. Three weeks later, Barksdale made good on his threat and ordered the bank closed. Chief Examiner to People's Southern One Cent Savings Bank, August 4, 1910; Richard C. Ker [*sic*] to Chief Examiner, August 24, 1910, vol. July–Aug.–Sept. 1910, SCC Banking Bureau Letters.

81. Chief Examiner to A[ndrew] W[illiam] E[rnest] Bassette, October 4, 1910, vol. Oct.–Sept. 1910, SCC Banking Bureau Letters. Compare the harsher tone of Bassette letter to those written to other banks that had more serious conditions: Chief Examiner to Bank of Holland, December 20, 1910; Chief Examiner to Bank of Jarretts, November 25, 1910; Chief Examiner to Powell's Valley Bank, October 21, 1910, vol. Oct.–Sept. 1910, SCC Banking Bureau Letters. Powell's Valley Bank's vice president and attorney challenged the examiners' assessments in Chief Examiner to Robert L. Pennington, Esq., November 14, 1910, vol. Oct.–Sept. [*sic*] 1910, SCC Banking Bureau Letters.

82. The black-owned banks that were placed in receivership in the last half of 1910 were Galilean Fishermen's Savings, Gideon Savings, Nickel Savings, and True Reformers Savings. The liquidated bank was Southern One Cent Savings, and the bank that ceased operations was Sussex-Surrey-Southampton Savings Bank–American Home and Missionary Banking Association. The fraternal banks (Knights of Gideon, Galilean Fishermen, and True Reformers) housed the funds of their orders. The Colored Knights of Pythias was the major depositor in Nickel Savings Bank, and the Order of Abraham held its funds in the People's Southern One Cent. Of the four black banks in Richmond, only the Mechanics Savings and the St. Luke Penny Savings remained open. "Case 255," 35; "Case 259," 37–38; "Report of the Chief Bank Examiner," 60–62, here 61, in *Virginia State Corporation Commission, Eighth Annual Report for Year Ending December, 1910* [. . .] (Richmond: Davis Bottom, 1910); Chief Examiner to Lawrence O. Murray, October 21, 1910, vol. Oct.–Sept. [*sic*] 1910, SCC Banking Bureau Letters.

83. See Chief Examiner to Sons and Daughters of Peace Penny, Nickel, and Dime Savings Bank, August 3, 1910; Chief Examiner to Mechanics Savings Bank, August 3, 29, 1910; Chief Examiner to St. Luke Penny Savings Bank, August 3, 1910; Chief Examiner to Crown Savings Bank, August 4, 1910; Chief Examiner to Brown Savings and Banking Company, August 4, 1910; Chief Examiner to Galilean Fisherman's Bank, September 10, 1910, vol. July–Aug.–Sept. 1910, SCC Banking Bureau Letters.
84. Bank No. 215, Examiner's Report of the Condition of Peoples Dime Savings Bank and Trust Association, Staunton, Va., Examined September 10, 1910, in Examiner's Reports, Banking Division, SCC nos. 209 to 233, First Year 1910–1911, vol. 8, Virginia State Corporation Commission record group 112, State Records Center, hereafter SCC Examiner's Reports.
85. *Hill's Directory, Staunton, Va., 1922–23* (Staunton, Va.: Hill Directory Co., [1923]); 1910 U.S. Census, Household of Cha[rle]s F. Points, Augusta 2-WD Staunton, series T624, roll 1650, p. 89; 1900 U.S. Census, Household of Thomas [E.] Jackson, Augusta 2-WD Staunton, series T623, roll 1740, p. 65.
86. On Walker's visits to the Women's Benefit Association (formerly Ladies of the Maccabees), see transcript of interviews with Mr. Anthony J. Binga, Mrs. Mamie Evelyn Walker Crawford, Mrs. Bernetta Young Plummer, Dr. Maggie Laura Walker, and Mr. Armstead Walker, February–October, 1981, National Park Service and Diann L. Jacox, Maggie L. Walker Oral History Project, vol. 2 (October 1986), NPS Walker House; Maggie Lena Walker Diary, 1918–1922, September 11, 1919, NPS Walker House. On the WBA, see Keith L. Yates, *An Enduring Heritage: The First One Hundred Years of North American Benefit Association (Formerly Woman's Benefit Association)* (Port Huron, Mich.: North American Benefit Association, 1992).
87. Division Clerk to Peoples Dime Savings, August 12, 1910. Also see Chief Examiner to Peoples Dime Savings Bank and Trust Association, July 15, 1910; Chief Examiner to Peoples Dime Savings, September 19, 1910, vol. July–Aug.–Sept. 1910, SCC Banking Bureau Letters.
88. On grading and color coding neighborhoods under the Home Owner's Loan Corporation in the 1930s, see Amy E. Hillier, "Redlining and the Home Owners' Loan Corporation," *Journal of Urban History* 29, no. 4 (May 2003): 394–420; N. D. B. Connolly, *A World More Concrete: Real Estate and the Remaking of Jim Crow South Florida* (Chicago: University of Chicago, 2014); actual maps, appraisers comments, and contemporary poverty data for Richmond at University of Richmond, Redlining Richmond, http://dsl.richmond.edu/holc/pages/home, accessed May 22, 2017.

   Real estate professionals, city planners, and civic leaders established practices that inured racial hierarchies to space well before the 1930s. See, for example, Andrew Wiese, *Places of Their Own: African American Suburbanization in the Twentieth Century* (Chicago: University of Chicago Press, 2004), 17–31, 40–41; David M. P. Freund, *Colored Property: State Policy and White Racial Politics in Suburban America* (Chicago: University of Chicago Press, 2007), esp. 1–98; Paige Glotzer, "Exclusion in Arcadia: How Suburban Developers Circulated Ideas about Discrimination, 1890–1950," *Journal of Urban History* 41, no. 3 (2015): 479–94.

   Segregated enclaves emerged as vibrant communities anchored by their Black Wall Streets, businesses and community institutions created by and catering to the needs of black communities. John Sibley Butler and Kenneth L. Wilson, *Entrepreneurial*

Enclaves in the African American Experience (Washington, D.C.: Neighborhood Policy Institute Publication Series, 1990).

89. Chief Examiner to Nickel Savings Bank, August 3, 1910, vol. July–Aug.–Sept. 1910, SCC Banking Bureau Letters.
90. Chief Examiner to St. Luke Penny Savings Bank, November 11, 1910, vol. Nov.–Dec. 1910, SCC Banking Bureau Letters.
91. The other remaining black bank in Richmond, the Mechanics Savings Bank, also built and opened a new bank building in 1911 at the corner of Clay and Third Streets. Alexander, *Race Man*, 170–71.
92. "Record of 1909," *IOSL Fiftieth Anniversary Report*, 35.
93. Cattelino, "Casino Roots," 68, 81.

4. RITUALS OF RISK AND RESPECTABILITY: GENDERED ECONOMIC PRACTICES, CREDIT, AND DEBT TO WORLD WAR I

1. A. J. Evans to Emmett C. Burke, December 4, 1910, emphasis in original, folder [5], box Letter Box, 1906–1911, Consolidated Bank and Trust Records, c. 1903–1993, hereafter CB&T Records, Special Collections, L. Douglas Wilder Library and Learning Resource Center, Virginia Union University; 1910 U.S. Census, William F. Evans household, Bristol County, Attleborough, sheet no. 26A, series T624, roll 574, p. 177.
2. Jessica R. Cattelino, "Casino Roots: The Cultural Production of Twentieth-Century Seminole Economic Development," in *Native Pathways: American Indian Culture and Economic Development in the Twentieth Century*, ed. Brian Hosmer and Colleen O Neill (Boulder: University Press of Colorado, 2004), 70–71, quote on 70.
3. Similarly, Louis Hyman highlights how small profits on credit cards quickly emerged as a primary profit center for financial institutions in the 1980s. The notion that small fees coupled with securitization and other financial innovations helped reorient financiers' attention from traditional investment reinforces how the St. Luke Bank's practices made financial sense. Louis Hyman, *Debtor Nation: The History of America in Red Ink* (Princeton, N.J.: Princeton University Press, 2011), esp. chap. 7, "Securing Debt in an Insecure World: Credit Cards and Capital Markets," 220–80. Quote from Nicholas Osborne, "Little Capitalists: The Social Economy of Saving in the United States, 1816–1914" (PhD diss., Columbia University, 2014), 184.
4. A. H. Ham, "Remedial Loans as a Factor in Family Rehabilitation," in *Proceedings of the National Federation of Remedial Loan Associations, Boston, Mass., June 12–13, 1911* (Baltimore, Md.: Lucas Brothers, 1912), 3–11, here 6. Also see the Russell Sage Foundation–sponsored investigations, primarily in New York City in 1908, including C. W. Wassam, *The Salary Loan Business in New York City* (New York: Russell Sage Foundation, 1908); Arthur H. Ham, *The Chattel Loan Business* [. . .] (New York: Charity Organization Society of New York, 1908).
5. An early twentieth-century social scientist suggested that remedial loan associations would have a positive impact in black communities. See John T. Emlen, "The Movement for the Betterment of the Negro in Philadelphia," *American Academy of Political and Social Science* 49 (September 1913): 81–92, here 91–92.

   Philanthropic loan societies ranked highest in reformers' preference as sources of credit and loans for the poor and working classes, followed by savings and loan associations, and then profit-minded capitalists as a last resort. Lenders in the last category made a profit but charged reasonable rates of interest. Unlike loan sharks, they openly advertised their rates and terms, observed legislation, and submitted themselves to the public scrutiny of regulators and auditors. See *Proceedings of the National Federation of Remedial Loan Associations.*

6. Michael Edward Easterly, "Your Job Is Your Credit: Creating a Market for Loans to Salaried Employees in New York City, 1885–1920" (PhD diss., University of California, Los Angeles, 2008), 9.
7. Technically, the St. Luke Bank was a member of the Virginia Bankers Association (VBA). James P. Branch of the National Merchants Bank extended an invitation to Walker to join the VBA. The St. Luke Bank does not show up in any of the extant records of the VBA proceedings either as a member bank or as a participant in its meetings. W. M. Habliston, "Annual Address of the President," *Proceedings of the Twelfth Annual Convention of the Virginia Bankers Association* [ ], *June 15–17, 1905* (Richmond: Everett Waddey, 1905), 17–21, here 19–20.
8. Beverly Lemire, "Petty Pawns and Informal Lending: Gender and the Transformation of Small-Scale Credit in England, Circa 1600–1800," in *From Family Firms to Corporate Capitalism: Essays in Business and Industrial History in Honour of Peter Mathias*, ed. Peter Mathias, Kristine Bruland, and Patrick Karl O'Brien (Oxford: Clarendon, 1998), 112–38, here 113.
9. Lemire, 113–19, 121–22; Melanie Tebbutt, *Making Ends Meet: Pawnbroking and Working-Class Credit* (Leicester, U.K.: Leicester University Press; New York: St. Martin's, 1983), 1, 11, 22, 35; Marie Eileen Francois, *A Culture of Everyday Credit: Housekeeping, Pawnbroking, and Governance in Mexico City, 1750–1920* (Lincoln: University of Nebraska Press, 2006), 8–9, 12, 44–45.
10. Tebbutt also makes the point that continued investment in burial insurance rather than life insurance suggests that working-class people valued a material affirmation for their saving (16–17, quote on 16). Consider also Francois, who writes, "Pawning also suggests that goods served as savings accounts or investments managed by housekeepers across the economic and ethnic spectrum" (46).
11. W. E. B. Du Bois, *The Philadelphia Negro: A Social Study* (Philadelphia: University of Philadelphia Press, 1899), 192.
12. On stereotypes of black consumers, see Ted Ownby, *American Dreams in Mississippi: Consumers, Poverty and Culture, 1830–1998* (Chapel Hill: University of North Carolina, 1998), esp. chap. 3, "You Don't Want Nothing: Goods, Plantation Labor, and the Meanings of Freedom, 1865–1920s," 90–97. For humorous news stories, see "A Sneak Thief's Goose," *Afro-American* (Baltimore, Md.), September 14, 1901, 4; "Real Charity," *Chicago Defender*, November 18, 1911, 2. On more serious warnings and investigations, see "Loan Sharks," *Afro-American* (Baltimore, Md.), December 14, 1907, 4.
13. "Conference Meeting for [Colored Charity Workers]," *Afro-American* (Baltimore, Md.), December 14, 1907, 8; "Washington YMCA After Loan Sharks," *Afro-American* (Baltimore, Md.), February 18, 1911, 1; "War Against Loan Sharks," *Chicago Defender*, February 3, 1912, 8; "How a Murder Suspect Is [. . .]," *Richmond Planet*, September 21, 1918, 7.
14. Robert Cornelius Raby, *The Regulation of Pawnbroking* (New York: Russell Sage Foundation, 1924), 17, 20, 60; Lemire, "Petty Pawns," 127–28; Tebbutt, *Making Ends Meet*, 11; Francois, *A Culture of Everyday Credit*, 45–46, 258–60; Wendy A. Woloson, *In Hock: Pawning in America from Independence Through the Great Depression* (Chicago: University of Chicago Press, 2009), 3, 87, 92–93.

15. "Richmond Grand Jury Makes Startling Disclosures," *Richmond Planet*, June 29, 1918, 2; "Public Believes Fay Will Escape," *Richmond Planet*, April 16, 1910, 2; Daniel Bluestone, "Charlottesville's Landscape of Prostitution, 1880–1950," *Buildings and Landscapes: Journal of the Vernacular Architecture Forum* 22, no. 2 (Fall 2015): 36–61, here 52; "A Brutal Tragedy," *Richmond Planet*, April 25, 1896, 1.
16. Joseph B. Earnest Jr., *The Religious Development of the Negro in Virginia* (Charlottesville, Va.: Michie, 1914), 164.
17. "[The Post Office Will Apply the Lottery Law]," *Richmond Planet*, December 11, 1897, 2.
18. The scholarship begs a full-length journal article or monograph on extralegal policy, lotteries, and gambling in the early to mid-twentieth-century South. On blacks and antebellum numbers games, see Shane White, Stephen Garton, and Stephen Robertson, *Playing the Numbers: Gambling in Harlem Between the Wars* (Cambridge, Mass.: Harvard University Press, 2010), 33–42. On women in the informal economy, see Victoria Wolcott, "Mediums, Messages, and Lucky Numbers: African-American Female Spiritualists and Numbers Runners in Inter-War Detroit," in *The Geography of Identity*, ed. Patricia Yeager (Ann Arbor: University of Michigan Press, 1996), 273–306; LaShawn Harris, *Sex Workers, Psychics, and Numbers Runners: Black Women in New York City's Underground Economy* (Urbana: University of Illinois Press, 2016).
19. When Dye died in 1918, newspapers reported that she had $12,000 in cash stashed in various places in her home and total assets of $100,000 (about $199,000 and $1.7 million respectively in 2017 dollars). Ad, "Fortune Teller," *Richmond Planet*, December 27, 1890, 1; ad, "[Madame Mace]," *Richmond Planet*, December 3, 1898, 2; ad, "[Madam Eldon]," *Richmond Planet*, August 21, 1909, 8. On Caroline Dye, see Robert D. Craig, "'Aunt Caroline' Dye (1843?–1918)," Encyclopedia of Arkansas History and Culture, last updated September 16, 2014, http://www.encyclopediaofarkansas.net/encyclopedia/entry-detail.aspx?entryID=14; James Logan Morgan, "She Put Newport on the Map: A Biography of Aunt Caroline Dye," *Stream of History* 5, no. 1 (January 1967): 17–18, 28–32, Jackson County Digital History Collection, http://cdm15320.contentdm.oclc.org/cdm/ref/collection/p15320coll1/id/54; "Old Negro Seer Had Much Money on Premises," (Little Rock) *Arkansas Democrat*, October 2, 1918, 4.
20. Ivan Light, "Numbers Gambling Among Blacks: A Financial Institution," *American Sociological Review* 42, no. 6 (December 1977): 892–904, here 896.
21. Gambling plays an important role in African American history. Enslaved and free blacks participated in sports and games on which others placed bets. The enslaved and free also played legal antebellum lotteries. Many leaned on the lotteries for extra income or to purchase their own freedom and the freedom of their loved ones. Enslaved people were sometimes the prizes in lotteries. Extralegal numbers games created by Caribbean and Afro-Latin immigrants evolved into modern state lotteries. Light, 896–98. Also see D. Wiggins, "Good Times on the Old Plantation: Popular Recreations of the Black Slave in Antebellum South, 1810–1860," *Journal of Sport History* 4, no. 3 (Fall 1977): 260–84, here 272–74; Jeff Forret, *Race Relations at the Margins: Slaves and Poor Whites in the Antebellum Southern Countryside* (Baton Rouge: Louisiana State University Press, 2006), 56–62; Neal E. Millikan, *Lotteries in Colonial America* (New York: Routledge, 201), 27–29.

    The lines between gambling, speculation, and insurance is an arbitrary and historically contingent one. Claude-Olivier Doron, "The Experience of 'Risk': Genealogy and Transformations," in *Routledge Handbook of Risk Studies*, ed. Adam Burgess, Alberto Alemanno, and Jens Zinn (Abingdon: Routledge, Taylor & Francis, 2016), 17–26; Frank Knight, *Risk, Uncertainty, and Profit* (1921; reprint, Mineola, N.Y.: Dover, 2006), 40–46; Lorraine J. Daston, "The Domestication of Risk: Mathematical Probability and Insurance 1650–1830," in *The Probabilistic Revolution*, vol. 1, *Ideas in History*, ed. Lorenz Krüger, Lorraine Daston, and Michael Heidelberger (Cambridge: Massachusetts Institute of Technology Press, 1987), 237–60.

Numbers runners were often compared to insurance agents collecting small weekly sums from clients. Shirley Stewart, *The World of Stephanie St. Clair. An Entrepreneur, Race Woman and Outlaw in Early Twentieth Century Harlem* (New York: Peter Lang, 2014), 83.

22. See Jonathan Levy, *Freaks of Fortune: The Emerging World of Capitalism and Risk in America* (Cambridge, Mass.: Harvard University Press, 2012), esp. chap. 1, "The Failure of the Freedman's Bank," 104–49; Linda English, "Recording Race: General Stores and Race in the Late Nineteenth-Century Southwest," *Southwestern Historical Quarterly* 110, no. 2 (October 2006): 192–217, esp. 194–98, 207–9; Douglas R. Egerton, "Slaves to the Marketplace: Economic Liberty and Black Rebelliousness in the Atlantic World," *Journal of the Early Republic* 26, no. 4 (Winter 2006): 617–39; Ownby, *American Dreams in Mississippi*, esp. 62–81; Dew, *Bond of Iron*, part 2, "Slaves," 171–239, here 171–72, 183–84; Juliet E. K. Walker, *The History of Black Business In America: Capitalism, Race, Entrepreneurship* (Chapel Hill: University of North Carolina Press, 2009), 109–22, 170–71; Marcus Anthony Allen, "Cautiously Capitalistic: Black Economic Agency at the Savings Bank of Baltimore, 1850–1900" (PhD diss., Morgan State University, 2013).
23. Easterly, "Your Job Is Your Credit," 11–12, 19–20.
24. Dan Bouk, *How Our Days Became Numbered: Risk and the Rise of the Statistical Individual* (Chicago: Chicago University Press, 2015); Jacqueline Agesa, Richard Agesa, and Woodrow Berry, "A History of Racial Exploitation in Life Insurance," *Franklin Business and Law Journal* no. 3 (September 2011): 1–21; Benjamin Alan Wiggins, "Managing Risk, Managing Race: Racialized Actuarial Science in the United States" (PhD diss., University of Minnesota, 2013); Paul Lawrie, "'To Make the Negro Anew': The African American Worker in the Progressive Imagination 1896–1928" (PhD diss., University of Toronto, 2011); Mary L. Heen, "Ending Jim Crow Life Insurance Rates," *Northwestern Journal of Law and Social Policy* 4, no. 360 (Fall 2009): 360–99, http://scholarlycommons.law.northwestern.edu/njlsp/vol4/iss2/3.
25. Bouk, 40, 40n29. On gender and risk in banking, insurance, and credit, see William C. Jordan, *Women and Credit in Pre-Industrial and Developing Societies* (Philadelphia: University of Pennsylvania Press, 1993); Anne Laurence, Josephine Maltby, and Janette Rutterford, eds., *Women and Their Money, 1700–1950: Essays on Women and Finance* (London: Routledge, 2009); Sharon Ann Murphy, *Investing in Life: Insurance in Antebellum America* (Baltimore, Md.: Johns Hopkins University Press, 2010), 39–45, 127–28; Lindsey Keiter, "Uniting Interests: The Economic Functions of Marriage in America, 1750–1860" (PhD diss., College of William and Mary, 2015); Sara Damiano, "Gender, Law, and the Culture of Credit in New England, 1730–1790" (PhD diss., Johns Hopkins University, 2015).
26. Cattelino, "Casino Roots," 68; David La Vere, "Minding Their Own Business: The Kiowa-Comanche-Apache Business Committee of the Early 1900s," in *Native*

Pathways: American Indian Culture and Economic Development in the Twentieth Century, ed. Brian Hosmer and Colleen O Neill (Boulder: University Press of Colorado, 2004), 52–65, here 53, 57; Jeffrey P. Shepherd, "Land, Labor, and Leadership: The Political Economy of Hualapai Community Building, 1910–1940," in Hosmer and O Neill, *Native Pathways*, 209–37, here 216–17.

27. Stephanie J. Shaw, *What a Woman Ought to Be and Do: African American Professional Women Workers During the Jim Crow Era* (Chicago: University of Chicago Press, 1996), 7, 245n2.
28. The seminal work on the politics of respectability is chap. 7, "The Politics of Respectability," in Evelyn Brooks Higginbotham, *Righteous Discontent: The Women's Movement in the Black Baptist Church, 1880–1920* (Cambridge, Mass.: Harvard University Press, 1993), 185–230. Also see Brittney C. Cooper, *Beyond Respectability: The Intellectual Thought of Race Women* (Urbana: University of Illinois Press, 2017).
29. Works on the carceral state, poverty activism, and the informal economy privilege the voices of women who rejected many of the normative strictures of respectability politics. They enacted respectability in ways that reflected the political, economic, and other constraints acting on them. See, for example, Talitha L. LeFlouria, *Chained in Silence: Black Women and Convict Labor in the New South* (Chapel Hill: University of North Carolina Press, 2015); Rhonda Y. Williams, *The Politics of Public Housing: Black Women's Struggles Against Urban Inequality* (New York: Oxford University Press, 2004); Harris, *Sex Workers*.
30. Rowena Olegario, *A Culture of Credit: Embedding Trust and Transparency in American Business* (Cambridge, Mass.: Harvard University Press, 2006), 85. In the absence of detailed financial information, merchants had long relied on character as a proxy for creditworthiness and as a marker of middle-class values. Credit reporting and enforcement systems created empirical measures of character to predict systematically a person's willingness and likelihood to repay debt. Until the late twentieth century, financial institutions still relied on both early nineteenth-century "calculated leaps of faith" and systematic and empirical tools. Some lenders still rely on relationship lending, particularly between banks and small firms. Josh Lauer, "The Good Consumer: Credit Reporting and the Invention of Financial Identity in the United States, 1840–1940," *Enterprise and Society* 11, no. 4 (December 2010): 689–94, "calculated" quote on 91; Olegario, *A Culture of Credit*, 81–82; Bruce G. Carruthers, "The Social Meaning of Credit, Value, and Finance," in *Money Talks: Explaining How Money Really Works*, ed. Nina Bandelj, Frederick F. Wherry, and Viviana A. Zelizer (Princeton, N.J.: Princeton University Press, 2017), 73–88, here 77; Allen N. Berger and Gregory F. Udell, "Small Business Credit Availability and Relationship Lending: The Importance of Bank Organisational Structure," *Economic Journal* 112, no. 477 (February 2002): F32–F53.
31. Time certificates of deposit, similar to thrift instruments, had fixed denominations, earned fixed amounts of interest, and had a redemption date. They had strict penalties if a customer withdrew the funds early but earned substantially higher rates of interest if customers kept them until maturity. Minutes of April 6, 1904, St. Luke Bank Board Minutes, 11, CB&T Records; Lillian H. Payne et al., to President et al., July 5, 1913, folder [4], box St. Luke's Penny Savings Correspondence, 1914–1932, CB&T Records.
32. William M. T. Forrester, *Ritual of the Independent Order of St. Luke Containing the Rules, Regulations, and Ceremonies of Degrees*, rev. (n.p.: 1894), 9.

33. The IOSL created six degrees for its members and three special degrees available only to past chiefs, or presidents, of the councils. A member could pursue the higher degrees for her own personal enlightenment and self-improvement, but if she aspired to leadership positions in the local council or state-level Right Worthy Grand Council, she was required to hold certain degrees. Only members who had ascended to the sixth degree could run for the highest council offices like right worthy chief, recording secretary, and treasurer. Forrester, 9. Also see William M. T. Forrester, *Ritual of the Independent Order of St. Luke Containing Form for Opening, Closing, Initiating, Consulting, and Consecrating of Subordinate Councils, Ceremonies for Installation of Officers and Funerals with Rules and Regulations*, rev. ed. (Richmond: St. Luke Herald, 1906).
34. In addition to her duties with the IOSL, she was also active in the community, serving as executive secretary for the Richmond Community House for Colored People, which Walker helped organize in 1915. In the early 1900s, Payne served as grand worthy inspectrix of the local and was on the executive board of the state Court of Calanthe, the women's auxiliary of the Colored Knights of Pythias. "Record of 1902," *Golden Jubilee Historical Report of the R[ight] W[orthy] G[rand] Council, I[ndependent] O[rder of] St. Luke, 1867–1917* (Richmond: Everett Waddey Co., [1917?]), box 14, folder 5, item A-0228, p. 25, Independent Order of St. Luke Records, hereafter *IOSL Fiftieth Anniversary Report*; "The Grand Opening [of the Pythian Castle and Calanthe Court Chamber]," *Richmond Planet*, October 13, 1900, 1; "Another Court of Calanthe Instituted," *Richmond Planet*, March 22, 1902, 1; 1930 U.S. Census, Henrico County, Monroe-WD, Richmond, Virginia, Enumeration District 116–57, sheet 1B, dwelling 9, family 16, Lillian Payne Household, National Archives and Records Administration (hereafter NARA), microfilm, T626, roll 2478, p. 243; 1920 U.S. Census, Henrico County, Monroe-WD, Richmond, Virginia, Enumeration District 144, sheet 25B, dwelling 390, family 490, Lillian Payne Household, NARA, microfilm, T625, roll 1911, p. 255.
35. On some of the varied financial activities of councils, see extant meetings minutes for Busy Bee Circle No. 570 [Blacksburg, Va.,] (Nov 8, 1920–March 14, 1938), folder 8, box 1, Independent Order of St. Luke Collection, 1877–1970, Special Collections, University Libraries, Virginia Polytechnic Institute and State University, Blacksburg, Virginia; St. Francis Council (n.d.), folder 6, box 1, Independent Order of St. Luke Collection.
36. The records at Virginia Union University do not include an extant minutes book for the finance committee. The executive committee minutes include details about the finance committee's recommendations, instructions, and requests, which offer some sense of the finance committee's priorities and logic. The executive committee minutes also include additional finance committee–related details, such as borrowers, loan amounts, and terms. See St. Luke's Penny Savings—Executive Committee Minutes, 1913, CB&T Records; extant borrowers' correspondence in Letter Box folders, CB&T Records.
37. S. A. Bright to Emmett C. Burke, March 5, 1907; February 7, 1907, folder Letter Box 1 A–C, box Letter Box 1, 1906–1907, CB&T Records.
38. Festus Perkins to Maggie Lena Walker, September 2, 1908, folder Letter Box D 1908 N–O, box Letter Box 1908, CB&T Records.
39. W. G. Singleton and L. H. Dickerson, Trustees, to St. Luke Penny Savings Bank, September 22, 1908, folder Letter Box D 1908 T, box Letter Box, 1908, CB&T Records;

fire insurance policy with Hamburg-Bremen Fire Insurance Company, folder Letter Box 2, 1906–1907 A, box Letter Box 1, 1906–1907, CB&T Records.

40. A. J. Chewing to Union Prospect Council, October 21, 1910, folder [8], box Letter Box, 1906–1911, CB&T Records.
41. All quotes in Samuel Burley, James Johnson, and Thornton Lecost, Finance Committee, to the President and Board of Directors of St. Luke's Bank, May 19, 1906, folder Letter Box 1 D–G, box Letter Box 1, 1906–1907, CB&T Records.
42. The IOSL adopted its earliest actuarial practices from the True Reformers in the mid-1890s. In the early years of the twentieth century, the IOSL improved its actuarial practices, including maintaining detailed records of the causes of deaths that noted the frequency of certain diseases. It used the information to launch health initiatives, improve its initial health screenings, and hire visiting nurses.
43. Mamie Carter [to Emmett C. Burke], November 24, 1910, folder [4], box Letter Box, 1906–1911, CB&T Records.
44. Arthur Bell [to Emmett C. Burke], August 26, 1911, folder [19], box Letter Box, 1906–1911, CB&T Records.
45. W. L. Young to Emmett C. Burke, October 17, 1906, folder Letter Box 1 M–Z, box Letter Box 1, 1906–1907, CB&T Records.
46. Richmond B. Garrett to Emmett C. Burke, January 17, 1907, folder Letter Box 1 D–G, box Letter Box 1, 1906–1907, CB&T Records.
47. Winnie S. B. Harrison to Emmett C. Burke, November 13, 1906, folder Letter Box 1 D–G, box Letter Box 1, 1906–1907, CB&T Records.
48. R. D. Pittman to Emmett C. Burke, November 21, 1907, folder Letter Box 1 M–Z, box Letter Box 1, 1906–1907, CB&T Records.
49. I borrow the notion of the materiality of fraternal practices and ritual from Corey D. B. Walker, *A Noble Fight: African American Freemasonry and the Struggle for Democracy in America* (Urbana: University of Illinois Press, 2008), 2–4. Also see comments on the marketplace in James C. Scott, *Domination and the Arts of Resistance: Hidden Transcripts* (New Haven, Conn.: Yale University Press, 1990), esp. chap. 5, "Making Social Space for a Dissident Subculture," 108–35.
50. Elsa Barkley Brown, "Uncle Ned's Children: Negotiating Community and Freedom in Postemancipation Richmond, Virginia," (PhD diss., Kent State University, 1994), 509.
51. Bayliss J. Camp and Orit Kent, "'What a Mighty Power We Can Be': Individual and Collective Identity in African American and White Fraternal Initiation Rituals," *Social Science History* 28, no. 3 (Fall 2004): 439–83, here 439.
52. An order's works were a valuable asset. In the late 1870s, Forrester created a distinct ritual for the IOSL based on the original Grand United Order of St. Luke in Baltimore and sold it to the local councils. William Browne of the True Reformers sold his ritual to the True Reformers for $40,000 in 1895. On Brown's sale, see David M. Fahey, ed., *The Black Lodge in White America: "True Reformer" Browne and His Economic Strategy* (Dayton, Oh.: Wright State University Press, 1994), 18, 22–23; William P. Burrell and D. E. Johnson, *Twenty-Five Years History of the Grand Fountain of the United Order of True Reformers, 1881–1905* (Richmond, Va.: Grand United Order of True Reformers, 1909), 200–206.
53. Alessandra Lorini, *Rituals of Race: American Public Culture and the Search for Racial Democracy* (Charlottesville: University Virginia Press, 1999), xiii; John M. Giggie, *After*

Redemption: Jim Crow and the Transformation of African American Religion in the Delta, 1875–1915 (New York: Oxford University Press, 2007), 73. I allude to the notion of rituals of perfection discussed in Martin Anthony Summers, *Manliness and Its Discontents: The Black Middle Class and the Transformation of Masculinity, 1900–1930* (Chapel Hill: University of North Carolina Press, 2004), 22, 41–42. On black fraternal rituals and civic participation, see Camp and Kent, "'What a Mighty Power We Can Be'"; Summers; Walker, *A Noble Fight*. My thinking on the interlocking roles of risk and ritual was inspired by Eidinow's work on curses and on conflicting and discursive conceptions of risk. See Esther Eidinow, *Oracles, Curses, and Risk Among the Ancient Greeks* (Oxford: Oxford University Press, 2007), esp. chap. 1, "Exploring Uncertainty," chap. 12, "Curses and Risks."

54. References to St. Helena and other elements of the rituals, scripts, and symbols are open to other interpretations. Forrester, *Ritual of the IOSL*, 10, 18, 21, 25–28, 35, 37, 38, 42; also see a password cipher on 52.

    Regrettably, images of many of the actual ritual implements and regalia are not extant. A few images are included in a mid-1920s St. Luke regalia catalog; see Independent Order of St. Luke, Regalia Catalog, item no. MAWA 99-2446, folder 14, box 1, IOSL Records, Maggie Lena Walker Historical Site, National Park Service, Richmond, Virginia, hereafter NPS Walker House.

55. On achieving balance between religious and secular values in commercial exchange, see Joel Kaye, *A History of Balance, 1250–1375: The Emergence of a New Model of Equilibrium and Its Impact on Medieval Thought* (Cambridge: Cambridge University Press, 2014), esp. chaps. 1, 2 in sec. "Equality and Equalization in the Economic Sphere."

    Out of several hundred loan application letters, only a fraction of those in which the writers reference their membership in the IOSL use the closing "Yours in L. P. C." or simply "L. P. C.," which suggests a special privilege in being able to use the IOSL motto.

56. Banking numbers Gertrude Woodruff Marlowe, *A Right Worthy Grand Mission: Maggie Lena Walker and the Quest for Black Economic Empowerment* (Washington, D.C.: Howard University Press, 2003), 173; "Report of the Right Worthy Grand Secretary-Treasurer, Maggie Walker," *IOSL Fiftieth Anniversary Report*, 49–54, membership numbers and quote 50.

57. Emmett C. Burke to Samuel D. Calloway, n.d., St. Luke's Penny Savings Letters, [1903–] 1914, 870, hereafter Cashier's Letter Book, 1903–1914; recession from Hugh Rockoff, "Until It's Over, Over There: The U.S. Economy in World War I," National Bureau of Economic Research Working Paper 10580, June 2004, http://www.nber.org/papers/w10580.

    The Cashier's Letter Book proved to be an invaluable resource in understanding the daily operations of the bank. Unfortunately, hundreds of pages in this book were faded beyond readability due to previous exposure.

58. On the development of probabilistic thinking in social and decision sciences, see Lorenz Kruger, Gerd Gigerenzer, and Mary S. Morgan, eds., *The Probabilistic Revolution*, vol. 2, *Ideas in the Sciences* (Cambridge: Massachusetts Institute of Technology Press, 1987). With regard to credit markets, see Carl Wennerlind, *Casualties of Credit: The English Financial Revolution, 1620–1720* (Cambridge, Mass.: Harvard University Press, 2011), esp. chap. 3, "The Epistemology of Credit," 83–122. With regard to monetizing life experiences, particularly ritualizing money and making financial instruments like life

insurance symbolic, see Viviana A. Zelizer, "Human Values and the Market: The Case of Life Insurance and Death in 19th-Century," *American Journal of Sociology* 84, no. 3 (November 1978): 591–610, esp. 591–94, 599–603.

59. Vinton would go on to become the first woman president of the Universal Negro Improvement Association. Henrietta Vinton Davis to Emmett C. Burke, November 28, December 5, 11, 1912, folder Letters 1912–1913 D, box Letters, 1912–1913, 2 of 2, CB&T Records; quotes in first undated letter and payment in second undated letter, Emmett C. Burke to Henrietta Vinton Davis, [February] 1913, Cashier's Letter Book, 1913, CB&T Records.
60. J. C. Carter to Emmett C. Burke, July 19, 1912, folder Letters 1912 C, box Letters, 1912–1913, 1 of 2, CB&T Records.
61. S. P. B. Steward to Emmett C. Burke, August 27, 1912, folder Letters 1912 C, box Letters, 1912–1913, 1 of 2, CB&T Records; full name and title from *1912 Richmond Directory*.
62. Dr. A. Moncrieffee Mitchell to Emmett C. Burke, October 25, 1906, folder Letter Box 1 H-L, box Letter Box 1, 1906–1907, CB&T Records.
63. Moncrieffee Mitchell to Emmett C. Burke, September 21, October 5, October 30, 1906; March 30, April 3, April 4, 1907, folder Letter Box 1 H–L, box Letter Box 1, 1906–1907, CB&T Records.
64. John J. Smallwood to Emmett C. Burke, February 20, 1907, folder Letter Box 1 M–Z, box Letter Box 1, 1906–1907, CB&T Records.
65. J. G. Harris to Emmett C. Burke, September 20, October 1, 1910, folder [8], box Letter Box, 1906–1911, CB&T Records. Full names from 1910 U.S. Census, John G. Harris household, Dinwiddie County, 6 WD Petersburg, sheet no. 92A, series T624, roll 1641, p. 241.
66. Minutes of January 15, 1913, Executive Committee Minutes, 1913 [January 15, 1913–October 27, 1913], unpaginated, CB&T Records.
67. Higginbotham, *Righteous Discontent*, 189.
68. Ellen Hartigan-O'Connor, *The Ties that Buy: Women and Commerce in Revolutionary America* (Philadelphia: University of Pennsylvania Press, 2009), 70, 97.
69. It is difficult to find specific statistics about women's use of banks in the early twentieth century, which would provide a more detailed sense of the scale of the St. Luke Bank's practices in the larger industry. Sheri J. Caplan, *Petticoats and Pinstripes: Portraits of Women in Wall Street's History* (Santa Barbara, Calif.: Praeger, 2013), 83–84.
70. Charles Jefferson to [Burke], August 17, 1908, folder Letter Box D 1908 J, box Letter Box, 1908, CB&T Records.
71. Bettie Ransome to [Emmett C. Burke], March 1, 1905, folder Letter Box B, 1906–1907 R, box Letter Box 1, 1906–1907, CB&T Records; Josephine D. Chambers Cannaday to Emmett C. Burke, July 18, 1912, folder Letters 1912 C, box Letters, 1912–1913, 1 of 2, CB&T Records; Belle Fitzhugh to Emmett C. Burke, December 18, 1906, folder Letter Box 1 D–G, box Letter Box 1, 1906–1907, CB&T Records.
72. Maggie E. Austin to Board of Directors, April 8, 1912, folder Letters 1912 A, box Letters, 1912–1913, 1 of 2, CB&T Records; employees being encouraged and number of mortgage loans in L[ily] H. Hammond, "A Woman Banker: Maggie Lena Walker," in *In the Vanguard of a Race* (New York: Council of Women for Home Missions and Missionary Education Movement, 1923), 108–18, here 113, 115; loan terms in David L. Mason, "Homeownership Is Colorblind: The Role of African American Savings and

Loans in Home Finance, 1880–1980," *Business and Economic History* Online 8 (2010): 2, http://www.thebhc.org/sites/default/files/mason.pdf; rates of homeownership in President's Conference on Home Building and Home Ownership, *Negro Housing: Report of the Committee on Negro Housing* [. . .] (Washington, D. C.: National Capitol, 1932), 85, 231.

73. References in this strongly worded letter suggest that Brown tried earlier to get a loan. Sarah Paige Brown to Emmett C. Burke, September 17, 1906, folder Letter Box 1 A–C, box Letter Box 1, 1906–1907, CB&T Records.
74. M. H. Bullock letter, June 14, 1906, folder Letter Box 1 A–C, box Letter Box 1, 1906–1907, CB&T Records.
75. For configurations of bourgeois white womanhood that valued calculated risk taking and independent enterprise outside the home, see Edith Sparks, *Capital Intentions: Female Proprietors in San Francisco, 1850–1920* (Chapel Hill: University of North Carolina Press, 2006). For enterprise in the home, particularly the conflation of home, work, and the marketplace for middle-class white women, see George Robb, *Ladies of the Ticker: Women and Wall Street from the Gilded Age to the Great Depression* (Champaign: University of Illinois Press, 2017); Wendy Gamber, *The Boardinghouse in Nineteenth-Century America* (Baltimore, Md.: Johns Hopkins University Press, 2007), esp. 5–8, though risk taking is not an essential variable in Gamber's narrative. A financial identity reflects some level of economic skill but also communicates moral and social values. See Josh Lauer, *Creditworthy: A History of Consumer Surveillance and Financial Identity in America* (New York: Columbia University Press, 2017), 46–47, 105–7.
76. "Negress Banker Says If Men Can, Women Can," *Columbus Journal*, September 16, 1909, quoted in Marlowe, *A Right Worthy Grand Mission*, 111.
77. Quoted in Marlowe, 65
78. On racial capitalism, see Cedric J. Robinson, *Black Marxism: The Making of the Black Radical Tradition* (Chapel Hill: University of North Carolina Press, 2000); Robin D. G. Kelley, "What Did Cedric Robinson Mean by Racial Capitalism?" *Boston Review*, January 12, 2017, http://bostonreview.net/race/robin-d-g-kelley-what-did-cedric-robinson-mean-racial-capitalism; Angela Davis, "Reflections on the Black Woman's Role in the Community of Slaves," *Black Scholar* 3, no. 4 (December 1971): 2–15.
79. The bank also earned extra money by discounting notes. It seldom discounted its own notes but did purchase other banks' and individuals' notes for a fraction of the principal amount. The last half of the Finance Committee Minutes Book of Second Street Savings Bank is dominated by lists of notes discounted; it is not implausible to deduce from the St. Luke Bank's fragmented record that it also aggressively engaged in the discounting market. Some letters specifically referencing discounting notes by the St. Luke Bank include J. Thomas Hewin to St. Luke Penny Savings Bank, July 3, 1912, folder Letters 1912 H, box Letters 1912–1913, 1 of 2, CB&T Records; Nelson Williams to Maggie Lena Walker, n.d., folder Letters 1912–1913 U–V, box Letters 1912–1913, 2 of 2, CB&T Records. See Second Street Savings Minutes of the Finance Committee, 1921–1925, CB&T Records.
80. Lillian H. Payne to Emmett C. Burke, December 31, 1906; January 22, 1907, folder Letter Box 1 M–Z, box Letter Box 1, 1906–1907, CB&T Records.
81. Johnson relied on his connection to the bank to ensure a steady stream of credit and loans to fund his lavish business and personal expenses. Johnson's creditors outside the St. Luke Bank were especially aggressive in seeking payment on Johnson's bounced

checks. Lenient quote in W. I. Johnson to Emmett C. Burke, August 16, 1912, folder Letters 1912 N, box Letters, 1912–1913, 1 of 2, CB&T Records; "Funeral Director William Isaac Johnson Dead," *Richmond Planet*, November 29, 1919, 1; Michael A. Plater, *African American Entrepreneurship in Richmond, 1890–1940: The Story of R. C. Scott* (New York: Garland, 1996), 15–16; W. C. Hegge [?] to St. Luke Penny Savings Bank, June 26, 1912, folder [Letters 1912] R, box Letters, 1912–1913, 1 of 2, CB&T Records; Duryee & Barwise to St. Luke Penny Savings Bank, January 3, 1911, October 28, November 16, December 21, 1912, folder Letters 1912–1913 D, box Letters, 1912–1913, 2 of 2, CB&T Records.

82. [Julia] Hayes to Mag[gie L. Walker], October 26, 1910, folder [5], box Letter Box, 1906–1911, CB&T Records.
83. One reason Hayes encountered financial problems is that she sometimes lent councils very small sums to help with their charters. When they did not reimburse her, her checks for personal expenses at the bank bounced. Quote in Julia Hayes to Emmett C. Burke, November 3, 1910, folder [8], box Letter Box, 1906–1911, CB&T Records; Hayes to [Walker], August 7, 1911, folder [23], box Letter Box, 1906–1911, CB&T Records.
84. Both quotes in Allisen Brown to Emmett C. Burke, folder Letter Box D 1908 S, box Letter Box 1908, CB&T Records; W. H. Brooks to Emmett C. Burke, March 4, 1907, folder Letter Box 1 A–C, box Letter Box 1, 1906–1907, CB&T Records.
85. Anderson Branch to Emmett C. Burke, undated, folder Letter Box 1 A–C, box Letter Box 1, 1906–1907, CB&T Records.
86. State of West Virginia, Harrisburg County, to Maggie Lena Walker and Emmett C. Burke, October 27, 1906, folder Letter Box 1 D–G, box Letter Box 1, 1906–1907, CB&T Records.
87. B. F. Turner to Emmett C. Burke, June 5, 1908, folder Letter Box D 1908 S, box Letter Box 1908, CB&T Records.
88. R. D. Lewis to Emmett C. Burke, November 27, 1908, emphasis added, folder Letter Box D 1908 J, box Letter Box, 1908, CB&T Records.
89. W. W. Moore to Emmett C. Burke, July 23, 1908, folder Letter Box D 1908 K–L, box Letter Box 1908, CB&T Records.
90. E. W. Brown to Emmett C. Burke, March 15, 1907, folder Letter Box 1 A–C, box Letter Box 1, 1906–1907, CB&T Records.
91. Brown to Burke, March 15, 1907. Also see Joseph Carie [?] to Emmett C. Burke, October 19, 1906, folder Letter Box 1 A–C, box Letter Box 1, 1906–1907, CB&T Records.
92. Emmett C. Burke to Maria Chatham, December 4, 1914, Cashier's Letter Book, 1903–1914, 975.
93. Mr. C. Trice to Maggie Lena Walker, December 24, 1906, folder Letter Box 1 M–Z, box Letter Box 1, 1906–1907, CB&T Records.
94. Charles E. Carr to Emmett C. Burke, June 19, 1912, folder Letters 1912 N, box Letters, 1912–1913, 1 of 2, CB&T Records.
95. The bank used its attorney James Hewin and other attorneys like W. C. Bibb. See Hewin to Board of Directors; W. C. Bibb, Attorney, to St. Luke Penny Savings Bank, September 8, 1911, folder [19], box Letter Box, 1906–1911, CB&T Records. L. T. Branch to St. Luke Penny Savings Bank, December 12, 1906, February 8, 1907; bill from L. T. Branch, December 6, 1906, folder Letter Box 1 A–C, box Letter Box 1, 1906–1907, CB&T Records. Though Branch advertised legal services, he was not a licensed

attorney; see *The Bulletin of the Commercial Law League of America* 27, no. 2 (February 22, 1922): 91, 173.

96. Quote in A. T. Laumany [?],West St. Louis Trust, to Emmett C. Burke, December 30, 1912; invoice dated January 6, 1913, for "Benson, Nellie," totaling $25.30, folder Letters 1912–1913 U–V, box Letters, 1912–1913, 2 of 2; Nellie F. Benson to Emmett C. Burke, August 24, 1912, folder Letters 1912 N, box Letters, 1912–1913, 1 of 2, CB&T Records.
97. Emmett C. Burke to Freedmen's Board of the Presbyterian Church, October 14, 1914, Cashier's Letter Book, 1903–1914, 929.
98. Emmett C. Burke to Squire Lacy, January 24, 1914, Cashier's Letter Book, 1903–1914, 575.
99. J. T. Hewin to Board of Directors, St. Luke Penny Savings Bank, February 6, 1918, folder [4], box St. Luke's Penny Savings Correspondence, 1914–1932, CB&T Records.
100. C. P. [?] Grandfield to St. Luke Penny Savings Bank, November 19, 1912, folder Letters, 1912–1913 W, box Letters, 1912–1913, 2 of 2, CB&T Records.
101. Weston's attorney, ironically, eventually arranged to have Weston's wages garnished. Grandfield to St. Luke Penny Savings Bank, November 19, 1912; W. R. Southward to St. Luke Penny Savings Bank, January 7, 14, 1913, Folder Letters, 1912–1913 W, Box Letters, 1912–1913, 2 of 2, CB&T Records; E. H. Watson to St. Luke Penny Savings Bank, n.d.; George B. White to St. Luke Penny Savings Bank, January 11, 1913, folder Letters 1912–1913 U–V, box Letters, 1912–1913, 2 of 2, CB&T Records; N. T. Lewis to St. Luke Penny Savings Bank, July 28, 1908, folder Letter Box D 1908 J, box Letter Box, 1908, CB&T Records.

5. "A GOOD, STRONG, HUSTLING WOMAN": FINANCING THE NEW NEGRO IN THE NEW ERA, 1920–1929

1. Maggie Lena Walker to Charlotte Hawkins Brown, January 5, 1917, Charlotte Hawkins Brown Papers, 1883–1961, microfilm (Wellington, Del.: Scholarly Resources, 1984).
2. Brown organized the Palmer Institute in 1902. She openly promoted it as a preparatory school for young women by the 1920s. In the 1930s, it became a popular finishing and boarding school with a curriculum that stressed classical education and foreign languages. Brown wrote a popular conduct book, *The Correct Thing to Do, to Say, to Wear* (Boston: Christopher Publishing House, 1941). Walker financially supported and raised money for Palmer and other schools for women and girls, including the National Training School for Women and Girls in Washington, D.C; Hartshorn Memorial College, a women's college in Richmond, which merged with a seminary to become Virginia Union University; and her close friend Mary McLeod Bethune's Daytona Literary and Industrial Training School for Negro Girls, which became Bethune-Cookman University, in Daytona, Florida.

   On Brown and the Palmer Institute, see Charles W. Wadelington and Richard F. Knapp, *Charlotte Hawkins Brown and Palmer Memorial Institute: What One Young African American Woman Could Do* (Durham: University of North Carolina Press, 1999); Katherine C. Reynolds, "Charlotte Hawkins Brown and Palmer Memorial Institute," in *Founding Mothers and Others: Women Educational Leaders During the Progressive Era*, ed. Alan R. Sadovnik and Susan F. Semel (New York: Palgrave, 2002), 7–17; North Carolina Department of Archives and History, Charlotte Hawkins Brown Museum, http://www.nchistoricsites.org/chb/, accessed September 20, 2017. On black women's industrial education in the period, see Victoria W. Wolcott, "'Bible, Bath, and Broom': Nannie Helen Burroughs's National Training School and African-American Racial Uplift," *Journal of Women's History* 9, no. 1 (1997): 88–110.

3. The IOSL often claimed one hundred thousand members, but that number was a public relations ploy. Gertrude Woodruff Marlowe, "Appendix A: Independent Order of St. Luke Membership Figures," in *A Right Worthy Grand Mission: Maggie Lena Walker and the Quest for Black Economic Empowerment* (Washington, D.C.: Howard University Press, 2003), 262–67, here 265.
4. Allan H. Spear, *Black Chicago: The Making of a Negro Ghetto, 1890–1920* (Chicago: University of Chicago Press, 1967); James R. Grossman, *Land of Hope: Chicago, Black Southerners, and the Great Migration* (Chicago: University of Chicago Press, 1989); Gilbert Osofsky, *Harlem: The Making of a Ghetto, Negro New York, 1890–1930* (1966; Chicago: Ivan R. Dee Publisher, 1996); James Gregory, *The Southern Diaspora: How the Great Migrations of Black and White Southerners Transformed America* (Chapel Hill: University of North Carolina Press, 2005); Joe W. Trotter Jr., *Black Milwaukee: The Making of an Industrial Proletariat, 1915–45*, 2nd ed. (1986; Urbana: University of Illinois, 2007), parts 1 and 2.
5. Darlene Clark Hine, "Rape and the Inner Lives of Black Women in the Middle West," *Signs* 14, no. 4 (Summer 1989): 912–20.
6. On the New Negro beyond the artistic movement known as the Harlem Renaissance, see David Levering Lewis, *When Harlem Was in Vogue* (New York: Alfred A. Knopf, 1981); Davarian L. Baldwin, *Chicago's New Negroes: Modernity, the Great Migration, and Black Urban Life* (Chapel Hill: University of North Carolina Press, 2007); Erin Chapman, *Prove It on Me: New Negroes, Sex, and Popular Culture in the 1920s* (New York: Oxford University Press, 2012); Shannon King, *Whose Harlem Is This, Anyway?: Community Politics and Grassroots Activism During the New Negro Era* (New York: New York University, 2015); Claudrena N. Harold, *New Negro Politics in the Jim Crow South* (Athens: University of Georgia Press, 2016).
7. Gerald Early, "The New Negro Era and the Great African American Transformation," *American Studies* 49, nos. 1/2 (Spring/Summer 2008): 9–19, here 10.
8. Professor Best, "War Activities of Blacks in Evansville," *Report of the Nineteenth Annual Convention of the National Negro Business League, Held in Atlantic City, NJ, August 21–23, 1918*, 223–25, here 225.
9. Ott notes that white, immigrant, and African American women were especially essential to grassroots investment movements for war loans and bonds during World War I. Julia C. Ott, *When Wall Street Met Main Street: The Quest for an Investors' Democracy* (Cambridge, Mass.: Harvard University Press, 2011), 81–84, quote on 82. See Nikki Brown, *Private Politics and Public Voices: Black Women's Activism from World War I to the New Deal* (Bloomington: Indiana University Press, 2006).
10. Scott Ellsworth, *Death in a Promised Land: The Tulsa Race Riot of 1921* (Baton Rouge: Louisiana State University Press, 1982); Alfred L. Brophy, *Reconstructing the Dreamland: The Tulsa Riot of 1921: Race, Reparations, and Reconciliation* (Oxford: Oxford University Press, 2002); Nan Elizabeth Woodruff, *American Congo the African American Freedom Struggle in the Delta* (Cambridge, Mass.: Harvard University Press, 2003), 74–109; William M. Tuttle, *Race Riot: Chicago in the Red Summer of 1919* (1970; Champaign: University of Illinois Press, 2009); Cameron McWhirter, *Red Summer: The Summer of 1919 and the Awakening of Black America* (New York: Henry Holt, 2011).

11. Ida B. Wells's full quote is "Nobody in this section of the country believes the old threadbare lie that Negro men rape white women," from "Free Speech," Memphis, Tenn., May 21, 1892, reprinted in Ida B. Wells-Barnett, *The Red Record: Tabulated Statistics and Alleged Causes of Lynching in the United States* (1895), https://www.gutenberg.org/files/14977/14977-h/14977-h.htm.
12. Cathy Bergin, "'Unrest Among the Negroes': The African Blood Brotherhood and the Politics of Resistance," *Race and Class* 57, no. 3 (January–March 2016): 45–58.
13. Interactive Map, "A Red Record: Revealing Lynching Sites in North Carolina and South Carolina," University of North Carolina, http://lynching.web.unc.edu/; "Negroes, Armed to Teeth, Fire upon All White Persons," *World News* (Roanoke, Va.), July 21, 1919, 1; McWhirter, *Red Summer*, 105; "Negro Riots Starts When Troops Return," *Nevada State Journal* (Reno), July 22, 1919, 8; Jan Voogd, *Race Riots and Resistance: The Red Summer of 1919* (New York: Peter Lang, 2008), 93–95.
14. Anne Stavney, "Mothers of Tomorrow: The New Negro Renaissance and the Politics of Maternal Representation," *African American Review* 32, no. 4 (Winter 1998): 533–61, here 535.
15. Stavney; Hazel V. Carby, "Policing the Black Woman's Body in an Urban Context," *Critical Inquiry* 18 (Summer 1992): 738–55; Angela Davis, *Blues Legacies and Black Feminism: Gertrude "Ma" Rainey, Bessie Smith, and Billie Holiday* (New York: Pantheon, 1998); Brown, *Private Politics and Public Voices*; Michelle R. Scott, *Blues Empress in Black Chattanooga: Bessie Smith and the Emerging Urban South* (Urbana: University of Illinois Press, 2008); Chapman, *Prove It on Me*.
16. I capitalize Black Wall Streets to encompass several black business districts before and beyond Tulsa as important centers of black business and finance. Davarian Baldwin notes that the Stroll, which stretched from about 26th to 39th on State Street in Chicago, was also known as "the black man's Broadway and Wall Street." Black Wall Streets were contested sites of race and public space. Jacqueline Najuma Stewart, *Migrating to the Movies: Cinema and Black Urban Modernity* (Berkeley: University of California Press, 2005), 9–11; Baldwin, *Chicago's New Negroes*, 22–26, quote on 25; Lewis, *When Harlem Was in Vogue*, 156; John Sibley Butler and Kenneth Wilson, "Entrepreneurial Enclaves in the African American Experience" *National Journal of Sociology* 2 (Winter, 1988): 128–66.
17. Abram Harris, *The Negro as Capitalist: A Study of Banking and Business Among American Negroes* (1936; College Park, Md.: McGrath, 1968), 178. Also see Abram L. Harris, *Race, Radicalism, and Reform: Selected Papers*, ed. William Darity Jr. (New Brunswick, N.J.: Transaction, 1989).
18. See contemporary debates about the black separate economy in E. Franklin Frazier, *Black Bourgeoisie* (New York: Collier, 1957); Carter G. Woodson, "Insurance Business Among Negroes," *Journal of Negro History* 14 (1929): 202–26; St. Clair Drake and Horace R. Cayton, *Black Metropolis: A Study of Negro Life in a Northern City*, rev. ed. (Chicago: University of Chicago Press, 1993); Paul K. Edwards, *The Southern Urban Negro as Consumer* (1935; College Park, Md.: McGrath, 1969); Merah S. Stuart, *An Economic Detour: A History of Insurance in the Lives of American Negroes* (New York: Wendell Malliett, 1940); Joseph A. Pierce, *Negro Business and Business Education: Their Prospect and Prospective Development* (New York: Harper and Brothers, 1947).

    The Communist-interpolated "black belt thesis" constructed blacks in the Deep South as an economically exploited proletariat. See Erik S. McDuffie, *Sojourning for*

Freedom: Black Women, American Communism, and the Making of Black Left Feminism (Durham, N.C.: Duke University Press, 2011), 43–45, 51–57.

19. Lou Turner, "Toward a Black Radical Critique of the Political Economy," *Black Scholar* 40, no. 1 (Spring 2010): 7–19, here 16–17; Zenia Kish and Justin Leroy, "Bonded Life: Technologies of Racial Finance from Slave Insurance to Philanthrocapital," *Cultural Studies* 29, no. 5 (March 2015): 630–51, here 645–46.
20. Claudrena Harold, *The Rise and Fall of the Garvey Movement in the Urban South, 1918–1942* (New York: Routledge; Taylor and Francis, 2007), 6.
21. Quoted in McDuffie, *Sojourning for Freedom*, 8, see 26–27.
22. Elise Johnson McDougald, "The Task of Negro Womanhood," in *The New Negro: An Interpretation*, ed. Alain Locke (1925; New York: Simon and Schuster, 1992), 369–82, here 369.
23. Jervis Alexander, *A. Philip Randolph: A Biographical Portrait*, reprint (Berkeley: University of California, 1986), 130–43; Sonnet H. Retman, "Black No More: George Schuyler and Racial Capitalism," *PMLA* 123, no. 5 (2008): 1448–64, here 1460–61; McDuffie, *Sojourning for Freedom*; Harold, *The Rise and Fall of the Garvey Movement*.
24. Chapman, *Prove It on Me*, 6–8; Tiffany M. Gill, *Beauty Shop Politics: African American Women's Activism in the Beauty Industry* (Urbana: University of Illinois Press, 2010), 33–36; Stewart, *Migrating to the Movies*, 132–35, 143. On corporate-sponsored activities in the financial industry, see Angel Kwolek-Folland, "The African American Financial Industries: Issues of Class, Race, and Gender in the Early Twentieth Century," *Business and Economic History* 23, no. 2 (Winter 1994): 85–106, here 101–4; Walter B. Weare, *Black Business in the New South a Social History of the North Carolina Mutual Life Insurance Company* (Urbana: University of Illinois Press, 1993), 134–37.
25. *Souvenir Programme Sixtieth Anniversary, Fifth Biennial Meeting Independent Order of St. Luke, August 15–18, 1927*, hereafter *IOSL Sixtieth Anniversary Program*, folder 12, box 1, Independent Order of St. Luke Records, Maggie Lena Walker Historical Site, National Park Service, Richmond, Virginia, hereafter NPS Walker House; Maggie Lena Walker Diary, September 29, 1918, NPS Walker House; memoranda September 1918; October 4, 1918; June 22–23, 1926, Maggie Lena Walker Papers, 1897–1935, NPS Walker House.
26. Quoted in Suzanne Lebsock, "Women Suffrage and White Supremacy: A Virginia Case Study," in *Visible Women: New Essays on American Activism*, ed. Nancy A. Hewitt and Suzanne Lebsock (Urbana: University of Illinois Press, 1993), 62–100, here 81.
27. The number of registered black women represented 12.5 percent of black women over twenty-one years of age in Richmond. Lesbock, 83, 84, 90, 97n57; Marlowe, *A Right Worthy Grand Mission*, 182; *From Municipal Housekeeping to Political Equality: The Virginia Suffrage Movement, 1870–1920, April 28–August 7, 1995*, folder 119, box 4, Betsy Brinson Papers, 1894–1999, Virginia Historical Society, Richmond, Virginia.
28. Lilia L. Garfield to Lillian Payne, February 25, 1929, folder 4, Lillian H. Payne Papers, 1907–1974, hereafter Payne Papers, Valentine Museum and Richmond History Center.
29. Circular letter from Maggie L. Walker to Organizing Deputies Working Under Jurisdiction of the RWG Council, IO of St. Luke, August 21, 1924, folder 3, Payne Papers.
30. Lillian H. Payne to Kindred Cohen, February 11, 1929; Lillian H. Payne to Della Allen, February 11, 1929; Mary C. Rose to Lillian H. Payne, March 20, 1929; Idah G.

Henderson to Lillian H. Payne, March 5, 1929; Andrew Maples to Lillian H. Payne, undated, folder 6, Payne Papers; Lillian H. Payne to Lillian Timsley, February 27, 1929, folder 16, Payne Papers.

31. Marlowe, *A Right Worthy Grand Mission*, 118.
32. In the renovation, Walker insisted that a sizeable number of the construction workers be black; half of the three hundred men who worked on the building were black. Marlowe, 118, 174.
33. Men who worked as clerks were feminized by their work if they stayed in a similar occupation without moving into a male-dominated field such as management or sales. Kwolek-Folland, "The African American Financial Industries," 90–91, 95–96.
34. Marlowe mentions only the IOSL as involving a daily devotional, but it is very likely that the same happened at the bank. Walker Diary, April 12, 19, 1920; March 20, 1921; September 13, 1926. Marlowe, *A Right Worthy Grand Mission*, 66; Mary White Ovington, *Portraits in Color* (New York, Viking, 1927), 130. See images of women clerks in *IOSL Sixtieth Anniversary Program*.
35. "Statement Showing Condition of Incorporated State Banks," *13th Annual Report* [. . .] *of the Incorporated State Banks Operating in Virginia,* [. . .] *1922* (Richmond: Commonwealth of Virginia, Department of Purchases and Supply, 1922), 11–27, here 23; "Comparative Assets of I. O. St. Luke," *IOSL Sixtieth Anniversary Program*.
36. Walker Diary, August 4, 1920; August 4, 1921.
37. Both quotes from Walker Diary, November 6, 1920.
38. Walker awarded Anderson a gold cross with three diamonds for twenty years of service in 1925. "Still disgruntled" quote from Walker Diary, February 29, 1921; March 20, 1921; Marlowe, *A Right Worthy Grand Mission*, 214.
39. Walker Diary, July 30, 1920; Marlowe, *A Right Worthy Grand Mission*, 189–90; "Bankett, Mrs. Lelia Williams," *Who's Who in Colored America* [. . .], *1941–1944*, 6th ed., ed. Thomas Yenser (Brooklyn, N.Y.: Who's Who in Colored America, 1942), 39.
40. The 1920s board minutes are not in the Consolidated Bank and Trust archive at Virginia Union University. "Virginian Holds Conference," *Broad Ax* (Chicago), June 20, 1925, 1; "St. Luke Leader," *Pittsburgh Courier*, July 30, 1927, 6; "Chicago Society," *Pittsburgh Courier*, July 9, 1927, 6; "Bankett, Mrs. Lelia Williams," *Who's Who*.
41. See various letters, Lillian H. Payne to Kindred Cohen, February 11, 1929; Payne to Della Allen, February 11, 1929; Mary C. Rose to Payne, March 20, 1929; Idah G. Henderson to Payne, March 5, 1929; Andrew Maples to Payne, undated; Supervising Deputies A. C. Russ, District Deputy, to Payne, May 19, 1929; A. F. Angel, Supervising Deputy, to Payne, April 5, 1929, folder 6, Correspondence, Heliotrope Council No. 160, Payne Papers; Lillian Payne and Various Virginia Groups, 1929–1930; Payne to Lillian Timsley, February 27, 1929, folder 16, Correspondence, Heliotrope Council No. 160, Payne Papers.
42. Walker Diary, January 12, 1926.
43. "Another Court of Calanthe Instituted," *Richmond Planet*, March 22, 1902, 1; "[Mrs. Lelia W. Bankett]," *Pittsburgh Courier*, June 16, 1928, 7.
44. Walker Diary, January 1, 1928.
45. Walker Diary, March 12, 1928.
46. "Personal Mention," *Pittsburgh Courier*, January 16, 1928, 7; ad, "Right Worthy Grand Council," *New York Age*, March 23, 1929, 2; "Great St. Luke Drive Closes Tuesday, April 16," *New York Age*, April 13, 1929, 10.

47. Marlowe, *A Right Worthy Grand Mission*, 264.
48. Janie Armistead to Maggie Walker, [February 1929]; Lillian H. Payne to Janie Armistead, February 20, 1929, folder 18, Correspondence, Lillian Payne and Little David Council No. 835, Payne Papers.
49. Fannie L. Nicholas to Lillian H. Payne, March 3, 1929, folder 6, Payne Papers.
50. Evie G. Henderson to Lillian H. Payne, February 3, 1929, folder 11, Payne Papers.
51. Quote in Evie G. Henderson to Lillian H. Payne, February 25, 1929, folder 11, Correspondence, Charlottesville, Va.–J. N. Baker, 1929, Payne Papers; Lillian Payne to J. N. Baker, January 3, 1929, folder 4, Correspondence, Charlottesville, Va.–J. N. Baker, 1929, Correspondence, Legal Reserves Division, Payne Papers.
52. "Big Finance Corporation Is Launched," *Pittsburgh Courier*, November 29, 1924, 13. Attendees at the banquet discussed the pressing need for credit. They considered starting a central black bank in Harlem, supported by the seventy-two black banks in the country, but they determined that this idea was not feasible. They instead considered creating a pool of capital for black banks and other businesses that could be used to fund mortgages and to help with business expansion and liquidity. See "Mammoth Financial Institution Launched," *Carolina Times* (Durham, N.C.), June 13, 1924, 1, folder 23, box 5, Charles Clinton Spaulding Papers, David M. Rubenstein Rare Book and Manuscript Library, Duke University, hereafter Spaulding Papers.
53. Very few women worked in high positions in black insurance companies and banks during the 1920s. They include Walker's close friend Mary McLeod Bethune, who served on the board of the Central Life Insurance in Tampa; Jessie Gillespie Herndon, vice president of the Atlanta Life Insurance Company; and Minnie Geddings Cox, secretary-treasurer of Mississippi Life Insurance Company until 1923 and vice president of the Delta Penny Savings Bank from 1916 to 1928, a bank she cofounded in 1903. A few women were prominent in burial insurance, such as Gertrude Pocte Geddes Willis in New Orleans; Mary Augusta Rayford Collins in Jackson, Mississippi; and Mame Stewart Josenberger in Fort Smith, Arkansas. Very few women served on the boards of black banks.
54. "Big Finance Corporation Is Launched."
55. "Big Finance Corporation Is Launched"; "The National Negro Finance Corporation," *Social Forces* 3, no. 2 (January 1925): 320; "Dr. Moton Addresses National Negro Finance Corporation," *Pittsburgh Courier*, July 9, 1927, 3; "Negro Business Men Consider Plans [to] Stabilize Negro Business," *Savannah Tribune*, [November 25, 1924], folder National Negro Finance Corporation, box 4 Clippings, hereafter NNFC Clippings, Spaulding Papers.
56. During World War I, Scott resigned his secretary position at Tuskegee to serve as special assistant to the secretary of war. On Emmett J. Scott's business philosophy, see Maceo Crenshaw Dailey Jr., "Neither 'Uncle Tom' Nor 'Accommodationist': Booker T. Washington, Emmett Jay Scott, and Constructionalism," *Atlanta History* 38, no. 4 (Winter 1995): 20–33.
57. In the 1960s, the National Negro Business League (NNBL) changed its name to the National Business League (http://nationalbusinessleague.org/). On the NNBL's history, see Louis Harlan, "Booker T. Washington and the National Negro Business League," in *Seven on Black: Reflections on the Negro Experience in America*, ed. William G. Shade and Roy C. Herrenkohl (Philadelphia: J. B. Lippincott, 1969), 73–91;

John H. Burrows, *The Necessity of Myth: A History of the National Negro Business League, 1900–1945* (Auburn, Ala.: Hickory Hill, 1988); Shennette Monique Garrett, "'He Ran His Business like a White Man': Race, Entrepreneurship, and the Early National Negro Business League in the New South" (MA thesis, University of Texas at Austin, 2006).

58. These white business titans also invested in black businesses and banks. Their outlays were modest compared to their wealth but represented major investments for black businesses. For example, Rosenwald was a majority stockholder in the Mound Bayou Cotton Seed Oil Mill in Mound Bayou, Mississippi, in 1912, and Rockefeller held 75 percent of the stock in the Dunbar National Bank opened in 1928 in Harlem. As for the Allied Finance's all-black officers, Edward Brown owned an insurance company, more than $1 million worth of real estate in New York City, and a small chain of theaters in Philadelphia; Pace was an executive in Standard Life of Atlanta before starting his own insurance company that eventually became Supreme Liberty Life Insurance in Chicago; and Nail joined Afro-American Realty in Harlem before starting his own real estate investment firm, Nail and Parker, in 1907 and was also on Black Swan Records' board. On Allied Finance, "Three and Three Quarter Million Dollar Corporation," *Tulsa Star*, January 22, 1921, 1; "Washington, D.C.," *New York Age*, June 9, 1923, 2.

59. Prospectus for the Allied Industrial Finance Corporation (digital copy), Allied Industrial Finance Corporation, manuscript 312, W. E. B. Du Bois Papers, 1803–1999, Special Collections and University Archives, University of Massachusetts Amherst Libraries, http://credo.library.umass.edu/view/full/mums312-b015-i327.

60. "Silver Jubilee Meeting of the National Negro Business League Attended by 6,000," *New York Age*, August 23, 1924, 1, 3; "National Negro Business League Holds Third Meeting in Durham [. . .]," *New York Age*, November 29, 1924, 1, 7; Burrows, *Necessity of Myth*, 112–13.

61. "Insurance Men Hear Plan to Aid Business Outlined," *Chicago Defender*, August 23, 1924, 4.

62. R. G. Dun and Company, formed in the 1840s, was a commercial rating firm that maintained credit information and other business-related details about entrepreneurs and companies. In the early 1930s, it merged to form Dun and Bradstreet Corporation, currently one of the world's largest commercial data and analytics companies. Floyd J. Calvin, "The-Digest [*sic*]," *Pittsburgh Courier*, August 16, 1924, 16; "A Financial Departure," *Chicago Defender*, September 20, 1924, 14; ad, National Negro Finance Corporation, *St. Luke Herald*, November 29, 1924, 1; "Negro Finance Corporation in Fine Shape," *St. Luke Herald*, November 29, 1924, 4, NNFC Clippings, Spaulding Papers.

63. *Forbes* estimated that Perry was worth $8 million (or about $117 million in 2017 dollars). His holding company, Service Corporation, held assets in excess of $2 million, including a construction company, a pharmacy, and a realty firm. Eric C. Walrond, "Largest Negro Commercial Enterprise in the World," *Forbes*, February 2, 1924. On the sale, see Shennette Garrett-Scott, "'To Do a Work That Would Be Very Far Reaching': Minnie Geddings Cox, the Mississippi Life Insurance Company, and the Challenges of Black Women's Business Leadership in the Early Twentieth-Century United States," *Enterprise and Society* 17, no. 3 (September 2016): 473–514, here 473, 496–502; Alexa Benson Henderson, "Heman E. Perry and Black Enterprise in Atlanta, 1908–1925," *Business History Review* 61, no. 2 (1987): 216–42, here 237–39; Stuart, *An Economic Detour*, 290–96.

64. Ad, National Negro Finance Corporation, undated clipping, folder 23, box 5, Spaulding Papers.
65. One of Perry's most ambitious investment deals involved a master-planned single-family residential subdivision outside Atlanta. An internal investigation by the Laura Spelman Rockefeller Memorial Foundation revealed that Perry had enlisted the help of the Interracial Commission in Atlanta to defuse white homebuyers' and real estate agents' opposition to the suburban development. White opponents succeeded in rezoning Perry's land holdings, which kept Perry from selling new tracts and completing construction on those already sold. Perry turned to outside lenders for capital, but they charged him exorbitant rates and gave him an unusually short window for repayment. Perry pledged more than $400,000 ($5.8 million in 2017 dollars) in assets, including Mississippi Life for $100,000; $249,000 in Standard Life shares; $100,000 in Citizens Trust Company shares; and the land itself, valued at $100,000. The actual value of the land appraised at only $50,000, but the value of the other pledged assets appraised for $646,000, far more than original estimates. Julius Rosenwald, John D. Rockefeller Jr., Arthur Curtis James, George Peabody, and Clarence Kelsey expressed interest in lending money to pay off Perry's creditors. They also renegotiated a high bonus fee charged by the creditor, Southeastern Trust. Given new source material, the events surrounding Standard Life deserve historical reconsideration. Memorandum of Interview, "Southern Trip," November 3–December 5, 1923, 2; Appraisal Memorandum, Lybrand, Ross Brothers, and Montgomery; Trevor Arnett to Raymond B. Fosdick (two letters on the same date), November 4, 1924; Alfred B. Dawson to Beardsley Ruml, November 15, 1924, folder Standard Life Part 1, Laura Spelman Rockefeller Memorial Collection, microfilm, series 3: Appropriations, 1917–1945 (New York: Rockefeller University, 1998), Scholarly Resources.
66. "Philanthropists' $500,500 Couldn't Save Standard Life," *Afro-American* (Baltimore), May 7, 1932.
67. Other AIFC board members who may have been involved in the loan arrangements include Harry Pace, who was also an officer in Perry's Standard Life; Charles Banks, a banker and financier in Mississippi and an associate of Minnie Geddings Cox; and Bert M. Roddy, a grocery store chain owner and cashier of Solvent Savings Bank in Memphis, the site of Mississippi Life's headquarters after 1920. In 1925, National Benefit Life Insurance of Washington, D.C., tried and failed to buy Standard Life to keep it from falling into the hands of a white company. The attempted purchase further weakened the already-impaired National Benefit and hastened its failure in 1931. W. Gomez to R. R. Moton, August 12, 1924, Robert Russa Moton Papers No. 2, Special Collections, Ford Motor Company Library, Tuskegee University, hereafter Moton Papers No. 2; "Standard Life is Gobbled Up," *Gazette* (Cleveland, Oh.), January 24, 1925, 1; "Philanthropists' $500,500 Couldn't Save Standard Life."
68. From its inception in the late 1800s, the black insurance industry stressed male protection of widows and children. In reality, women policyholders typically outnumbered men. For example, an 1897 survey of a poor and working-class neighborhood in New York revealed that only 15 percent of black fathers and more than half of black mothers held fraternal insurance. Gustavus Adolphus Steward, "Something New Under the Sun," *Opportunity* 3, no. 25 (January 1925): 20–22; Shennette Garrett-Scott, "Daughters of Ruth: Black Women in Insurance in the New South, 1890s–1930s" (PhD diss., University of Texas at Austin, 2011), 33–34, 47, 77–78.

69. Quoted in George Cross van Dosen to J. Edgar Hoover, March 19, 1921, in *The Marcus Garvey and Universal Negro Improvement Association Papers*, vol. 3, *September 1920–August 1921*, ed. Robert A. Hill (Durham, N.C.: Duke University Press, 2014), hereafter *Garvey Papers*, 255–65, here 257.
70. Editorial letter by Marcus Garvey, March 5, 1921, *Garvey Papers*, 3:240–41, here 241.
71. Editorial letter by Marcus Garvey, March 5, 1921; Government's Exhibit 30, "The Negro Must Evolve from a Dependent [. . .]," *Negro World*, March 6, 1920, 7478–85; Exhibit 60, "An Appeal to the Colored People of New York [. . .]," 7690–712, *Marcus Garvey v United States*, no. 8317, Ct. App., 2nd Cir., February 2, 1925; "Universal Negro Catechism," *Garvey Papers*, 3:302–20, here 316; Lewis, *When Harlem Was in Vogue*, 37, 40; Marcus Garvey, "Articles," reprinted in *Marcus Garvey: Life and Lessons, a Centennial Companion to the Marcus Garvey and Universal Negro Improvement Association Papers*, ed. Robert A. Hill and Barbara Bair (Berkeley: University of California Press, 1987), 35–110, here 92–94.
72. Members did have access to the UNIA properties: Liberty Hall and two office buildings at 54–56 West 135th Street, which housed the UNIA and Black Star Line offices. Editorial letter by Marcus Garvey, October 11, 1920, *Garvey Papers*, 3:50–51; Garvey, "Articles," 43, 93–94; Government's Exhibit 30, "The Negro Must Evolve from a Dependent [. . .]."
73. A. Philip Randolph, a civil rights activist and committed socialist, was founder and president of the Brotherhood of Sleeping Car Porters, editor of *The Messenger*, and architect of the March on Washington Movement in the 1930s. Marcus Garvey and members of the Universal Negro Improvement Association promoted black economic self-determination and hoped to establish an independent nation-state in Africa. Alexander, *A. Philip Randolph*, 130–43; Tomas Fernandez Robaina, "Marcus Garvey in Cuba: Urrutia, Cubans, and Black Nationalism," in *Between Race and Empire: African-Americans and Cubans Before the Cuban Revolution*, ed. Lisa Brock and Digna Casteñada Fuertes (Philadelphia: Temple University Press, 1998), 120–28; Harold, *The Rise and Fall of the Garvey Movement*.
74. Madam C. J. W. (Sarah Breedlove) Walker (1867–1919), no relation to Maggie Lena Walker, created an international beauty products manufacturing empire that earned annual revenues of more than $1 million in the early decades of the twentieth century. "African Fundamentalism" was a kind of manifesto that laid out the fundamental principles of the UNIA's vision and objectives. The full title is "African Fundamentalism. A Racial Hierarchy and Empire for Africans African's Faith Must Be Confidence in Self His Creed: One God. One Aim. One Destiny." Marlowe, *A Right Worthy Grand Mission*, 224; Harold, *The Rise and Fall of the Garvey Movement*, esp. chap. 4, "Virginian Garveyism, 1918–1942," 91–114.
75. Editorial, *St. Luke Herald*, May 17, 1924, quoted in Hill, *Garvey Papers*, September 1922–August 1924, 5:585n6.
76. Mary G. Rolinson, *Grassroots Garveyism: The Universal Negro Improvement Association in the Rural South, 1920–1927* (Chapel Hill: University of North Carolina Press, 2007), quote on 3, 50–55.
77. Judith Stein, *The World of Marcus Garvey: Race and Class in Modern Society* (Baton Rouge: Louisiana State University Press, 1986); Tony Martin, "Women in the Garvey Movement," in *Garvey: His Work and Impact*, ed. Rupert Lewis and Patrick Bryan

(Mona, Jamaica: Institute of Social and Economic Research, 1988); Barbara Bair, "True Women, Real Men: Gender, Ideology, and Social Roles in the Garvey Movement," in *Gendered Domains: Rethinking Public and Private in Women's History*, ed. Dorothy O. Helly and Susan Reverby (Ithaca, N.Y.: Cornell University Press, 1992); Ula Y. Taylor, *The Veiled Garvey: The Life and Times of Amy Jacques Garvey* (Chapel Hill: University of North Carolina Press, 2002). On white capitalists' support of the NNBL and controversies around that support, see Burrows, *The Necessity of Myth*, 105–10; Garrett, "'He Ran His Business like a White Man,'" 12–13, 70–71, 92–93, 96–100.

78. "'The Business of America Is Business' A Famously Unfair Misquote," This Day in Quotes (blog), January 15, 2017, http://www.thisdayinquotes.com/2010/01/business-of-america-is-business.html; Bruce Barton, *The Man Nobody Knows* (New York: Bobbs-Merrill, 1925); William Z. Ripley, *Main Street and Wall Street* (New York: Little, Brown, 1927).
79. Prospectus for the Allied Industrial Finance Corporation, 6, 8.
80. "National Negro Finance Corporation [Prospectus]," 7, folder National Negro Finance Corporation, 1924, box 166, Spaulding Papers.
81. Newspaper quoted in "National Negro Finance Corporation [Prospectus]," 6.
82. On New Proprietorship, the popular movement that encouraged ordinary people to invest in corporate stocks, see Ott, *When Wall Street Met Main Street*, 151–53; NNIA questions in "Insurance Men Hear Plan to Aid Business Outlined," *Chicago Defender*, August 23, 1924, 4.
83. The AIFC offered preferred and common classes of stock. It paid a 15 percent commission to any fiscal agent and promised an ambitious 8 percent dividend. To buy $130 worth of stock (ten preferred and five common shares), an investor only needed to put twenty dollars down and pay ten dollars per month for eleven months. The lowest-level investor could buy six preferred and three common shares for seventy-eight dollars with thirteen dollars down and five dollars per month for thirteen months. Prospectus for the Allied Industrial Finance Corporation; W. Gomez to Mrs. E. S. Sanders, William H. Carter, Albert D. Foster, Pauline Young, James E. Scott, September 7, 1925, folder 919, National Negro Finance Corp., box 123, Moton Papers No. 2. For details about blacks trading on Wall Street in the 1920s, see Gregory S. Bell, *In the Black: A History of African Americans on Wall Street* (New York: John Wiley, 2002), 24–26. Unfortunately, Bell's work does not provide adequate footnotes to verify the histories given.
84. "National Negro Finance Corporation [Prospectus]," 7.
85. Calvin, "The-Digest."
86. Editorial, "[How the Rascals]," *Gazette* (Cleveland, Oh.), November 7, 1925, 2.
87. P[?]. E. Tobias to Robert R. Moton, June 12, 1924, 3, emphasis in original, folder T Correspondence 1924–1925, box 5, Albon L. Holsey Papers, Special Collections, Ford Motor Company Library, Tuskegee University, hereafter Holsey Papers.
88. In the early years of the twentieth century, Negro captains of industry proselytizing the gospel of success were not above invoking racial stereotypes and prejudices to establish themselves both as worthy of citizenship and as legitimate leaders of a self-reliant community. Drawing distinctions between themselves and, in their characterizations, the troublesome island native, the anarchist immigrant, and the untrustworthy Jew, black entrepreneurs hoped to integrate themselves into the new industrial and imperial order. By the 1920s, some of the rhetoric of the buy black movement turned even

more bigoted. Advocates were not above accusing Jews and other ethnic and immigrant groups along with white Americans of preying on the black consumers and actively undermining the black group economy.

89. Burrows, *Necessity of Myth*, 113–14, 116–117; Weare, *Black Business in the New South*, 120–21; "Gomez, Wanti W. [Louis Jones]," Notable Kentucky African Americans Database, accessed October 6, 2017, http://nkaa.uky.edu/nkaa/items/show/2202; F. B. Ransom to W. Gomez, October 21, 1925, folder 919 National Negro Finance Corp., box 123, Moton Papers No. 2; W. Gomez to Albon S. Holsey, March 29, 1925, folder F Correspondence 1924–1925, box 1, Holsey Papers; "Dr. Moton Addresses National Negro Finance Corporation"; "September 30, 1927 Statement National Negro Finance Corporation," folder 935 National Negro Finance Corp., box 124, Moton Papers No. 2; James T. Carter to NNFC, October 11 (with attachment), December 18, 1928; Carter to C. C. Spaulding, January 7, 1929, folder 1, box 1, Rencher Nicholas Harris Papers, 1851–1980, Rubenstein Rare Book and Manuscript Library, Duke University.
90. William H. Jones, *Recreation and Amusement Among Negroes in Washington, D.C. . . .* (Washington, D.C.: Howard University Press, 1927), 161, quoted in Shane Vogel, *The Scene of Harlem Cabaret: Race, Sexuality, Performance* (Chicago: University of Chicago, 2009), 134; Lewis, *When Harlem Was in Vogue*, 103–8; "Entertainment and Harlem," *Encyclopedia of the Harlem Renaissance*, ed. Aberjhani West and Sandra L. West (New York: Facts on File, 2003), 102–4.
91. Ad, "A Series of New Negro Lectures," *Richmond Planet*, April 10, 1920, 9; "Blue Triangle Notes," *Richmond Planet*, May 28, 1921, 3; "Grand Concert of Song," *Richmond Planet*, November 20, 1920, 2; "St. Lukes Grand Jubilee and Soiree," *Washington, D.C. Bee*, May 2, 1914, 5.
92. The ratio was 142 women emigrants to every one hundred men. Marlowe, *A Right Worthy Grand Mission*, 87; Schomburg Center for the Study of Black Culture, "The Northern Migration," In Motion: The African-American Migration Experience, http://www.inmotionaame.org/migrations/landing.cfm?migration=7; Kevin McGruder, *Race and Real Estate: Conflict and Cooperation in Harlem, 1890–1920* (New York: Columbia University Press, 2015), 18–28; Marcy S. Sacks, *Before Harlem: The Black Experience in New York City Before World War I* (Philadelphia: University of Pennsylvania Press, 2006). On black women's migration experiences, see Tera Hunter, *To 'Joy My Freedom: Southern Black Women's Lives and Labors After the Civil War* (Cambridge, Mass.: Harvard University Press, 1997); Lillian Serece Williams, *Strangers in the Land of Paradise: The Creation of an African American Community, Buffalo, New York, 1900–1940* (Bloomington: Indiana University Press, 1999).
93. Petersburg Directory for 1882; 1900 U.S. Census, household of Robert H. Jones, Borough of Manhattan, sheet 6A; Maggie Lena Walker to Charity Jones, October 7, 1903, Cashier's Letter Book, 201, Consolidated Bank and Trust Records, c. 1903–1993, hereafter CB&T Records; "Report of Stockholders, 1904," folder Letter Box E 1904, box Letter Box 1908, CB&T Records; "Card of Thanks," *New York Age*, October 28, 1909; "[Mrs. John Brewer]," *New York Age*, March 15, 1917; "'Mother' of Order of St. Luke's in New York City Died July 19th and Hundreds View Body in Casket," *New York Age*, July 27, 1929, 1; Marlowe, 136n133. Marlowe mistakenly notes Pittsburgh as Jones's birthplace.
94. "Philip A. Payton, Jr. and the Afro-American Realty Company," in *The Negro in Business*, ed. Booker T. Washington (Boston: Hertel, Jenkins, and Jones, 1907), 197–205,

here 198; McGruder, *Race and Real Estate*, 51, 53–54; Dailey, "Booker T. Washington and the Afro-American Realty Company," 187, 188, 198n1.

95. Blacks earned about $109 per month and paid about $55.70 per month, or 51 percent of their monthly income, for a four-room apartment in Harlem. Whites, by contrast, earned about $131 per month but paid an average of $32.43 per month for similar accommodations, about 24 percent of their incomes. About one-quarter of blacks in Harlem relied on lodgers compared to 12 percent of whites. Lewis, *When Harlem Was in Vogue*, 108.
96. "Negro Invasion Threat Angers Flat Dwellers," *New York Times*, July 21, 1906, 2.
97. "Court Names Receiver to Take Charge of Affairs of St. Luke Finance Corporation in N.Y.," *New York Age*, July 20, 1929, 1–2, here 1.
98. "Court Names Receiver"; "St. Luke Stockholders Inc.," *New York Age*, April 12, 1930, 1; "Local Members of the I. O. of St. Luke in 9th Anniversary," *New York Age*, November 5, 1927, 10; Lester A. Walton, "Property Worth $300,000 Owned by New York Society," *Pittsburgh Courier*, July 26, 1924, 13; McGruder, *Race and Real Estate*, 81; Marlowe, *A Right Worthy Grand Mission*, 41–42.
99. I was not able to find additional biographical details about most of these women. "St. Luke Stockholders Inc."; Walton, "Property Worth $300,000"; 1920 U.S. Census, Laura Nixon Household, Manhattan Assembly District 19, New York, New York, Enumeration District 1350, roll T625_1221, p. 5B.
100. "St. Luke Stockholders Inc."; Walton, "Property Worth $300,000."
101. Strivers' Row was a section of brownstones in Harlem from 138th to 139th Street. Blacks living in this neighborhood were thought to have arrived in elite society. Walton, "Property Worth $300,000"; ad, "Casanova," *New York Tribune*, April 1, 1900, 10.
102. Charity Jones lived in one of the two remaining apartments. "St. Luke's Assembly," *Afro-American* (Baltimore, Md.), May 16, 1925, 3; "St. Luke Banquet," *New York Amsterdam News*, May 11, 1927, 18; "St. Andrews Buys Historical Low Real Estate," *New York Amsterdam News*, November 7, 1923, 9; ad, "Look! Look! Look! Who's with Us!," *New York Amsterdam News*, March 7, 1923, 4; "Greet Ex-Mayor of Port of Spain," *New York Amsterdam News*, May 4, 1927, 1; "Brotherhood of Sleeping Car Porters Rally Tonight," *New York Amsterdam News*, August 22, 1927, 2; Gerald Horne, *Black Liberation/Red Scare: Ben Davis and the Communist Party* (Newark: University of Delaware, 1994), 51–52; King, *Whose Harlem Is This, Anyway?*, 72.
103. That same year, New York Mayor Jimmy Walker required establishments in which three or more people would be dancing or musicians would be playing instruments to procure a dance hall or cabaret license. The goal of the license was to make it easier for law enforcement to police and surveil speakeasies and clubs, especially in Harlem. Police heavily patrolled licensed Harlem clubs, and city officials made it difficult for black concerns to procure dance hall licenses. Eli Kerry and Penn Bullock, "The Racist Legacy of NYC's Anti-Dancing Law," *Thump*, March 8, 2017, https://thump.vice.com/en_us/article/z45g5e/nyc-cabaret-law-racism-discrimination-history; Tom Davin, "Conversation with James P. Johnson," in *Voices from the Harlem Renaissance*, ed. Nathan Irvin Huggins (1976; New York: Oxford University Press, 1995), 324–35, here 328; King, *Whose Harlem Is this, Anyway?*, 147n100; "Local I. O. of St. Lukes [*sic*] to Dedicate Remodeled Building Before Grand Council Convening," *New York Age*, August 15, 1925, 1.

104. All quotes in "Ministers in Meeting Denounce YMCA and Certain Orders as Demoralizing to Christian Ideals and Community Welfare," *New York Age*, May 16, 1925, 1, 3, here 3.

105. LaShawn Harris, *Sex Workers, Psychics, and Numbers Runners: Black Women in New York City's Underground Economy* (Urbana: University of Illinois Press, 2016), 60.

106. Harris, 57–60. On policy in Harlem, see Harris; Shane White, Stephen Garton, and Stephen Robertson, *Playing the Numbers: Gambling in Harlem Between the Wars* (Cambridge, Mass.: Harvard University Press, 2010); Lewis, *When Harlem Was in Vogue*.

107. Most of the employees (fourteen) worked in the restaurant, the St. Luke Club Dining Room. "Local I. O. of St. Lukes."

108. "Local I. O. of St. Lukes."

109. "Court Names Receiver."

110. "Court Names Receiver"; Pace, "The Business of Banking Among Negroes," 184; Mehrsa Baradaran, *The Color of Money: Black Banks and the Racial Wealth Gap* (Cambridge, Mass.: Harvard University Press, 2017), 77–79; "Negro Finance Corporation Has a Capital of a Million," clipping, folder 23, box 5, Spaulding Papers.

Men and women who engaged in the extralegal and illegal economy often gave generously to charitable causes, helped institutions and individuals, and funded legitimate businesses. See Robert E. Weems Jr., *Black Business in the Black Metropolis: The Chicago Metropolitan Assurance Company, 1925–1985* (Bloomington: Indiana University Press, 1966); White, Garton, and Robertson, *Playing the Numbers*; Harris, *Sex Workers*; Baldwin, *Chicago's New Negroes*, 45–51; Juliet E. K. Walker, *The History of Black Business in America: Capitalism, Race, Entrepreneurship* (Chapel Hill: University of North Carolina Press, 2009), 235–38.

111. "Court Names Receiver," 2.

112. "Court Names Receiver," 1.

113. "Parent Body Disclaims Financial Operations of St. Luke in N.Y.," *New York Age*, July 20, 1929, 1.

114. From 1921 to 1922, black depositors increased more than 12 percent, according to a Department of Labor report from thirteen states and the District of Columbia. Their average deposit accounts fell from $95.63 to $83.03 in the same period. The clipping does not provide a comparison to depositors in other racial and ethnic groups. "Trend of Deposits Savings of Negro Workers, as Indicated by Savings Banks' Reports from Typical Industrial and Business Centers," *Star of Zion*, September 28, 1922, 1.

115. *Fifteenth Census of the U.S.: 1930, Population*, vol. 5, *General Report on Occupations* (Washington, D.C.: Government Printing Office, 1933), table 2; *Negroes in the United States, 1920–1932* (Washington, D.C.: Government Printing Office, 1935), table 27, extrapolated from Kwolek-Folland, "The African American Financial Industries," 92.

EPILOGUE

1. Both the Second Street Savings and the Commercial Bank and Trust opened in 1920.

2. For example, all three institutions jointly financed a $30,000 first mortgage for Sixth Mt. Zion Church. Gertrude Woodruff Marlowe, *A Right Worthy Grand Mission: Maggie Lena Walker and the Quest for Black Economic Empowerment* (Washington, D.C.:

Howard University Press, 2003), 243, 257n35; Jesse E. Fleming, "A History of Consolidated Bank and Trust Company" (MA thesis, Rutgers University, 1972), 42–47; "Endorse Bank Merger," *Pittsburgh Courier*, December 28, 1929, 1; "Richmond, Va., Banks Merge," *Chicago Defender*, January 24, 1931, 2; 1927–29 Federal Tax Returns, untitled folders, St. Luke's Penny Savings Correspondence, 1914–1932, Consolidated Bank and Trust Records, c. 1903–1993, Special Collections, L. Douglas Wilder Library, Virginia Union University, hereafter CB&T Records. On Mechanics Savings closure, see Ann Field Alexander, "Collapse," in *Race Man: The Rise and Fall of the "Fighting Editor," John Mitchell* (Charlottesville: University of Virginia Press, 2002), 185–204.

3. In 1933, the five women directors were Lillian Bazeley, Lillian Payne, Maggie Maclin Smith, Maggie Lena Walker, and Rosa E. Watson. Shareholder records for Second Street are incomplete. Women represented less than 20 percent of Commercial Bank's more than two hundred shareholders. At least thirty-eight women held 193 of the bank's eight hundred shares. One investor, Olivia Orange, held an unusually large amount with seventy-two shares. Fleming, "A History of Consolidated Bank and Trust Company," 46; Minutes of January 17, 1933, Consolidated Bank Board of Directors Meeting Minutes, 1933–1943, CB&T Records; "Commercial Bank and Trust Co. List of Stockholders [. . .], February 1923," Mss3 B7327 a FA1, sec. 4, Subsidiary Companies, Merchants National Bank, Richmond, Va., folder Lists of Stockholders in Richmond Area Banks, 1923, box 246, Branch & Company, Richmond, Va., Records, 1837–1976, Virginia Historical Society.
4. Some black bankers saw Hoover's National Credit Corporation (NCC) as a chance to interact on equal terms with other banks. For example, Richard R. Wright Sr., founder and president of the Citizens' and Southern Banking Company in Philadelphia, encouraged black bankers to join the NCC. Roosevelt folded Hoover's Reconstruction Finance Corporation (RFC) into his New Deal program. Title 3 of the Emergency Banking Act (1932) authorized the RFC to make investments in banks through bank purchases of a special class of preferred stock. Richard R. Wright Sr., "People's Money Must Be Safe at Any Cost," *Philadelphia Tribune*, November 26, 1931, 9, 15, here 9; "Federal Home Loan Bank Board Will Prove Boon," *Wyandotte Echo* (Kansas City, Kans.), August 26, 1932, 1. See Memorandum, Warren J. Lockwood to B. T. McGraw, Re: Information for Article on Minority Group Resources in Home Financing, April 11, 1949, FHA Commissioner's Correspondence and Subject File, 1938–1958, folder Mortgagees—Leading Institutions, box 4, record group 31, Records of the Federal Housing Administration, National Archives and Records Administration.
5. Fleming, "A History of Consolidated Bank and Trust Company," 56–57.
6. Carol Hazard, "Consolidated Bank to Become Premier Bank," *Richmond Times-Dispatch*, March 4, 2011, https://www.richmond.com/business/consolidated-bank-to-become-premier-bank/article_3b794b82-c1bc-5862-982a-01fe7aaef43d.html; "New Chief Executive Hopes to Revive Century-Old African-American Bank," *Index-Journal* (Greenwood, S.C.), January 4, 2004, 30, https://www.newspapers.com/newspage/70539303/; "Description of Business," in Premier Financial Bancorp, Inc., form 10-K, December 31, 2016, 4–19, here 5, https://www.last10k.com/sec-filings/pfbi.
7. Sandra Phillips, "The Subprime Mortgage Calamity and the African American Woman" *Review of Black Political Economy* 39, no. 2 (June 2012): 227–37; John Leland, "Baltimore Finds Subprime Crisis Snags Women," *New York Times*, January 15, 2008, http://www.nytimes.com/2008/01/15/us/15mortgage.html; Avis Jones-DeWeever,

"Losing Ground: Women and the Foreclosure Crisis," National Council of Jewish Women, n.d., http://www.ncjw.org/content_1441.cfm, accessed January 25, 2017. Also see Suparna Bhaskaran with New Jersey Communities United, ISAIAH, and ACCE Institute, *"Pinklining": How Wall Street's Predatory Products Pillage Women's Wealth, Opportunities and Futures*, June 2016, https://d3n8a8pro7vhmx.cloudfront.net/acce-institute/pages/100/attachments/original/1466121052/acce_pinklining_VIEW.pdf?1466121052.

Selected Bibliography

PRIMARY SOURCES

Manuscript Collections

Consolidated Bank and Trust Records. C. 1903–1993. Special Collections. L. Douglas Wilder Library and Learning Resource Center. Virginia Union University.

David M. Rubenstein Rare Book and Manuscript Library. Duke University.

Harris, Rencher Nicholas. Papers. 1851–1980.

Spaulding, Charles Clinton. Papers.

John Shaw Pierson Civil War Collection. Rare Books and Special Collections. Firestone Library. Princeton University.

Munford, Mary-Cooke Branch. Papers. 1881–1935. Library of Virginia. Richmond, Va.

National Park Service. Maggie Lena Walker Historical Site. Richmond, Va.

Independent Order of St. Luke. Records.

Maggie L. Walker Oral History Project.

Walker, Maggie Lena. Papers. 1897–1935.

Special Collections. Ford Motor Company Library. Tuskegee University.

Holsey, Albon L. Papers.

Moton, Robert Russa. Papers. No. 2.

Special Collections. University Libraries. Virginia Polytechnic Institute and State University.

Blacksburg [Virginia] Odd Fellows Records. 1902–1969.

Independent Order of St. Luke Collection. 1877–1970.

State Records Center. Library of Virginia. Richmond, Va.

Virginia Constitutional Convention (1901–1902). Records, 1901–1902.

Virginia State Corporation Commission. Record Group 112.

Valentine Museum and Richmond History Center. Richmond, Va.
Payne, Lillian H. Papers. 1907–1974.
Vertical Files.
Virginia Historical Society. Richmond, Va.
Brinson, Betsy. Papers. 1894–1999.
Branch & Company, Richmond, Va. Records. 1837–1976.

Published Primary Sources, Microfilm, and Digital Collections

Adams, F. Colburn. *"White Man Bery Unsartin"; "Nigger Haint Got No Friends, No How": The Blackest Chapter in the History of the Republican Party: The Men Who Robbed and Combined to Rob the Freedmen of Their Hard Earnings.* Washington, D.C.: Judd and Detweiler, 1878.

American Freedmen's Inquiry Commission. *Preliminary Report Touching the Condition and Management of Emancipated Refugees* [. . .]. New York: J. F. Trow, 1863.

Brooks, Charles H. *The Official History and Manual of the Grand United Order of Odd Fellows in America.* Philadelphia, 1902.

Brown, Charlotte Eugenia (Hawkins), 1883–1961. Papers. 1900–1961. Watertown, Mass.: General Microfilm Co., 1984. Microfilm.

Browne, William Washington, and D. Webster Davis. *The Life and Public Services of Rev. William Washington Browne.* Philadelphia: AME Book Concern, 1910.

Burrell, William P., and D. E. Johnson. *Twenty-Five Years History of the Grand Fountain of the United Order of True Reformers, 1881–1905.* Richmond, Va.: Grand Fountain of True Reformers, 1909.

Bush, A. E., and P. L. Dorman, eds. *History of the Mosaic Templars of America: Its Founders and Officials.* Little Rock: Central Printing, 1924. http://www.mosaictemplarspreservation.org/history_mosaic/history.pdf.

Dabney, Wendell P. *Maggie L. Walker and The I[ndependent] O[rder] of Saint Luke: The Woman and Her Work.* Cincinnati: Dabney, 1927.

Delany, Martin R. *The Condition, Elevation, Emigration, and Destiny of the Colored People of the United States.* 1852. Reprint. New York: Arno, 1968.

Dodson, Jualynne E. *Engendering Church: Women, Power, and African Methodism.* Lanham, Md.: Rowman and Littlefield, 2002.

Douglass, Frederick. *Life and Times of Frederick Douglass: His Early Life as a Slave, His Escape from Bondage, and His Complete History to the Present Time.* Hartford, Conn.: Park, 1882.

Du Bois, W. E. B. Papers. 1803–1999. Special Collections and University Archives, University of Massachusetts Amherst Libraries. Microfilm.

——. *The Philadelphia Negro: A Social Study.* Philadelphia: University of Philadelphia Press, 1899.

——, ed. *Some Efforts of American Negroes for Their Own Social Betterment.* Atlanta University Publications 3. Atlanta: Atlanta University Press, 1898.

Eaton, John, and Ethel Osgood Mason. *Grant, Lincoln, and the Freedman: Reminiscences of the Civil War with Special Reference to the Work for the Contrabands and Freedman of the Mississippi Valley.* New York: Longmans, Green, 1907.

Forrester, William M. T. *Ritual of the Independent Order of St. Luke Containing Form for Opening, Closing, Initiating, Consulting, and Consecrating of Subordinate Councils,*

Ceremonies for Installation of Officers and Funerals with Rules and Regulations. Revised. Richmond: St. Luke Herald, 1906.

——. *Ritual of the Independent Order of St. Luke Containing the Rules, Regulations, and Ceremonies of Degrees.* Revised. N.p.: 1894.

Freedman's Savings and Trust Company. Letters Received by the Commissioners. 1870–1914. Part 1: Correspondence, Loans, and Bank Books. Bethesda, Md.: UPA collection from LexisNexis, 2005–. Microfilm.

Grand Fountain United Order of True Reformers. *1619–1907: From Slavery to Bankers.* Richmond: Reformers, [1907?]. https://hdl.handle.net/2027/emu.010000576508.

Handy, James. *Scraps of African Methodist Episcopal History.* Philadelphia: AME Book Concern, [1902].

Laura Spelman Rockefeller Memorial Collection. Series 3: Appropriations. 1917–1945. Rockefeller University. Microfilm.

The Marcus Garvey and Universal Negro Improvement Association Papers. Ed. Robert A. Hill. Durham, N.C.: Duke University Press, 2014.

McDougald, Elise Johnson. "The Task of Negro Womanhood." In *The New Negro: An Interpretation*, ed. Alain Locke, 369–82. 1925. Reprint. New York: Simon and Schuster, 1992.

Miscellaneous Negro Newspapers. Committee on Negro Studies of the American Council of Learned Societies. Library of Congress, Washington, D.C. Microfilm.

Raby, Robert Cornelius. *The Regulation of Pawnbroking.* New York: Russell Sage Foundation, 1924.

Records of the National Negro Business League. Part 1: Annual Conference Proceedings and Organizational Records. 1900–1919. Bethesda, Md. Microfilm.

Registers of Signatures of Depositors in Branches of the Freedman's Savings and Trust Company. 1865–1874. National Archives and Records Administration, Washington, D.C. Microfilm.

Taylor, Susie King. *Reminiscences of My Life in Camp with the 33d United States Colored Troops, Late 1st S.C. Volunteers.* Boston, 1902.

Walrund, Eric C. "The Largest Negro Commercial Enterprise in the World." *Forbes*, February 2, 1924.

War of the Rebellion: Compilation of the Official Records of the Union and Confederate Armies. Washington, D.C.: General Printing Office, 1894.

Washington, Booker T. *The Future of the American Negro.* Boston: Small, Maynard, 1902.

SECONDARY SOURCES

Books and Chapters

Alexander, Ann Field. *Race Man: The Rise and Fall of the "Fighting Editor," John Mitchell.* Charlottesville: University of Virginia Press, 2002.

Bair, Barbara. "True Women, Real Men: Gender, Ideology, and Social Roles in the Garvey Movement." In *Gendered Domains: Rethinking Public and Private in Women's History*, ed. Dorothy O. Helly and Susan Reverby, 154–65. Ithaca, N.Y.: Cornell University Press, 1992.

Baldwin, Davarian L. *Chicago's New Negroes: Modernity, the Great Migration, and Black Urban Life.* Chapel Hill: University of North Carolina Press, 2007.

Baradaran, Mehrsa. *The Color of Money: Black Banks and the Racial Wealth Gap*. Cambridge, Mass.: Harvard University Press, 2017.

Bay, Mia. "'If Iola Were a Man': Gender, Jim Crow and Public Protest in the Work of Ida B. Wells." In *Becoming Visible: Women's Presence in Late Nineteenth-Century America*, ed. Janet Floyd, R. J. Ellis, and Lindsey Traub, 105–28. New York: Rodopi, 2001.

Berlin, Ira, and Philip D. Morgan, eds. *The Slave's Economy: Independent Production by Slaves in the Americas*. 1991. Reprint. London: Frank Cass, 1995.

Berry, Mary Frances. *My Face Is Black Is True: Callie House and the Struggle for Ex-Slave Reparations*. New York: Knopf, 2005.

Bouk, Dan. *How Our Days Became Numbered: Risk and the Rise of the Statistical Individual*. Chicago: Chicago University Press, 2015.

Burrows, John H. *The Necessity of Myth: A History of the National Negro Business League, 1900–1945*. Auburn, Ala.: Hickory Hill, 1988.

Butler, John Sibley. *Entrepreneurship and Self-help Among Black Americans: A Reconsideration of Race and Economics*. Revised. New York: State University of New York Press, 2005.

Butler, John Sibley, and Kenneth L. Wilson. *Entrepreneurial Enclaves in the African American Experience*. Washington, D.C.: Neighborhood Policy Institute Publication Series, 1990.

Cattelino, Jessica R. "Casino Roots: The Cultural Production of Twentieth-Century Seminole Economic Development." In *Native Pathways: American Indian Culture and Economic Development in the Twentieth Century*, ed. Brian Hosmer and Colleen O Neill, 66–90. Boulder: University Press of Colorado, 2004.

Chapman, Erin. *Prove It on Me: New Negroes, Sex, and Popular Culture in the 1920s*. New York: Oxford University Press, 2012.

Collier-Thomas, Bettye. *Jesus, Jobs, and Justice: African American Women and Religion*. New York: Alfred A. Knopf, 2010.

Connolly, N. D. B. *A World More Concrete: Real Estate and the Remaking of Jim Crow South Florida*. Chicago: University of Chicago Press, 2014.

Dailey, Jane Elizabeth. *Before Jim Crow: The Politics of Race in Postemancipation Virginia*. Chapel Hill: University of North Carolina Press, 2000.

Dodson, Jualynne E. *Engendering Church: Women, Power, and the AME Church*. Lanham, Md.: Rowman and Littlefield, 2002.

Dossett, Kate. "Luxuriant Growth: The Walkers and Black Economic Nationalism." In *Bridging Race Divides: Black Nationalism, Feminism, and Integration in the United States, 1896–1935*, 107–49. Gainesville: University Press of Florida, 2008.

Eidinow, Esther. *Oracles, Curses, and Risk Among the Ancient Greeks*. Oxford: Oxford University Press, 2007.

Engs, Robert Francis. *Freedom's First Generation: Black Hampton, Virginia, 1861–1890*. New York: Fordham University Press, 2004.

Fahey, David M., ed. *The Black Lodge in White America: "True Reformer" Browne and His Economic Strategy*. Dayton, Oh.: Wright State University Press, 1994.

Fairlie, Robert W. *Ethnic and Racial Entrepreneurship: A Study of Historical and Contemporary Differences*. New York: Garland, 1996.

Farmer-Kaiser, Mary. "'The Women Are the Controlling Spirits': Freedwomen, Free Labor, and the Freedmen's Bureau." In *Freedwomen and the Freedmen's Bureau: Race, Gender, and Public Policy in the Age of Emancipation*, 64–94. New York: Fordham University Press, 2010.

Fields, Barbara Jeanne. *Slavery and Freedom on the Middle Ground: Maryland During the Nineteenth Century*. New Haven, Conn.: Yale University Press, 1985.

Francois, Marie Eileen. *A Culture of Everyday Credit: Housekeeping, Pawnbroking, and Governance in Mexico City, 1750–1920*. Lincoln: University of Nebraska Press, 2006.

Frankel, Noralee. *Freedom's Women: Black Women and Families in Civil War Era Mississippi*. Bloomington: University of Indiana Press, 1999.

Frazier, E. Franklin *Black Bourgeoisie*. 1957. New York: Collier, 1962.

Freund, David M. P. *Colored Property: State Policy and White Racial Politics in Suburban America*. Chicago: University of Chicago Press, 2007.

Garon, Sheldon M. *Beyond Our Means: Why America Spends While the World Saves*. Princeton, N.J.: Princeton University Press, 2012

George, Carol V. R. "Widening the Circle: The Black Church and the Abolitionist Crusade, 1830–1860." In *Antislavery Reconsidered: New Perspectives on the Abolitionists*, ed. Michael Fellman, 75–95. Baton Rouge: Louisiana State University Press, 1979.

Germain, Richard N. *Dollars Through the Doors: A Pre-1930 History of Bank Marketing in America*. Westport, Conn.: Greenwood, 1996.

Gerteis, Louis. *From Contraband to Freedman: Federal Policy Toward Southern Blacks, 1861–1865*. Westport, Conn.: Greenwood, 1973.

Giggie, John M. *After Redemption. Jim Crow and the Transformation of African American Religion in the Delta, 1875–1915*. New York: Oxford University Press, 2007.

Gill, Tiffany M. *Beauty Shop Politics: African American Women's Activism in the Beauty Industry*. Urbana: University of Illinois Press, 2010.

Glymph, Thavolia. *Out of the House of Bondage: The Transformation of the Plantation Household*. New York: Cambridge University Press, 2008.

Gruchy, Allan G. *Supervision and Control of Virginia State Banks*. New York: Appleton-Century, 1937.

Habermas, Jurgen. *The Structural Transformation of the Public Sphere: An Inquiry into a Category of Bourgeois Society*. Trans. Thomas Burger. Cambridge: Massachusetts Institute of Technology Press, 1989.

Hale, Grace Elizabeth. "'For Colored' and 'For White': Segregating Consumption in the South." In *Jumpin' Jim Crow: Southern Politics from Civil War to Civil Rights*, ed. Jane Dailey, Glenda Elizabeth Gilmore, and Bryant Simon, 162–82. Princeton, N.J.: Princeton University Press, 2000.

Harlan, Louis. "Booker T. Washington and the National Negro Business League." In *Seven on Black: Reflections on the Negro Experience in America*, ed. William G. Shade and Roy C. Herrenkohl, 73–91. Philadelphia: J. B. Lippincott, 1969.

Harold, Claudrena N. *New Negro Politics in the Jim Crow South*. Athens: University of Georgia Press, 2016.

——. *The Rise and Fall of the Garvey Movement in the Urban South, 1918–1942*. New York: Routledge; Taylor and Francis, 2007.

Harris, Abram. *The Negro as Capitalist: A Study of Banking and Business Among American Negroes*. 1936. College Park, Md.: McGrath, 1968.

Harris, LaShawn. *Sex Workers, Psychics, and Numbers Runners: Black Women in New York City's Underground Economy*. Urbana: University of Illinois Press, 2016.

Hermann, Janet Sharp. *The Pursuit of a Dream*. New York: Oxford University Press, 1981.

Higginbotham, Evelyn Brooks. *Righteous Discontent: The Women's Movement in the Black Baptist Church, 1880–1920*. Cambridge, Mass.: Harvard University Press, 1993.

Hunter, Tera. *To 'Joy My Freedom: Southern Black Women's Lives and Labors After the Civil War*. Cambridge, Mass.: Harvard University Press, 1997.

Hyman, Louis. *Debtor Nation: The History of America in Red Ink*. Princeton, N.J.: Princeton University Press, 2011.

Jones, Jacquelyn. "A Spirit of Enterprise: The African-American Challenge to the Confederate Project in Civil War-Era Savannah." In *African American Life in the Georgia Lowcountry: The Atlantic World and the Gullah Geechee*, ed. Philip D. Morgan, 188–223. Athens: University of Georgia Press, 2010.

Jones, Martha S. *All Bound Up Together: The Woman Question in African American Public Culture, 1830–1900*. Chapel Hill: University of North Carolina Press, 2007.

Katznelson, Ira. *When Affirmative Action Was White: An Untold History of Racial Inequality in Twentieth-Century America*. New York: W. W. Norton, 2005.

Kelley, Blair L. M. *Right to Ride: Streetcar Boycotts and African American Citizenship in the Era of "Plessy v Ferguson."* Chapel Hill: University of North Carolina Press, 2010.

King, Shannon. *Whose Harlem Is This, Anyway?: Community Politics and Grassroots Activism During the New Negro Era*. New York: New York University, 2015.

Lauer, Josh. *Creditworthy: A History of Consumer Surveillance and Financial Identity in America*. New York: Columbia University Press, 2017.

Lemire, Beverly. "Petty Pawns and Informal Lending: Gender and the Transformation of Small-Scale Credit in England, Circa 1600–1800." In *From Family Firms to Corporate Capitalism: Essays in Business and Industrial History in Honour of Peter Mathias*, ed. Peter Mathias, Kristine Bruland, and Patrick Karl O'Brien, 112–38. Oxford: Clarendon, 1998.

Levy, Jonathan. *Freaks of Fortune: The Emerging World of Capitalism and Risk in America*. Cambridge, Mass.: Harvard University Press, 2012.

Lewis, David Levering. *When Harlem Was in Vogue*. New York: Alfred A. Knopf, 1981.

Light, Ivan H. *Ethnic Enterprise in America: Business and Welfare Among Chinese, Japanese and Blacks*. Berkeley: University of California Press, 1972.

Lorini, Alessandra. *Rituals of Race: American Public Culture and the Search for Racial Democracy*. Charlottesville: University Virginia Press, 1999.

Marable, Manning. *How Capitalism Underdeveloped Black America: Problems in Race, Political Economy, and Society*. Revised. Cambridge, Mass.: South End, 2000.

Marlowe, Gertrude Woodruff. *A Right Worthy Grand Mission: Maggie Lena Walker and the Quest for Black Economic Empowerment*. Washington, D.C.: Howard University Press, 2003.

McDuffie, Erik S. *Sojourning for Freedom: Black Women, American Communism, and the Making of Black Left Feminism*. Durham, N.C.: Duke University Press, 2011.

McGruder, Kevin. *Race and Real Estate: Conflict and Cooperation in Harlem, 1890–1920*. New York: Columbia University Press, 2015.

Murphy, Sharon Ann. *Investing in Life: Insurance in Antebellum America*. Baltimore, Md.: Johns Hopkins University Press, 2010.

Newby-Alexander, Cassandra L. *An African American History of the Civil War in Hampton Roads*. Charleston, S.C.: History, 2010.

O'Donovan, Susan Eva. "Black Women and the Domestication of Free Labor." In *Becoming Free in the Cotton South*, 162–207. Cambridge: Harvard University Press, 2007.

Olegario, Rowena. *A Culture of Credit: Embedding Trust and Transparency in American Business*. Cambridge, Mass.: Harvard University Press, 2006.

Osthaus, Carl R. *Freedmen, Philanthropy, and Fraud: A History of the Freedman's Savings Bank*. Urbana: University of Illinois Press, 1976.

Ott, Julia C. *When Wall Street Met Main Street: The Quest for an Investors' Democracy*. Cambridge, Mass.: Harvard University Press, 2011.

Ownby, Ted. *American Dreams in Mississippi: Consumers, Poverty and Culture, 1830–1998*. Chapel Hill: University of North Carolina Press, 1998.

Pierce, Joseph A. *Negro Business and Business Education: Their Prospect and Prospective Development*. New York: Harper, 1947.

Robb, George. *Ladies of the Ticker: Women and Wall Street from the Gilded Age to the Great Depression*. Champaign: University of Illinois Press, 2017.

Robertson, Nancy Marie. "'The Principles of Sound Banking and Financial Noblesse Oblige': Women's Departments in U.S. Banks at the Turn of the Twentieth Century." In *Women and Their Money, 1700–1950: Essays on Women and Finance*, ed. Anne Laurence, Josephine Maltby, and Janette Rutterford, 243–53. London: Routledge, 2009.

Robinson, Cedric J. *Black Marxism: The Making of the Black Radical Tradition*. Chapel Hill: University of North Carolina Press, 2000.

Rockman, Seth. *Scraping By: Wage Labor, Slavery, and Survival in Early Baltimore*. Baltimore, Md.: Johns Hopkins University Press, 2009.

Rolinson, Mary G. *Grassroots Garveyism: The Universal Negro Improvement Association in the Rural South, 1920–1927*. Chapel Hill: University of North Carolina Press, 2007.

Rose, Willie Lee. *Rehearsal for Reconstruction: The Port Royal Experiment*. Indianapolis: Bobbs-Merrill, 1964.

Rothstein, Richard. *The Color of Law: A Forgotten History of How Our Government Segregated America*. New York: Liveright, 2017.

Shaw, Stephanie J. *What a Woman Ought to Be and Do: African American Professional Women Workers During the Jim Crow Era*. Chicago: University of Chicago Press, 1996.

Stanley, Amy Dru. "The Labor Question and the Sale of Self." In *From Bondage to Contract: Wage Labor, Marriage, and the Market in the Era of Slave Emancipation*, 60–97. Cambridge: Cambridge University Press, 1998.

Stewart, Jacqueline Najuma. *Migrating to the Movies: Cinema and Black Urban Modernity*. Berkeley: University of California Press, 2005.

Stewart, Shirley. *The World of Stephanie St. Clair. An Entrepreneur, Race Woman and Outlaw in Early Twentieth Century Harlem*. New York: Peter Lang, 2014.

Stuart, Merah S. *An Economic Detour: A History of Insurance in the Lives of American Negroes*. New York: Wendell Malliett, 1940.

Summers, Martin Anthony. *Manliness and Its Discontents: The Black Middle Class and the Transformation of Masculinity, 1900–1930*. Chapel Hill: University of North Carolina Press, 2004.

Taylor, Ula Y. *The Veiled Garvey: The Life and Times of Amy Jacques Garvey*. Chapel Hill: University of North Carolina Press, 2002.

Tebbutt, Melanie. *Making Ends Meet: Pawnbroking and Working-Class Credit*. Leicester, U.K.: Leicester University Press, 1983.

Walker, Corey D. B. *A Noble Fight: African American Freemasonry and the Struggle for Democracy in America*. Urbana: University of Illinois Press, 2008.

Walker, Juliet E. K. *The History of Black Business In America: Capitalism, Race, Entrepreneurship*. Chapel Hill: University of North Carolina Press, 2009.

Weare, Walter B. *Black Business in the New South a Social History of the North Carolina Mutual Life Insurance Company*. Urbana: University of Illinois Press, 1993.

Weems, Robert E., Jr. *Black Business in the Black Metropolis: The Chicago Metropolitan Assurance Company, 1925–1985*. Bloomington: Indiana University Press, 1966.

White, Deborah Gray. *Ar'n't I a Woman? Female Slaves in the Plantation South*. 1985. Revised. New York: W. W. Norton, 1995.

White, Shane, Stephen Garton, and Stephen Robertson. *Playing the Numbers: Gambling in Harlem Between the Wars*. Cambridge, Mass.: Harvard University Press, 2010.

Williams, Eric Eustace. *Capitalism and Slavery*. Chapel Hill: University of North Carolina Press, 1944.

Williams, Lillian Serece. *Strangers in the Land of Paradise: The Creation of an African American Community, Buffalo, New York, 1900–1940*. Bloomington: Indiana University Press, 1999.

Woodward, C. Vann. *The Strange Career of Jim Crow: A Commemorative Edition*. New York: Oxford University Press, 2002.

Yee, Shirley. *Black Women Abolitionists: A Study in Activism, 1828–1860*. Nashville: University of Tennessee Press, 1992.

Yohn, Susan. "'Let Christian Women Set the Example in Their Own Gifts': The 'Business' of Protestant Women's Organizations." In *Women and Twentieth-Century Protestantism*, ed. Virginia Brereton and Margaret Bendroth, 213–35. Urbana: University of Illinois Press, 2002.

Journals and Periodicals

Brown, Elsa Barkley. "Constructing a Life and a Community: A Partial Story of Maggie Lena Walker." *OAH Magazine of History* 7, no. 4 (Summer 1993): 28–31.

——. "Womanist Consciousness: Maggie Lena Walker and the Independent Order of Saint Luke." *Signs* 14 (1989): 610–33.

Butler, John Sibley, and Kenneth Wilson. "Entrepreneurial Enclaves in the African American Experience." *National Journal of Sociology* 2 (Winter 1988): 128–66.

Camp, Bayliss J., and Orit Kent. "'What a Mighty Power We Can Be': Individual and Collective Identity in African American and White Fraternal Initiation Rituals." *Social Science History* 28, no. 3 (Fall 2004): 439–83.

Campbell, John. "'As a Kind of Free Man': Slaves' Market-Related Activities in the South Carolina Upcountry, 1800–1860." *Slavery and Abolition* 12, no. 1 (June 2008): 131–69.

Dailey, Maceo C., Jr. "Neither 'Uncle Tom' nor 'Accommodationist': Booker T. Washington, Emmett Jay Scott, and Constructionalism." *Atlanta History* 38, no. 4 (Winter 1995): 21–33.

Davis, Angela. "Reflections on the Black Woman's Role in the Community of Slaves." *Massachusetts Review* 13, nos. 1/2 (Winter–Spring 1972): 81–100.

Davis, John Martin. "Bankless in Beaufort: A Reexamination of the 1873 Failure of the Freedman's Savings Branch at Beaufort, South Carolina." *South Carolina Historical Magazine* 104, no. 1 (2003): 25–55.

Du Bois, W. E. B. "Negroes and the Crisis of Capitalism in the U.S." *Monthly Review* 4, no. 12 (April 1953); reprint, 54, no. 11 (April 2003). https://monthlyreview.org/2003/04/01/negroes-and-the-crisis-of-capitalism-in-the-united-states/.

Garrett-Scott, Shennette. "'To Do a Work That Would Be Very Far Reaching': Minnie Geddings Cox, the Mississippi Life Insurance Company, and the Challenges of Black Women's Business Leadership in the Early Twentieth-Century United States." *Enterprise and Society* 17, no. 3 (September 2016): 473–514.

Gilbert, Abby L. "The Comptroller of the Currency and the Freedman's Savings Bank." *Journal of Negro History* 57, no. 2 (April 1972): 125–43.

Glotzer, Paige. "Exclusion in Arcadia: How Suburban Developers Circulated Ideas About Discrimination, 1890–1950." *Journal of Urban History* 41, no. 3 (2015): 479–94.

Heen Mary L. "Ending Jim Crow Life Insurance Rates." *Northwestern Journal of Law and Social Policy* 4, no. 360 (Fall 2009): 360–99. http://scholarlycommons.law.northwestern.edu/njlsp/vol4/iss2/3.

Henderson, Alexa Benson. "Heman E. Perry and Black Enterprise in Atlanta, 1908–1925." *Business History Review* 61, no. 2 (Summer 1987): 216–42.

Hine, Darlene Clark. "Rape and the Inner Lives of Black Women in the Middle West." *Signs* 14, no. 4 (Summer 1989): 912–20.

Josiah, Barbara P. "Providing for the Future: The World of the African American Depositors of Washington, D.C.'s Freedmen's Savings Bank, 1865–1874." *Journal of African American History* 89, no. 1 (Winter 2004): 1–16.

Kelley, Robin D. G. "What Did Cedric Robinson Mean by Racial Capitalism?" *Boston Review*, January 12, 2017. http://bostonreview.net/race/robin-d-g-kelley-what-did-cedric-robinson-mean-racial-capitalism.

Kish, Zenia, and Justin Leroy. "Bonded Life: Technologies of Racial Finance from Slave Insurance to Philanthrocapital." *Cultural Studies* 29, no. 5 (March 2015): 630–51.

Kwolek-Folland, Angel. "The African American Financial Industries: Issues of Class, Race, and Gender in the Early Twentieth Century." *Business and Economic History* 23, no. 2 (Winter 1994): 85–106.

Light, Ivan. "Numbers Gambling Among Blacks: A Financial Institution." *American Sociological Review* 42, no. 6 (December 1977): 892–904.

Meier, August, and Elliott Rudwick. "Negro Boycotts of Segregated Streetcars in Virginia, 1904–1907." *Virginia Magazine of History and Biography* 81 (October 1973): 479–87.

Retman, Sonnet H. "Black No More: George Schuyler and Racial Capitalism." *PMLA* 123, no. 5 (2008): 1448–64.

Watkinson, James D. "William Washington Browne and the True Reformers of Richmond, Virginia." *Virginia Magazine of History and Biography* 97, no. 3 (July 1989): 375–98.

Zelizer, Viviana A. "Human Values and the Market: The Case of Life Insurance and Death in 19th-Century." *American Journal of Sociology* 84, no. 3 (November 1978): 591–610.

Dissertations and Theses

Allen, Marcus Anthony. "Cautiously Capitalistic: Black Economic Agency at the Savings Bank of Baltimore, 1850–1900." PhD diss., Morgan State University, 2013.

Brown, Elsa Barkley. "Uncle Ned's Children: Negotiating Community and Freedom in Postemancipation Richmond, Virginia." PhD diss., Kent State University, 1994.

Fleming, Jesse E. "A History of Consolidated Bank and Trust Company." MA thesis, Rutgers University, 1972.

Garrett, Shennette Monique. "'He Ran His Business Like a White Man': Race, Entrepreneurship, and the Early National Negro Business League in the New South." MA thesis, University of Texas at Austin, 2006.

Garrett-Scott, Shennette. "Daughters of Ruth: Enterprising Black Women in Insurance in the New South, 1890s to 1930s." PhD diss., University of Texas at Austin, 2011.

Osborne, Nicholas. "Little Capitalists: The Social Economy of Saving in the United States, 1816–1914." PhD diss., Columbia University, 2014.

Sledge, Stephen B. "The Bitter Fruit of Secession: The Union Army's Wartime Occupation of Southeastern Virginia." PhD diss., George Mason University, 2012.

Weis, Tracey M. "Negotiating Freedom: Domestic Service and the Landscape of Labor and Household Relations in Richmond, Virginia, 1850–1880." PhD diss., Rutgers University, 1994.

Index

Italicized page numbers indicate a figure.